Colonial Buganda and the End of Empire

Colonial Buganda was one of the most important and richly documented kingdoms in East Africa. In this book, Jonathon Earle offers the first global intellectual history of the Kingdom, using a series of case studies, interviews and previously inaccessible private archives to offer new insights concerning the multiple narratives used by intellectuals. Where previous studies on literacy in Africa have presupposed 'sacred' or 'secular' categories, Earle argues that activists blurred European epistemologies as they reworked colonial knowledge into vernacular debates about kingship and empire. Furthermore, by presenting Catholic, Muslim and Protestant histories and political perspectives in conversation with one another, he offers a nuanced picture of the religious and social environment. Through the lives, politics and historical contexts of these African intellectuals, Earle presents an important argument about the end of empire, making the reader rethink the dynamics of political imagination and historical pluralism in the colonial and postcolonial state.

JONATHON L. EARLE is Assistant Professor of History at Centre College and Chair of the African and African American Studies Program.

T0371512

African Studies Series

The African Studies series, founded in 1968, is a prestigious series of monographs, general surveys and textbooks on Africa covering history, political science, anthropology, economics and ecological and environmental issues. The series seeks to publish work by senior scholars as well as the best new research.

Editorial Board:

Other titles in the series are listed at the back of the book.

Colonial Buganda and the End of Empire

Political Thought and Historical Imagination in Africa

JONATHON L. EARLE
Centre College, Danville, Kentucky

CAMBRIDGE
UNIVERSITY PRESS

CAMBRIDGE
UNIVERSITY PRESS

University Printing House, Cambridge CB2 8BS, United Kingdom

One Liberty Plaza, 20th Floor, New York, NY 10006, USA

477 Williamstown Road, Port Melbourne, VIC 3207, Australia

314-321, 3rd Floor, Plot 3, Splendor Forum, Jasola District Centre, New Delhi - 110025, India

79 Anson Road, #06-04/06, Singapore 079906

Cambridge University Press is part of the University of Cambridge.

It furthers the University's mission by disseminating knowledge in the pursuit of education, learning and research at the highest international levels of excellence.

www.cambridge.org
Information on this title: www.cambridge.org/9781108404365
DOI: 10.1017/9781108264723

© Jonathon L. Earle 2017

First published 2017
First paperback edition 2020

A catalogue record for this publication is available from the British Library

ISBN 978-1-108-41705-1 Hardback
ISBN 978-1-108-40436-5 Paperback

To Jennifer

Contents

Illustrations

Maps

Table

Figures

Acknowledgements

I wish to begin by thanking Professors Derek R. Peterson and John M. Lonsdale. Derek and John served as my two doctoral supervisors, during which they expertly guided the early stages of this project. They have continued to offer critical insights and encouragement along the way. Their presence and historical insights continue to deeply inspire my work. My research has also been enriched by numerous conversations. I especially wish to thank: Christopher Bayly, who sadly passed away before this book was published, Felicitas Becker, Florence Brisset-Foucault, Joel Cabrita, Shane Doyle, Holger Bernt Hansen, Holly Hanson, Peter Hoesing, Emma Hunter, John Iliffe, Samwiri Lwanga-Lunyiigo, Abdu Kasozi, Neil Kodesh, Julie MacArthur, Marissa Mika, Yolana Pringle, Richard Reid, Emily Rodes, Ethan Sanders, China Schertz, David Smith, Rhiannon Stephens, Aidan Stonehouse, Andrea Stultiens, Carol Summers, Edgar Jack Taylor, Amos Tubb, Michael Twaddle, Megan Vaughan, Kathleen Vongsathorn and Emma Wild-Wood. Sections of this book were presented at workshops or conferences in Baltimore, Cambridge (UK), Indianapolis, Kampala, Mukono, New Haven, San Francisco, South Bend, Oxford and Washington, DC. Any shortcomings in this work are my own.

The completion of this book depended upon the support of many friends and colleagues in eastern Africa. I am particularly indebted to Ssalongo George Mpanga Lutwama, whose friendship, diligence and brilliance as a research assistant has been invaluable. Through countless conversations about the intricacies of Luganda grammar and Ganda cultural practices, to thousands of hours of conjoined field research, Mpanga has given himself to this project in ways that warrant my deepest appreciation and admiration. For their support and friendship over the past 15 years, I am grateful to Jonathan Mayo and Kenneth Hopson. For their unyielding embrace, I am also indebted to Illakut David Livingstone and the Atekok Itudai clan. I also wish to thank the City Language Centre (Kampala) for their excellent instruction in Ateso and Luganda. I am thankful for my wonderful colleagues at Centre College, the Faculty Development Committee and the administration of the College for their encouragement and support.

Without the early support of *Owekitiibwa* David Ntege this project would not have got off the ground so smoothly. I also owe much to *Omulamuzi* A.D. Lubowa and William S. Kajubi, who passed away before I could publish this work. Through hours of conversation on numerous occasions, these two significantly influenced my understanding of Buganda's late colonial politics – of what was at stake and the character of the claims that were circulating throughout central Uganda in the 1950s and 1960s.

I am particularly indebted to a handful of people in Uganda and Great Britain, whose interest in my work made it all possible. These individuals have provided countless hours of conversation, access to rare sources and critical engagement. For their friendships and belief in this project, I wish to thank *Omulangira* Kassim N. Kakungulu, Ambassador Maurice Kiwanuka, Sekinalya Hussein Mayanja, Uthman Mayanja, Peter Mulira, Edward N. Musazi and Moses Bwete.

I have also benefited from the insights of many friends, colleagues and mentors in Uganda, the United Kingdom and the United States, including: Hon Rhoda Kalema, Hugo Barlow, Elizabeth Musazi, Hon Kintu Musoke, Neal Ascherson, George Shepherd, Sam Kiwanuka, George Kasedde Mukasa, Michael Kibwika-Bagenda, Aggrey Mulira (who has sadly passed), Eva Mulira, Hon Ham-Mukasa Mulira, James Mulira, Sarah Mulira, Jack Kironde, Michael and Rae Grace, *Ow'abakyala* Mariam Mayanja, Nasser L. Mayanja, Eisah Kakyama Mayanja, Asiya Kakyama, Sheikh Abdu Obeid Kamulegeya, Al-Hajj Isa Lukwago, Al-Hajj Mustafa Mutiaba, Sheikh Anas A. Kalisa, Sheikh Isaac Ssettuba, Sheikh Burhan Ssebayigga, Ssemujju I. Nganda, Imelda Kiwanuka, Josephine Kiwanuka, Simon Mwebe, L. Mathias Tyaba, Kusemererwa James, Gaetano Steers, Sam Dick Kasolo, Samuel Mugwisa and Ambassador Semakula Kiwanuka.

For their time and assistance with archival sources, I wish to thank: Okello Ajum A. (Uganda National Archives), Christine Byaruhanga (Uganda Christian University), Father Charles (Rubaga Diocesan Archives), Joellen Elbashir (Howard University), Ivana Frlan (University of Birmingham), Marilyn Glanfield (Cambridge Centre of African Studies), Patrick B. Male (Budo, King's College), François

Richard (Archives of the Society of Missionaries of Africa), Amy Staples (National Museum of African Art) and Outa William (Soroti District Archives).

I am also grateful for the critical comments offered by my two anonymous reviewers, and the support, patience and encouragement of the series editors and Maria Marsh at Cambridge University Press.

Throughout the mid-twentieth century, communities in Buganda used different proverbs to talk about the importance of love and family. One saying noted, '*Okwagala*: *kulya magezi*', 'Love: it eats [is beyond] understanding'. During the duration of this project, the love and support of my family has surpassed my ability to describe it. This includes the unwavering support of the Earles, Lancasters and Thomases. I express my love and gratitude for Kiah Aguti, Jacob Osingada and Karis Ruth, who have inspired my imagination and filled this long process with tremendous joy. Most of all, I offer my deepest appreciation to Jennifer Atekit, who has been a relentless supporter. Her love and steady support has surely surpassed all understanding. To her, I dedicate this book.

Abbreviations: Archives and Private Papers

MA	Archives des Missionnaires d'Afrique Rome
NAP	Ascherson, Neal, Papers Copies in Personal Possession
BNA CO	British National Archives, Colonial Office Records Series Kew Gardens, London
BLA	Buganda Lukiiko Archives, Minutes, 1894–1918 Copies in Personal Possession
EBP	Bwete, Erieza, Papers Copies in Personal Possession
CCAS	Centre of African Studies, Cambridge, Archives University of Cambridge
CMS	Church Missionary Society Papers, Cadbury Research Library University of Birmingham
JLEP	Earle, Jonathon L., Papers Copies in Personal Possession
EEPA	Eliot Elisofon Photographic Archives Smithsonian National Museum of African Art Washington, DC
LFP	Fallers, Lloyd A., Papers, Special Collections Research Center University of Chicago

HMG	Grace, Canon Harold Myers and Mollie, Papers
	Copies in Personal Possession
ICS	Institute of Commonwealth Studies
	University of London
KCBA	King's College, Budo, Archives
	Budo, Uganda
KCCA	King's College, Cambridge, Archives
	Cambridge
BKMKP	Kiwanuka, Benedicto K.M., Papers
	Copies in Personal Possession
MUA	Makerere University Africana Archives
	Kampala
HML	Mukasa, Hamu, Library
	Kwata Mpola House
	Mukono, Uganda
MUA HMP	Mukasa, Hamu, Papers
	Makerere University Africana Archives
	Kampala
CCAS MP	Mulira, Eridadi M.K., Papers, Centre of African Studies
	University of Cambridge
IKML	Musazi, Ignatius K., Library
	Copies in Personal Possession
CMAA	Museum of Archaeology and Anthropology
	University of Cambridge
NARA AI	National Archives and Records Administration
	Washington, DC
SINP	Nganda, Ssemujju Ibrahim, Papers
	Copies in Personal Possession

RHOP   Perham, Dame Margery F., Papers
Bodleian Library of Commonwealth and African Studies
Rhodes House, University of Oxford

ARP   Richards, Professor Audrey, Papers
London School of Economics

RCMS   Royal Commonwealth Society Collections
University Library, University of Cambridge

RMCA SA   Royal Museum for Central Africa, Henry M. Stanley Archives
Tervuren, Brussels

RDA   Rubaga Diocesan Archives
Kampala

SOAS   School of Oriental and African Studies
Archives and Special Collections
London

UCU BA   Uganda Christian University Archives
Archives of the Bishop of Uganda
Mukono, Uganda

UML   Uganda Museum, Library
Kampala

UNAL   Uganda National Archives, Library
Entebbe

UNA SMP   Uganda National Archives, Secretariat Minute Papers
Entebbe

Maps

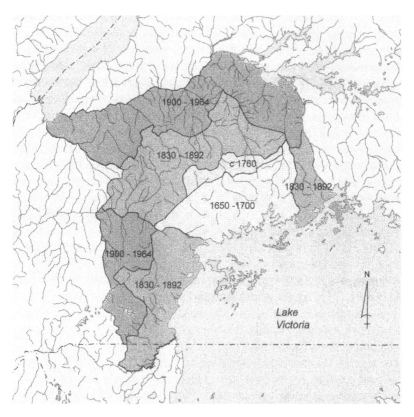

Map 0.1 Buganda Kingdom, seventeenth century onward
Adapted: Henri Médard, *Le Royaume Du Buganda Au XIXe Siècle* (2007)

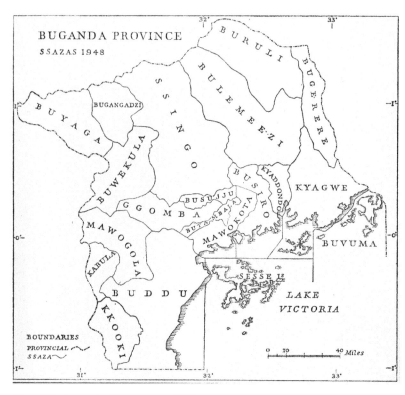

Map 0.2 Buganda Counties, c. 1950
Adapted: *Buganda and British Overrule*, ed. By D.A. Low and R.C. Pratt
(1960)

Introduction: Power and History Writing in Colonial Buganda

[Men and women] make their own history, but they do not make it just as they please in circumstances they choose for themselves; rather they make it in present circumstances, given and inherited. Tradition from all the dead generations weighs like a nightmare on the brain of the living. And just when they appear to be revolutionising themselves and their circumstances, in creating something unprecedented, in just such epochs of revolutionary crisis, that is when they nervously summon up the spirits of the past, borrowing from them their names, marching orders, uniforms, in order to enact new scenes in world history, but in this time-honoured guise and with this borrowed language.

Karl Marx[1]

This book is an intellectual history of the eastern African kingdom of Buganda. It uses material drawn from approximately one hundred semi-structured interviews and thirty-three private and institutional archives to explore the genealogies of political thought in late colonial Uganda. In doing so, it proposes three contributions to the historiography of eastern Africa. First, it shows the degree to which competing activists interwove literacy with precolonial regional histories to imagine dissenting visions of society and kingship in postwar Buganda. Whereas previous studies of colonial literacy in Africa have tended to focus on either 'sacred' or 'secular' literary practices, this volume argues that Ganda activists reworked their texts in ways that significantly blurred European religious and political epistemologies. Second, this book investigates how Buganda's colonial intellectuals used their texts and pasts differently to imagine alternative political futures during the concluding years of formal empire. In ways that have been glossed over in Buganda's nationalist historiography

---

[1] Karl Marx, 'The Eighteenth Brumaire of Louis Bonaparte', in *Marx: Later Political Writings*, ed. by Terrell Carver (Cambridge: Cambridge University Press, 1996), pp. 31–127 (p. 32).

and much of Uganda's postcolonial commentary, I argue that multiple political and historical narratives circulated throughout colonial Buganda. There did not exist one particular way of conceptualising or talking about power or social belonging in mid-twentieth-century southern Uganda. As opposed to explaining the end of empire in terms of centralised resistance following the First and Second World Wars, which has preoccupied previous studies, this work suggests that the end of empire was precipitated by political outcomes shaped by historiographical and ideational pluralism. In colonial Buganda, there did not exist a single historical vision around which the state's colonial order could be sustained over time. Finally, as opposed to seeing Buganda's colonial intellectuals as belonging strictly to a class of missionary-educated elites, as previous works on African intellectuals have suggested, this book argues that activists throughout the late colonial period laboured extensively to present themselves as able mediators of distant political pasts. Buganda's colonial intellectuals were fundamentally political historians, innovators who spliced regional historiographies with new types of source material to recast older ways of thinking about mobility, solidarity and power.

As previously unexplored private archives were unearthed during the course of my research, they began to highlight the prominence of political pluralism in colonial Buganda and the extent to which the classifications used in previous studies on colonial literacy needed to be reworked. After living in eastern Africa for two years, I began my doctoral research in Uganda in 2009. Building upon archival work that had been conducted in the United Kingdom during the previous year, I now returned with a list of approximately one hundred activists who had significantly shaped the processes of decolonisation in Buganda. The list included women and men, nationalists and patriots, and politicians committed to different religious traditions: spirit priests, Muslims, Protestants, Catholics and revivalists. In addition to cultivating meaningful relationships with these former activists and their surviving families, it was my hope to identify private collections that could offer intimate insight into Buganda's shifting intellectual landscapes throughout the postwar period.

One of the key activists whom I was interested to learn more about was the Catholic intellectual Benedicto Kiwanuka, Uganda's first elected prime minister. Like many other politicians during the period, Kiwanuka struggled to successfully navigate Uganda's tumultuous postcolonial politics. In the late 1950s he was one of the few Ganda intellectuals who openly argued that Buganda should be fully incorporated into a centrally governed state, whereas many Baganda advocated for Buganda's special status or the kingdom's secession from Uganda. As Uganda's chief justice in the early 1970s, he publicly challenged Idi Amin's government. In retaliation, military operatives assassinated him in late 1972. But in Uganda's Protestant historiography, which has informed much of the existing academic literature on colonial Buganda, very little had been written about Kiwanuka's political and historical imagination. From what vernacular historiographies did Kiwanuka draw to articulate his liberal vision? As a barrister who had studied law in London, to what extent did he adapt European legal theory to contest Buganda's monarchy? As a devout Catholic, how did he rework the Bible and Church traditions to complicate claims that were being circulated by Protestant and Muslim intellectuals? To address these types of questions it was necessary to identify sources that were not readily available in institutional archives.

From interviews that I conducted in Uganda with elderly members of Kiwanuka's political party, the Democratic Party, it appeared that Kiwanuka's private papers had been destroyed after his assassination. After all, many of Uganda's high-profile activists burned or submerged their records during the 1970s and 1980s to protect themselves and their families.[2] In time, though, I eventually got in touch with Prime Minister Kiwanuka's son, Ambassador Maurice Kiwanuka, to ascertain if in fact the papers actually existed. Following extensive conversations, I learned that after Kiwanuka was murdered most of his private records, including volumes from his personal library, were hidden and placed under lock and key. After a series of discussions, I was directed to a medical dispensary in the outskirts of Kampala where the collection was stored. As I soon discovered, Kiwanuka's tin-trunk archive included approximately 4,905 pages of material that was organised into eighty-three folders. It also contained over 900 pages of loose manuscripts, including course notebooks from Kiwanuka's studies in London in the early 1950s.

---

[2] One anonymous interlocutor whom I interviewed, who had been a prominent member of Buganda's parliament in the 1960s, recalled burning hundreds of files just outside of his home to protect himself and his family during the Luwero conflict.

The collection provides extensive insight into Kiwanuka's political thought. Through letters, diary entries, government correspondence, party reports and annotated newspapers and books, I was able to begin to understand the inner workings of Kiwanuka's public activism and historical vision. What I was particularly interested to find was the extent to which Kiwanuka wove Europe's classical liberal histories with Catholic theology to recast Buganda's vernacular historiographies. Kiwanuka's papers and annotated library show that he moved comfortably between historical sources that have often been compartmentalised in European intellectual history and much of the writing on colonial literacy in Africa, a point to which I will return below. By way of introduction, though, I wish first to present two case studies that illustrate Kiwanuka's coterminous use of European political history and Catholic writings.

The king of Buganda was exiled for two years in London in the mid-1950s, which I explore more fully in Chapter 3. The exile of *Kabaka* Muteesa II was Uganda's anti-colonial crisis. It precipitated the formation of numerous political parties and defined the constitutional terms under which Uganda secured her independence in the early 1960s. During this momentous occasion, Kiwanuka was critically studying constitutional history as a law student in London. His remaining study notebooks from 1952 to 1953 illuminate the content from which he drew to reflect on Buganda's uncertain monarchy.

Kiwanuka studied contractual, Roman and constitutional law during his course work.[3] Notes from his course on constitutional law show that Kiwanuka was actively thinking in the mid-1950s about 'the nature of federalism',[4] 'supremacy of the Constitution',[5] 'right of personal freedom'[6] and the 'Relation Between Parliamentary Sovereignty and the Rule of Law'.[7] Kiwanuka's textbook annotations focused particularly on the history of the constitutionalisation of European monarchies and the creation of nation-states in the late 1700s. Kiwanuka's underlined sections show that he studied the historian Frederic Swann's

---

[3] BKMKP [Course Notes]: 'Law of Contract', 9 October 1952–12 May 1953; 'Roman Law', 27 February 1953–c. 3 May 1953; 'Constitutional Law', 14 October 1952–12 May 1953.

[4] BKMKP [Course Notes] 'Constitutional Law', np.

[5] Ibid., np.

[6] Ibid., np.

[7] Ibid., np.

1923 discussion on 'Limited Monarchy'.[8] The underlined sections are Kiwanuka's:

The King knows no party. The King is nowadays raised quite above party strife. He is neither Whig nor Tory, Liberal nor Conservative. It was not always thus. But during and since Queen Victoria's long reign, our Sovereigns have, with great wisdom, shown no bias to the one side or the other in politics, and it is now an accepted rule that the Crown must not be drawn into the arena of political warfare. This impartial attitude of the Ruling Monarch enables all of us, whatever our particular shade of political opinion, to bury our differences, and unite in loyal adherence to the Throne.[9]

For reasons that are more fully explored below and throughout this book, the authority of Buganda's colonial monarchy was tied to Protestant control of the state. And Swann's summary presented Kiwanuka with political alternatives, the possibility of recreating a kingdom, previously divided along denominational fault lines, 'above party strife'.

The timbre of Kiwanuka's annotations translated easily into public discourse. His papers show that in May 1953 he addressed an audience of Baganda in London. The speech was delivered at a party to celebrate the graduation of the Protestant Joseph Luyambazi-Zake, who was graduating from law school. Luyambazi-Zake was a member of a prominent Protestant family and in the mid-1950s he served as a representative on the Namirembe Conference, which was tasked with redrafting Buganda's constitution (Chapter 3). During the speech, Kiwanuka argued that it had been problematic to develop political communities in Buganda according to religious devotion and bias, especially for non-Protestants: '[In the past] it has been the custom of us Baganda to see that we dissociate [. . .] from those other people who do not belong to our religion. [. . .]'[10] Kiwanuka proceeded to analyse the religious history of Buganda. Christian missionaries taught Baganda, he argued, to create political authority according to religious traditions. In the colonial state, religious devotion problematically predetermined political mobility and social interaction. Kiwanuka

---

[8] BKMKP Library Frederic Swann, *English Citizenship* (London: Longmans, Green and Co., 1923).
[9] Ibid., p. 3.
[10] BKMKP [Course Notes] 'Roman Law', np, [c. May 1953]. Kiwanuka's speech was drafted between two lectures delivered in May in his course notebook.

referenced an allegedly idyllic time before Christianity and Islam dominated kingdom politics: 'It is high time that we who are called grandsons of that mythical man known as Kintu [the first king of Buganda] joined our ranks and worked together as real brothers.'

By conjuring Kintu, Kiwanuka was in fact adapting his coursework in classical liberalism. In the eighteenth century, European intellectuals worked to reconstitute divine rights and monarchical authority; universal rights and republican conceptions of democracy were common alternatives. For Kiwanuka, political authority in Buganda needed to be divorced from the Church of Uganda, in ways that he noted from Swann and others. And now, to an audience comprised of children whose fathers and grandfathers had created the Protestant state that he was now assessing, citing Kintu was the most straightforward way to begin to pull away the layers of Buganda's partisan colonial history and to reimagine political solidarities. 'If we work apart we shall be doomed to failure as a nation,' Kiwanuka concluded, 'but together we shall surmount all obstacles.' Swann's political history and the story of Kintu were used to remember a time when authority in the state was not tied to Protestant confession.

Two months after addressing Luyambazi-Zake's guests, Kiwanuka began to read what would become one of the most annotated books from his studies in London: Richard Crossman's *Government and the Governed: A History of Political Ideas and Political Practice*. Kiwanuka's annotations show that he had become familiar with European political thought prior to returning to Uganda in the mid-1950s. He was especially interested in the writings of John Locke and Jean-Jacques Rousseau. Kiwanuka reflected on Locke's *Two Treatises of Government*, in which Locke argued that 'rulers should be sometimes liable to be opposed when they grow exorbitant in the use of their power, and employ it for the destruction, and not the preservation, of the properties of their people.'[11] Drawing from Crossman, Kiwanuka noted that 'Locke abolishes sovereignty and replaces it with a division of powers between the legislature and the executive (i.e., the new constitutional monarch)'.[12]

Whereas with Locke Kiwanuka observed the language of the division of monarchical and state power and the protection of rights and

[11] Ibid., p. 71, underscore.
[12] Ibid., p. 74, underscore.

liberty, 'a safeguard for rational man against the wilfulness of princes',[13] with Rousseau he scrutinised the themes of social equality and contractual power: General Will and Social Contract. That Rousseau 'reacted [. . .] violently as he did to the tyranny of absolute monarchy' was 'VIP' for Kiwanuka.[14] He underscored Rousseau's argument 'that bourgeois civilization would destroy the social organism and atomize society into a collection of propertied individuals',[15] much as it had in Buganda after the invention of private land (*mailo*) in 1900. With Uganda in mind, Kiwanuka annotated: '[Rousseau] was right!'[16] Crossman suggested that Rousseau imagined 'the restoration of a primitive natural community which is bound together by its moral sentiments, and whose law is the expression of those moral sentiments and of a new common will', which Kiwanuka noted was also 'VIP'.[17] A preferable society, 'the Will of the Community as a whole', highlighted Kiwanuka, is one 'in which every individual takes part [. . .]'.[18] For Rousseau and Kiwanuka the creation of equitable societies required the recovery of pristine pasts, periods that exhibited 'beautiful primitive qualities' before becoming 'contorted and defiled by the imposition of civilization'.[19] Kiwanuka drew from Rousseau to conceptualise a liberal kingdom, a state within which communities were not unsettled by religious – namely, Protestant – politics (Figure I.1).

Kiwanuka, though, did not only adapt Europe's constitutional canon to rethink Buganda's Protestant hierarchy. Following his return to Uganda, he became the president of the Democratic Party (DP), Uganda's foremost Catholic movement. In late 1959, Kiwanuka turned to Catholic tradition to develop the material culture of the party. In July, Kiwanuka began conceptualising the logo of the DP in conversation with the Verona missionary Father Tarcisio Agostoni, whose mission was based in Gulu. The two wished to develop a symbol based upon the cruciform monstrance (Figure I.2), an image located in

---

[13] Ibid., p. 71, underscore.
[14] Ibid., p. 111, annotation. The full range of Kiwanuka's marginalia indicates that he used the abbreviation VIP to signify a Very Important Point, and not only a Very Important Person.
[15] Ibid., p. 115, underscore.
[16] Ibid., p. 115, annotation.
[17] Ibid., p. 113, annotation.
[18] Ibid., p. 114, underscore.
[19] Ibid., p. 112, underscore.

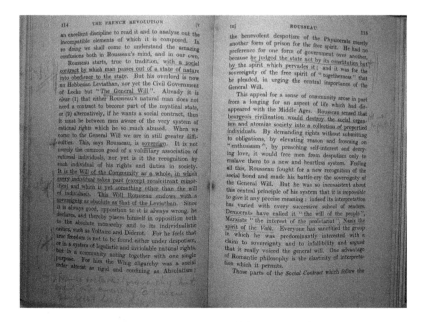

Figure I.1 H.S. Crossman, *Government and the Governed: A History of Political Ideas and Political Practice* (London: Christophers, 1952), annotated 2 July 1953, pp. 114–15

Annotations 1–2: 'VIP'

Annotation 3: 'France overthrew monarchy but went into anarchy because new bourgeois leadership.'

Annotation 4: 'He was right!'

Source: BKMKP Library

the Catholic missal. The artistic representation structured time and the natural world around Jesus Christ, 'the Sun of Justice'. The 'Sun of Justice' conveyed a particular order: the Gregorian and Catholic calendars, days, hemispheres, equinoxes and solstices. On 8 July 1959, Kiwanuka received a letter from Father Agostoni, who reflected on the Party's emblem. The Verona missionary hoped to recreate 'the Sun with the rays all over Uganda with the initial of Truth & Justice [. . .]',[20] which he suggested represented *amazima n'obwenkanya* (truth and justice). Truth, it was noted, 'is the light of the intellect to

---

[20] BKMKP CM/32 Tarcisio Agostoni to Benedicto Kiwanuka, 8 July 1959.

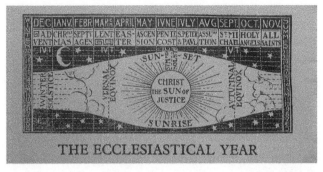

THE ECCLESIASTICAL YEAR

Figure I.2 *Saint Andrew Daily Missal* (Bruges: Liturgical Apostolate Abbey of St-André, 1957), p. x
Source: BKMKP Library

give one truth, [. . .] to enlighten one's mind'. Kiwanuka had disclosed to Agostoni earlier that he had hoped to market DP as 'light' and to portray opposing political parties 'as darkness'. 'What is best', replied Agostoni, 'than the sun's symbol'. The Sun signified political justice and implied that 'the sun is equal for all: it rises for all and sets down for all'. It reminded Ugandans that 'the Father in heaven loves all men indistinctly', that 'God let the sun to rise over the good and over the sinner in the same time without distinction [. . .]'. Without the Sun, 'there is no life, not heat, no crops, no rain no light on earth [. . .]'. In turn, 'the D.P. will be the life for the country, the heat (the love); will provide for economics and for industry; is the one to awaken people from the sleep and to open their eyes as the sun in the morning [*sic*]'.

The letter reminded Kiwanuka of the Party's divine mandate and its relationship to natural and moral genesis: Sun, light, redemption and development. Just as God demonstrated his love and purposes through the created world and the Church, it was asserted, Kiwanuka would administer political order in Uganda through the Democratic Party. The parallels were powerful, and during the following month, at the Party's Annual General Meeting, Kiwanuka translated the content of his and Agostoni's correspondence onto the front page of the conference programme. Kiwanuka noted that the 'Democratic Party is for Justice and Truth for the African People. D.P. is the Sun of the Country. D.P. is the Light of Uganda. D.P. is the Mother of Civilization. D.P. is the Backbone of Government of the Future of Uganda'. And

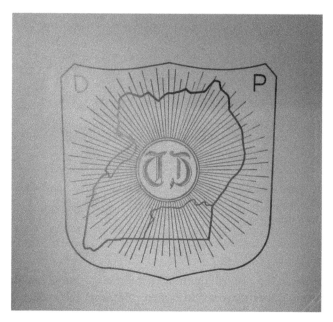

Figure I.3 DP Emblem, 1959
Source: BKMKP Sundry Corresp. + Lukiiko Matters

just as Christ's monstrance (presence) and the Sun's light provided life indiscriminately, 'D.P. is Just for All; D.P. is Good for All; D.P. is Fair to All'.[21] The Party's official emblem incorporated the missal's monstrance (star cluster) (Figure I.3). Two large letters replaced 'Christ the Sun of Justice', 'TJ', the abbreviation for truth and justice, which generously blanketed Uganda. In the opposing corners, the letters 'D' and 'P' were positioned.

Kiwanuka's movement between classical liberalism and Catholic theology problematises much of the existing literature on colonial literacy in Africa, which has largely followed the modernist distinction between 'sacred' and 'secular' classifications of knowledge production. Whereas academic approaches have tended to place 'religious' and 'political' texts and ideologies into separate spheres, Uganda's late

---

[21] BKMKP Sundry Corresp. + Lukiiko Matters 'Democratic Party Annual General Meeting: Programme', 7–9 August 1959.

colonial intellectuals read and reworked multiple genres of literature in ways that were largely disconnected from the intellectual historiographies of Europe. And while it is hard to imagine that Kiwanuka used Rousseau to organise his prayer life, the fluidity of these epistemological boundaries in political argumentation necessitates the revision of current models of interpretation. I will now outline the two approaches that have been characteristic of previous studies, and propose a convergent methodology.

Reconceptualising the 'Sacred' and 'Secular' in African Colonial Literacy

The history of biblical and religious literature in Africa constitutes a robust field of study. The historian Paul Landau first challenged historians of southern Africa to take seriously how Tswana Christians used their bibles to refigure power in early colonial Bechuanaland,[22] which redirected Jean and John Comaroff's preoccupation with European missionaries.[23] Since his important study, scholars have continued to explore how Christians throughout sub-Saharan Africa used the Bible to reconstitute authority in the twentieth century. Adrian Hastings argued that the 'Bible provided, for the Christian world at least, the original model of the nation', and suggested that without the Bible 'and its Christian interpretation and implementation, it is arguable that nations and nationalisms, as we know them – including Africa – could never have existed'.[24] Similar to Hastings, J.D.Y. Peel suggested that Bible translation played a crucial part in the creation of Yoruba national identity. More than their European counterparts could have imagined, argued Peel, African agents defined themselves principally in the language of biblical narration.[25] And in her important new work on

---

[22] Paul S. Landau, *The Realm of the Word: Language, Gender and Christianity in a Southern African Kingdom* (Portsmouth, NH: Heinemann Educational Publishers, 1995), pp. xvii–xix.

[23] Jean and John Comaroff, *Of Revelation and Revolution: Christianity, Colonialism, and Consciousness in South Africa*, 2 vols (Chicago: University of Chicago Press, 1991), I.

[24] Adrian Hastings, *The Construction of Nationhood: Ethnicity, Religion and Nationalism* (Cambridge: Cambridge University Press, 1997), p. 4.

[25] J.D.Y. Peel, *Religious Encounter and the Making of the Yoruba* (Bloomington, IN: Indiana University Press, 2003), p. 155.

textual practices in southern Africa, Joel Cabrita argues that 'reading, writing, and performing sacred texts enabled Nazaretha believers to claim spiritual and social authority, both within the church and more broadly within twentieth-century and present-day South Africa'.[26]

A separate body of literature, by contrast, following Paul Gilroy's seminal book in the early 1990s, has worked to identify discursive continuities across the Black Atlantic.[27] These studies have often reinforced important international political connections. In his work on Nigeria's colonial intellectual history, Philip Zachernuk shows how Nigeria's colonial elites conversed with Africans and the African diaspora in North America, the West Indies and London, the latter of which was the centre of activity for the Trinidadian Henry Sylvester Williams, who founded the African Association in Great Britain in 1897.[28] Whereas previous studies had problematically cast African intellectuals in an ongoing struggle between tradition and modernity, judging the 'intelligentsia either for converting or for failing to convert effectively from the African to the Western [. . .]',[29] Zachernuk persuasively argues that the intellectual lives of western Africans were far more sophisticated and integrative. Throughout the colonial period, 'the Nigerian intelligentsia exploited, selected, and adapted British and African American ideas about Africa as they attempted to work within accepted bounds of thought to construct their own worldview'.[30] Other important works have followed Zachernuk's study.[31]

While both of these currents of scholarship offer indispensable insights into Africa's intellectual histories, they have mostly followed the modernist biases of the social sciences,[32] maintaining the

---

[26] Joel Cabrita, *Text and Authority in the South African Nazaretha Church* (Cambridge: Cambridge University Press), p. 1.

[27] Paul Gilroy, *The Black Atlantic: Modernity and Double-Consciousness* (Harvard University Press, 1993).

[28] Philip S. Zachernuk, *Colonial Subjects: An African Intelligentsia and Atlantic Ideas* (Charlottesville, VA: University Press of Virginia, 2000), pp. 62–7.

[29] Ibid., p. 5.

[30] Ibid., pp. 15–16.

[31] Robert Trent Vinson, *The Americans are Coming!: Dreams of African American Liberation in Segregationist South Africa* (Athens: Ohio University Press, 2012); Ethan R. Sanders, 'The African Association and the Growth and Movement of Politics in Mid-Twentieth Century East Africa' (unpublished PhD thesis, University of Cambridge, 2012).

[32] John Milbank, *Theology and Social Theory: Beyond Secular Reason* (Oxford: Blackwell Publishers, 1990).

epistemological and textual boundaries of ostensibly sacred or secular categories.[33] Whereas the first body of scholarship has surprisingly little to say about the adaptation of secular literature, the second overlooks the force of theological production. While this distinction has been problematised in separate studies,[34] it has not been fully reworked in the scholarship on colonial literacy in Africa. We know, moreover, surprisingly little about how colonial intellectuals reworked the canons of European liberalism into local, vernacular political debates.[35]

This book shows that political thinkers in 1950s southern Uganda, such as Kiwanuka, utilised colonial literacy in ways that have not been fully synthesised by historians of Africa. In twentieth-century Buganda, the textual and epistemological boundaries between supposedly 'sacred' and 'secular' ideologies and types of literature were anything but rigid. Colonial and transnational knowledge was especially malleable and private archives show that local activists drew just as comfortably from their prayer books as they did from Jean-Jacques Rousseau. This challenges historians and social scientists to begin to rethink the intersection of colonial knowledge production and reading practices, until now laden with arbitrary distinctions between supposedly separate forms of religious and secular analytic classifications. The integration of these two respective approaches offers new possibilities for understanding the intellectual histories of late colonial eastern Africa and, as I will now show, novel ways of pluralising the history of nationalism in eastern Africa.

'Let me begin by speaking of the past': The Historiographies of Political Change in Colonial Buganda

Monarchical political historiography provided a powerful resource for debating Buganda's colonial order. Prior to the late 1800s, Buganda

---

[33] Daniel Magaziner's book is the exception: Daniel Magaziner, *The Law and the Prophets: Black Consciousness in South Africa, 1968–1977* (Athens: Ohio University Press, 2010).

[34] Stephen Ellis and Gerrie ter Haar, *Worlds of Power: Religious Thought and Political Practice in Africa* (London: Hurst & Company, 2004).

[35] I have in mind Christopher Bayly's work on the history of liberalism in India as a useful, comparative framework: 'Rammohan Roy and the Advent of Constitutional Liberalism in India, 1800–30', *Modern Intellectual History*, 4 (2007), 25–41.

had become a highly sophisticated state, a process that has been richly explored elsewhere.[36] Over a period of 300 years, Ganda statebuilders worked with military chiefs, priests and clan heads to expand the territorial sovereignty of Buganda. From the mid-1840s to the early 1890s, the practice of state power in Buganda was tied to the widening influence of Islam in the royal court, which was first mediated through the guidance of Omani traders from Zanzibar (Chapter 4). Through the adaptation of coastal material culture, the construction of mosques and the state-sanctioned distribution of qur'ans, Buganda's Muslim kings strove to centralise power during a period of expanding long-distance trade throughout eastern Africa.[37] How communities later remembered this period was central to the legitimisation of Christian authority in colonial Buganda.

The arrival of Christian missionaries in the 1870s undermined allegiances in Buganda's Muslim state, where superior weaponry enabled Ganda Christians to reorganise political power. To undermine the integrity of Islamic politics, Christian chiefs in the early 1900s used the Bible to create new types of political language, religious lexicography with which Muslim specialists were not familiar. The production of new types of religious knowledge reinforced the regulation of labour and resources in a Protestant protectorate.

Following the decline of Muslim power throughout the late 1880s and early 1890s, Buganda's colonial state was restructured around the charisma of towering Protestant personalities, most notably *Katikkiro* Sir Apolo Kaggwa and *Ssekibobo* Hamu Mukasa (Figure I.4). Protestant chiefs used missionary literacy to rewrite Buganda's past and to imagine new forms of political organisation and religious orthodoxy. Protestant power resulted in the social marginalisation

---

[36] The most recent works include Richard J. Reid, *Political Power in Pre-Colonial Buganda: Economy, Society and Welfare in the Nineteenth Century* (Oxford: James Currey, 2002); Holly E. Hanson, *Landed Obligation: The Practice of Power in Buganda* (Portsmouth, NH: Heinemann, 2003); Henri Médard, *Le Royaume du Buganda Au XIXe Siècle: Mutations Politiques et Religieuses D'un Ancien Etat d'Afrique de l'Est* (Paris: Karthala, 2007); Neil Kodesh, *Beyond the Royal Gaze: Clanship and Public Healing in Buganda* (Charlottesville, VA: University of Virginia Press, 2010).

[37] The best study on long-distance trade in eastern Africa and eastern African consumerism is Jeremy Prestholdt, *Domesticating the World: African Consumerism and the Genealogies of Globalization* (Berkeley, CA: University of California Press, 2008).

Figure I.4 Left to right: Hamu Mukasa and Apolo Kaggwa, London, 1902
Source: Courtesy of Hamu Mukasa Family Archive, Mukono, Uganda.
I wish to thank Andrea Stultiens and History in Progress Uganda for provid-
ing a high-resolution copy of this image.

of precolonial priests as well as Catholic and Muslim converts. In
consequence, historical debate and colonial politics in Buganda were
intensely religious in character. Christian chiefs and colonial cartogra-
phers restructured Buganda's precolonial counties according to religious devotion,[38] and chieftaincies and land were distributed according
to religious allegiances (Table I.1).

No historian utilised Arabic and English literacy more effectively
than Apolo Kaggwa, who governed Buganda throughout the regency
of *Kabaka* Daudi Chwa from the late 1800s up until the mid-1920s.

---

[38] BNA MP K122 'Map of Uganda Protectorate Showing Distribution of
Chieftainships among Adherents of Different Religions in the Kingdom of
Uganda' [early 1900s].

Table I.1 *Buganda Land Distributions, c. 1900*

Protestant counties	Area (square miles)	Catholic counties	Area (square miles)
Bugerere	246.0	Buddu	2 604.0
Bulemeezi	1 442.0	Bugangazzi	944.0
Buruli	1 682.0	Busujju	216.0
Busiro	343.0	Buvuma	122.0
Ggomba	702.0	Buwekula	1 024.0
Kabula	262.0	Buyaga	1 028.0
Kooki	736.0	Mawogola	374.0
Kyaddondo	162.0	Mawokota	306.0
Kyaggwe	1 584.0	**Sub-Total**	**6 618.0**
Ssese	264.0	*Per cent*	*40.4%*
Ssingo	2 122.0		
Sub-Total	**9 545.0**	**Muslim County**	
Per cent	*58.2%*	Butambala	230.0
		Sub-Total	**230.0**
		Per cent	*1.4%*
Total			**16 393.0**

UNA SMP 44/255 'Report on the Kingdom of Buganda, 1907–8'.

In the late 1800s, Kaggwa began writing the most influential political history of Buganda in the twentieth century, *Bassekabaka be Buganda, The Deceased Kings of Buganda*. The book would become, argues one historian, the most highly read book in colonial Buganda, besides the Bible.[39] In the 1960s, John Rowe observed that '[m]any Baganda who have no other book, cling tenaciously to their battered copy of *Basekabaka* [. . .]'.[40] Kaggwa's history was the cornerstone of Protestant historiography in colonial Uganda. In it he presented a past that legitimised military intervention to remove Buganda's Muslim chiefs and kings from power. As Michael Twaddle has shown, 'the imposition of colonial rule is rewritten

[39] John Rowe, 'Myth, Memoir, and Moral Admonition: *Luganda* Historical Writing, 1893–1969', *Uganda Journal*, 33 (1969), 17–40, 217–19 (pp. 21–2).
[40] Ibid., p. 21.

in *Basekabaka*, not only to heighten the importance of the military contributions of Kaggwa and his associates, but to Christianize retrospectively the whole anti-Muslim campaign as a kind of holy crusade'.[41] Kaggwa's chronicle inspired colonial policy and, as I show throughout the following chapters, cast a certain historical vision that dissenting Baganda were challenged to refocus throughout decolonisation.

In many ways, though, the writings of Hamu Mukasa were more comprehensive than Kaggwa's and more important in reinforcing Protestant control of the state (Chapter 2). For the county chief of Kyaggwe, who traced his lineage through one of Buganda's earliest clans, *Enjovu* (Elephant), the language of political progress (*-kukulaakulana*) offered one way of talking about social stability following cyclical violence in the late nineteenth century.[42] By the late 1890s, argued Mukasa to a largely European readership following the Second World War, the *kabaka* 'was no different than Hitler'.[43] The kingdom was frequently at war and Buganda's monarchs were known as *'Nnabeffululabiswa'*, red ants that emptied out termite hills. Mukasa used proverbial nomenclature to demonstrate that citizens in Buganda and rulers throughout eastern Africa were often forced to surrender to the arbitrary will of Buganda's precolonial conquering kings – a pattern that had to be stopped.[44] The burden ostensibly fell to Buganda's late-nineteenth century Christian chiefs.

The standardisation of the history of nineteenth-century violence was tied to the reconfiguration of colonial power. In April 1917, Baganda living in Nairobi published a letter to Mukasa in *Ebifa mu Buganda*, the organ of the Church of Uganda. The letter was written to critique Uganda's colonial courts and the development of colonial customs (*obulombolombo*) following Buganda's religious wars in the 1890s.[45] 'The leadership of the regents seventeen years ago resulted

---

[41] Michael Twaddle, 'On Ganda Historiography', *History in Africa*, 1 (1974), 85–100 (p. 87). See also John Rowe, 'Eyewitness Accounts of Buganda History: The Memoirs of Ham Mukasa and His Generation', *Ethnohistory*, 36 (1989), 61–71.

[42] In Luganda and Lugisu, songs of war often described the cyclical character of violence. Examples include *Emmuli Emmuli* and *Orugaamba*.

[43] Ham Mukasa, 'The Rule of the Kings of Buganda', *Uganda Journal*, 10 (1946), 136–43 (p. 136).

[44] Ibid., p. 137.

[45] *Abaganda abe Nairobi*, '*Ebaluwa eyava mu Baganda abali eNairobi*', *Ebifa mu Buganda*, 123 (1917), 80.

in peace,' argued the diaspora, 'but their leadership is now bad.'[46] For Mukasa, by contrast, the restructuring of Buganda's kingdom around its Protestant chiefs was necessary to establish long-term political stability in the state. Similarly, Apolo Kaggwa, early in his premiership, wrote that British and Ganda collaboration resulted in political security. To one colonial official, Kaggwa wrote: 'Nowadays in our country all is peace and quiet. We are at rest, there are no disturbances and bad events and all the important Europeans who work here in Buganda are very good, we have made friends with them and get along with them.'[47]

It is not without reason, then, that the capital of Anglicanism in Buganda was called *Namirembe*, the place of peace. The archaeology of colonial power was enshrined in the public architecture of Protestantism. In Luganda, the etymology of *Namirembe* was politically instructive. Its meaning derived from –*mulembe*, and simply referred to a 'period; era; epoch; century'.[48] In the form of a proverb it was used to suggest that 'things come and go' (*emirembe ngalo*), literally, 'generations are fingers'. And to introduce his three-volume history, *Simuda Nyuma* (Do not turn back; move forward), Mukasa began the first volume by using the language of *emirembe ngalo*:

Thus you, each who reads this book listen to our Luganda proverb, which says 'The generations (of the) fingers', the meaning of that proverb being this, that each generation [*mulembe*] which comes, in turn exceeds (the former) in wisdom because it progresses (a step forward) [as fingers increase in length on the hand]. So you, Muganda, do you not know that the people who were born in the reign of Suna surpassed those born under Kamanya? And that those born under Mukabya [Muteesa I] surpassed in wisdom the ones born under Suna? Let me start by speaking of the past where first we were in our ignorance, where we were passing by good things, whereas now we pass by bad things on account of (our) progress.[49]

---

[46] '*Okufuga okweda okwa Baregenti nga bakyafuga, ensi yali mirembe mu myaka egiise nga 17, naye kakano bafuga bubi.*'

[47] Apolo Kaggwa to Captain Frederick Lugard, 4 July 1896, in *The Mind of Buganda: Documents of the Modern History of an African Kingdom*, ed. by D.A. Low (London: Heinemann Educational, 1971), p. 31.

[48] John D. Murphy, *Luganda-English Dictionary* (Washington, DC: Catholic University of America Press, 1972), p. 367.

[49] LFP 54/7/1–2 Handwritten English translation: Ham Mukasa, *Simuda Nyuma: Ebiro bya Mutesa* (London: Society for the Promotion of Christian Knowledge, 1938).

Figure I.5 Hamu Mukasa, Mukono, Kyaggwe, c. 1920s
Source: Courtesy of Hamu Mukasa Family Archive, Mukono, Uganda.
I wish to thank Andrea Stultiens and History in Progress Uganda for providing a high-resolution copy of this image.

Mukasa used his history to give moral order to Uganda's colonial project. Kings come and go; one regiment of power replaces another. Political peace was made possible by Whigish progress. To his diasporic critics, Mukasa argued that Buganda's newfound leadership resulted in peace and honour in the kingdom (*gyemirembe nekitibwa*), and that Buganda's colonial king was honourable on account of his trustworthy assistants (*Kabaka wafe kyava abera nekitibwa ekirungi ekiriko ababezi abesigwa*).[50] The politics of the 1800s had been uncertain, he continued, a time when kings subjected chiefs and commoners to unnecessary labour and force.[51] In consequence, Mukasa concluded, it

[50] Ham Mukasa, *Ebyokunyonyola ebaluwa ya Baganda abali eNairobi, Ebifa mu Buganda*, 124 (1917), 87–92 (pp. 89–90).
[51] Ham Mukasa, 'The Life of Ham Mukasa', in *The Wonderful Story of Uganda*, trans. by Ven Archdeacon Walker (London: Church Missionary Society, 1904), pp. 173–208 (p. 187).

was necessary for Christian chiefs to '[divide] out the country amongst ourselves, and we took the chieftainships' (Figure I.5).[52]

There were, however, other ways of talking about stability and political inclusion in the colonial state, and dissimilar recollections of the nineteenth century. Mukasa's obsession with political progress did not quell debates surrounding how power and monarchical authority were allegedly created and practised, or how the successions of power and kingship were to be negotiated in the twentieth century. If anything, it exacerbated arguments and the possibility of political alternatives. When colonial officials invested Muteesa II in 1942, they announced the sovereignty of 'the undoubted Kabaka of this country of Buganda'.[53] Colonial investiture liturgy aimed to direct the loyalty of Buganda's subjects toward their young monarch: 'After the Proclamation has been made, the people are to signify their willingness and joy by loud and repeated acclamations, all with one voice crying out: GOD SAVE KABAKA MUTESA.'[54] Colonial rulers – Britons and Protestant Baganda – hoped to guarantee stable successions by creating uncontested monarchs who governed alongside progressive chiefs. Imperial economies required programmatic and predictable power.[55] But the practice of political stability surrounding succession was a myth of colonial powerbrokers and a stark deviation from how power was practised prior to the twentieth century. In Buganda's eighteenth-century kingship, princely rivals assassinated seven out of eight kings.[56] Buganda's late nineteenth-century kingdom was destabilised by a series of succession wars.[57] And as Christopher Wrigley has shown, '[n]one of the *kabakas* whose dates are historically known lived beyond what would now be called early middle age: Muteesa I died at about forty-five, Mwanga II at thirty-seven, Daudi Chwa at

---

[52] Ibid., p. 196. See also Ham Mukasa, 'Makerere College', *Uganda Herald*, 25 July 1945, in *The Mind of Buganda*, pp. 127–31 (p. 130).

[53] MUA KY/2 'Arrangements for the Coming of Age of His Highness the Kabaka Mutesa II', 19–22 November 1942, p. 24.

[54] Ibid.

[55] Eric J. Hobsbawm, *Nations and Nationalism since 1780: Programme, Myth, Reality* (Cambridge: Cambridge University Press, 1990).

[56] Benjamin C. Ray, *Myth, Ritual, and Kingship in Buganda* (Oxford: Oxford University Press, 1991), p. 162.

[57] John M. Gray, 'The Year of the Three Kings of Buganda', *Uganda Journal*, 14 (1949), 15–52.

forty-four [. . .]'.[58] Colonial and Ganda administrators standardised the liturgies of investiture; they could not determine what constituted laudable kingship among rural and urban communities. The imposition of colonial rule could only be pressed so far.

The complexity of Buganda's vernacular historiographies, compounded by the challenge of nation-building following the Second World War, fostered a robust academic historiography. Much of this earlier literature was shaped by Kaggwa's and Mukasa's interpretations of Ganda power. In the 1960s, scholars with the East African Institute of Social Research (EAISR) worked to illuminate 'traditional' patterns of authority in colonial Buganda. The American political scientist David Apter published *The Political Kingdom of Uganda* in 1961, a work from which scholars have continued to draw. During a time when various factions were competing to control Uganda's postcolonial state, Apter suggested that the kingdom of Buganda was a 'modernizing autocracy', a 'secular monarchy geared for adaptation and innovation and built around a central hierarchical system of authority'.[59] During the same period, Lloyd Fallers and Audrey Richards published *The King's Men*, a collaborative work of the EAISR that presented to its audiences a 'neo-traditional kingdom' built around particular substructures and patterns of authority. Drawing from the methodologies of functional anthropology, it was argued that decolonisation in Buganda was driven by social patterns and structures that were applicable to '*[a]ll* Baganda'.[60] According to this approach, the contingencies of local activism were believed to reflect foundational sociological arrangements.

Nearly one decade later, Professor Tony Low produced his influential history, *Buganda in Modern History*. More than his predecessors, Low emphasised sociological diversity within Buganda's kingdom. He argued that anti-colonial nationalism in Buganda reflected broader tensions between monarch (*kabaka*), appointed chiefs (*bakungu*), clan

---

[58] Christopher Wrigley, *Kingship and State: The Buganda Dynasty* (Cambridge: Cambridge University Press, 1996), p. 229.

[59] David E. Apter, *The Political Kingdom in Uganda: A Study of Bureaucratic Nationalism*, 2nd edn (Princeton: Princeton University Press, 1967), pp. 8–9.

[60] Audrey I. Richards, 'Traditional Values and Current Political Behaviour', in *The King's Men: Leadership and Status in Buganda on the Eve of Independence*, ed. by Lloyd A. Fallers (London: Oxford University Press, 1964), pp. 294–335 (p. 314). Emphasis added.

heads (*bataka*) and commoners or peasants (*bakopi*), each of which had competing political and economic interests. But Low's approach was still reductionistic. He argued that the emergence of political parties following the Second World War was driven by largely fixed sociological tensions.[61]

This first generation of nationalist scholars provided important insights into the complexities of Buganda's precolonial and twentieth-century monarchy. Such scholars often lived for several years in eastern Africa with well-trained research assistants, while working alongside key political activists. But this early cohort of pioneering researchers often cast the history of anti-colonial dissent in Buganda according to rigid political phases and static sociological patterns to explain what was believed to be Buganda's inevitable and necessary journey toward democratisation. The histories of nationalism from this period were overtly teleological: they argued that African interlocutors and negotiators were blank slates upon which the likes of Uganda's late colonial governor, Andrew Cohen, reinforced a postcolonial vision instituted by Westminster bureaucrats with little contestation.

By the 1980s, though, African scholarship had become more directly influenced by the linguistic turn, which compelled historians of Buganda to direct their attention toward the importance of political discourse. It was Holly Hanson who first argued that the affective language of love shaped debates over power and good governance from the kingdom's early past into the 1920s. She persuasively writes that in the 'Ganda practice of power, visible expressions of love and affection created relationships of mutual obligation between people with authority and those they ruled'.[62] And more recently, Carol Summers has examined how Ganda generational sensibilities shaped political imagination in the postwar period. 'For Bataka activists [those who self-identified with Buganda's clans]', she writes, 'the politics of grandfathers and grandsons resonated with older Ganda visions of family, moral responsibility, and good behaviour.'[63] Summers concludes that an emerging generation of dissenting politicians in the 1940s

---

[61] D.A. Low, *Buganda in Modern History* (Berkeley, CA: University of California Press, 1971).

[62] Hanson, *Landed Obligation*, p. 3.

[63] Carol Summers, 'Grandfathers, Grandsons, Morality, and Radical Politics in Late Colonial Buganda', *The International Journal of African Historical Studies*, 38 (2005), 427–47 (p. 428).

demonstrated an intentional rudeness that evoked the language of social ritual 'tied to an effort to build new sorts of public sociability to replace the older elite private networks'.[64] According to this approach, the language of 'youth' provided political organisers with rhetorical capital to articulate new visions of social order in late colonial Buganda.

The scholarship of Hanson and Summers provides powerful insights into Buganda's late nineteenth and mid-twentieth century past. Indeed, my understanding of Buganda's modern history has been enriched by the innovative work of these scholars. But these analyses have often underscored a particular discourse that is then used to explain how politics and opposition supposedly functioned throughout the kingdom as a whole. I argue that the intellectual history of colonial Buganda was far more complicated. There did not exist one particular narrative around which Baganda organised or talked about power – such as love (Hanson) or generational discourse (Summers). I wish to open the creative possibilities with which Ganda intellectuals in the colonial period addressed the most important political questions of the day. *Buganda*, and the kingdom's place in Uganda and international politics, looked very differently for individual activists throughout the colonial period. This book proposes an expansive framework for exploring the intellectual histories of southern Uganda. To do this, I use a collection of intellectual biographies to show the extent to which Buganda constituted an ideational kingdom: a polemical arena characterised by ambiguity and plurality. Baganda in the 1950s advocated for considerably different types of modernity, kingship, nationalism and political belonging. To do so, they revised dissimilar regional histories by reworking conflicting religious traditions and global intellectual histories that were cultivated through textual engagement and international experiences.

Historical Pluralism and the End of Empire

My approach in this book – that late colonial Buganda constituted an ideational kingdom – builds upon the earlier work of John Lonsdale. It was John Lonsdale who first showed the extent to which late colonial politics in central Kenya were propelled by changing moral arenas of

---

[64] Carol Summers, 'Radical Rudeness: Ugandan Social Critiques in the 1940s', *Journal of Social History*, 39 (2006), 741–70 (p. 741).

political debate.[65] Kikuyu nationalism, he suggests, like other nationalisms throughout late colonial Africa, reflected a broader contest of moral knowledge shaped by debates concerning wealth, poverty and civic virtue.[66] In colonial Buganda, similarly, I argue, communities developed competing conceptions and articulations of power, good governance and the past – and in ways that were often at odds.[67] Communities in Buganda's northern frontier, for instance, in places such as Bulemeezi (Chapter 1), had a different relationship to the kingdom's capital and Buganda's territorial neighbours than activists in Kooki, a tributary kingdom whose rulers continued to negotiate regional power between western and central Uganda into the 1900s (Chapter 2). Chiefs in the eastern county of Kyaggwe, by contrast, were challenged to navigate political topographies with their Basoga, Bagisu and Iteso neighbours in ways that communities in the western county of Buddu did not.[68] In turn, activists developed different ways of talking about the expectations of kingship and laudable monarchs. Throughout the nineteenth century, as Neil Kodesh has shown, these differences were expressed in competing regional histories, varying histories of clanship and dissimilar proverbs and songs.[69] As Richard Reid's work has also demonstrated, Buganda's nineteenth-century capital found itself constantly under pressure from competing, regionally specific political and economic centres throughout central Uganda.[70] In the colonial period, literacy provided a powerful resource for

[65] John Lonsdale, 'The Moral Economy of Mau Mau: The Problem', in *Unhappy Valley: Conflict in Kenya and Africa*, ed. by Bruce Berman and John Lonsdale (London: James Currey, 1992), pp. 265–314 (p. 267).

[66] John Lonsdale, 'The Moral Economy of Mau Mau: Wealth, Poverty and Civic Virtue in Kikuyu Political Thought', in *Unhappy Valley: Conflict in Kenya and Africa*, ed. by Bruce Berman and John Lonsdale (London: James Currey, 1992), pp. 315–504. See also John Lonsdale, 'Moral Ethnicity and Political Tribalism', in *Inventions and Boundaries: Historical and Anthropological Approaches to the Study of Ethnicity and Nationalism*, ed. by Preben Kaarsholm and Jan Hultin (Roskilde: International Development Studies, Roskilde University, 1994), pp. 131–50.

[67] The best study on Buganda's peripheral politics is Aidan Stonehouse, 'Peripheral Identities in an African State: A History of Ethnicity in the Kingdom of Buganda Since 1884' (unpublished PhD, University of Leeds, 2012).

[68] HML Hamu Mukasa, *Journey to Bukedi by Saza Chiefs*, 15 December 1917–18 January 1918.

[69] Kodesh, *Beyond the Royal Gaze*.

[70] Reid, *Political Power in Pre-Colonial Buganda*.

competing activists from these different regions to work toward standardising precolonial, provincial historiographies and the mythologies of clanship and kingship. Surrounding and following Uganda's independence, the complexity of these opposing claims only intensified.

The extent to which historical pluralism shaped the politics of colonial Buganda raises larger questions about the end of colonial empires. It also suggests more sophisticated ways of thinking about the place of intellectuals in Africa's colonial historiography. I will now address the first area, before turning to the second in the following section.

Over the past fifty years, scholars have offered a number of ways of thinking about the social, international and economic forces that culminated in the proliferation of anti-colonial nationalisms throughout Asia, Africa and the Atlantic world.[71] Following Elie Kedourie's work on European political philosophy,[72] it was Ernest Gellner who argued that the concept of nationalism was a distinctive product of modernity and industrial capitalism.[73] For Gellner, colonial Africa was predominantly governed by white, industrial administrations that governed within well-defined political units that wished to control large labour populations.[74] In time, he argued, anti-colonial nationalism was the result of 'summation' politics: the convergence of aggrieved communities brought about by the centralising and marginalising impact of industrialisation.[75]

If for Gellner nationalism was largely the outcome of the imposition of modernity upon local communities, it was Eric Hobsbawm, following E.P. Thompson's powerful social history of the English working class,[76] who aimed to rethink the history of nationalism by giving 'adequate attention to the view from below'.[77] By the 1950s, argued Hobsbawm, communities throughout Asia and Africa employed the

---

[71] A helpful review of this literature is Norman Etherington, *Theories of Imperialism: War, Conquest and Capital* (London, Croom Helm, 1984).

[72] Elie Kedourie, *Nationalism* (London: Hutchinson, 1960).

[73] This analysis draws from John Breuilly's (Breuilly, John, 'Introduction', in *Ernest Gellner, Nations and Nationalism*, 2nd edn (Ithaca: Cornell University Press, 2008), pp. xiii–liii).

[74] Ernest Gellner, *Nations and Nationalism*, 2nd edn (Ithaca: Cornell University Press, 2008), p. 80.

[75] Ibid.

[76] E.P. Thompson, *The Making of the English Working Class* (New York: Vintage Books, 1963).

[77] Hobsbawm, *Nations and Nationalisms*, pp. 10–11.

political and programmatic resources available to them in 'detecting the empty moral space at the centre of triumphant economic – and political – capitalist liberalism, as it destroyed all bonds between individuals except those based on Adam Smith's "propensity to barter" and to pursue their personal satisfactions and interests'.[78] In this respect, anti-colonial nationalism was a 'means of mobilizing the masses in traditional societies against modernization, either capitalist or socialist, or more precisely against the outsiders who imported it'.[79] The primary resource with which communities reimagined themselves in relation to these particular industrial contexts, Benedict Anderson would argue, was print technology. He contended that the 'convergence of capitalism and print technology on the fatal diversity of human language created the possibility of a new form of imagined community, which in its basic morphology set the stage for the modern nation'.[80]

Building upon this body of modernist scholarship, scholars of late colonial Africa and Asia have tended to frame the question of the end of empire in relation to the character of imperial administrative ambiguities and the force of political solidarities. In his work on Africa's postwar politics, Frederick Cooper suggests that colonial rule 'collapsed not because of an all-out assault from a clearly defined colonized people, but because the imperial system broke apart at its internal cracks, as Africans selectively incorporated into political structures based on citizenship or self-determination seized the initiative and escalated their demands for power'.[81] For Cooper, anti-colonial movements largely succeeded because they pried open political fissures that existed within the practice of empire.[82]

From the 1980s onward, similarly, subaltern scholars have highlighted the ambiguities that surrounded imperial power in late colonial southern Asia. Asian nationalists, for instance, observes Partha Chatterjee, reworked British histories of modernity to argue that

---

[78] Eric J. Hobsbawm, *The Age of Extremes: A History of the World, 1914–1991* (New York: Pantheon, 1994), p. 201.

[79] Ibid.

[80] Benedict Anderson, *Imagined Communities*, revised edn (London: Verso, 2006), p. 46.

[81] Frederick Cooper, *Africa since 1940: The Past of the Present* (Cambridge: Cambridge University Press, 2002), p. 66.

[82] Frederick Cooper, *Colonialism in Question: Theory, Knowledge, History* (Berkeley, CA: University of California Press, 2005), p. 204.

'colonial institutions of power were not modern enough, that the conditions of colonial rule necessarily limited and corrupted the application of the true principles of a modern administration'.[83] When Chatterjee talks about India's national history writing, however, he seems to have in mind an identifiable nationalist historiography (as opposed to focusing on the proliferation of competing local historiographies). For Chatterjee, Indian history writers subscribed to 'more or less the same views on historiography'.[84] It is only in a secondary sense that he begins to talk about the place of local pasts within the region's larger nationalist historiography.[85]

What this book contends, though, is that the end of empire in colonial B/Uganda was not primarily the outcome of the emergence of class consciousness among colonial labourers, the force of political party unification, the result of internal cracks within imperial administration or the power of an all-encompassing historiographical project that amalgamated dissenters for the purpose of common protest. In colonial southern Uganda, the logic and practice of empire was unsustainable precisely because there did *not* exist a single, all-inclusive narrative around which political power could be legitimised or instituted.

The sheer amount of vernacular historical argumentation that circulated the region throughout the nineteenth and twentieth centuries presented a formidable, disparate array of hurdles to overcome for aspiring rulers, in both the colonial and postcolonial periods. The historical manufacturing of Apolo Kaggwa and Britain's imperial historians could synthesise only so much. Further, the end of empire in postwar Buganda was not principally the result of a centralised kingship that naturally facilitated political resistance, as previous studies have intuitively proposed,[86] or the outcome of the sweeping republican alternatives of Milton Obote's Uganda People's Congress, as other historians have argued.[87] Colonial Buganda contained, simultaneously,

---

[83] Partha Chatterjee, *The Nations and Its Fragments* (Princeton, NJ: Princeton University Press, 1993), p. 15.

[84] Ibid., p. 109. See also Partha Chatterjee, *The Black Whole of Empire: History of a Global Practice of Power* (Princeton, NJ: Princeton University Press, 2012), pp. 240–55.

[85] Chatterjee, *The Nations and Its Fragments*, pp. 113–15.

[86] The force of Buganda's ostensibly unifying and modernising kingship has shaped much of the existing literature, following David Apter.

[87] Kenneth Ingham, *Obote: A Political Biography* (London: Routledge, 1994).

multiple historical times and periodisations. As Achille Mbembe has argued, political spaces across late colonial and postcolonial Africa often encompassed 'multiple *durées* made up of discontinuities, reversals, inertias, and swings that overlay one another, interpenetrate one another, and envelope one another: an *entanglement*'.[88] The assorted and amorphous character of southern Uganda's vernacular historiographies – not historiography – constituted a multifaceted arena of competing claims that were not easily fused or managed.

The Historical Gaze of Africa's Intellectuals

Before outlining the respective historiographical and ideational projects that are explored in this book, I wish to briefly describe how I am using the term *intellectual* – and how this book proposes to contribute to the existing literature on African intellectuals. Who exactly were Buganda's colonial *intellectuals*?

At one level, the actors upon which this book focuses provide insight into a particular class of urban men who used literacy and missionary education to shape local politics and assert new types of authority and patriarchy. This particular way of viewing African intellectuals is employed by Toyin Falola's work on nationalism, which underscores the impact of European education on the formation of a distinctive class of activists across the continent.[89] In western Africa, for both Falola and Philip Zachernuk, this class was 'defined as those men and women born in Nigeria or of African descent who concerned themselves with the past, present, and future problems of Nigeria as an appendage first of the Atlantic economy and latterly of the British Empire'.[90] The intelligentsia, in turn, 'were set apart from the unlettered bulk of colonial society and had particular characteristics and interests because of this. They were the products of the colonial system,

---

[88] Achille Mbembe, *On the Postcolony* (Berkeley, CA: University of California Press, 2001), p. 14. Italics are Mbembe's. See also Dipesh Chakrabarty's discussion on time: Dipesh Chakrabarty, *Provincializing Europe: Postcolonial Thought and Historical Difference* (Princeton, NJ: Princeton University Press, 2007), pp. 15–16.

[89] Toyin Falola, *Nationalism and African Intellectuals* (Rochester: University of Rochester Press, 2001), pp. 5–28.

[90] Zachernuk, *Colonial Subjects*, p. 12.

created to provide the clerical and other skills required by the colonial government, missions, and commercial firms'.[91]

While this understanding of Africa's colonial intellectuals is helpful, it is also limited. As I will show, Buganda's colonial elites clearly navigated and helped shape the production of European education in Uganda. These were also 'men of the world', who had spent time in southern and western Africa, Asia and Europe. But these were not the only spaces within which they operated. Private archives in southern Uganda show that late colonial elites were involved in far-reaching historical conversations that were framed by regional, peripheral discourses. In this respect, the distinction between urban elites and rural peasants is stifling, a point that Emma Hunter has recently explored in her work on intellectual life in colonial Tanzania.[92] Seeing Africa's colonial intellectuals as belonging to a restrictive class of elite literati presupposes sociological torpidity or economic isolation. Indeed, due to the circulation of competing histories, the long history of clanship, regional kingships, the emergence and expansion of long-distance trade, and migration from the sixteenth-century onward, intellectual life was dynamic and fluid in colonial southern Uganda.

But the study of *colonial* intellectuals has also tended to be restrained by its suggested periodisation. For reasons that are understandable, previous studies have tended to concentrate on what elites were doing in the twentieth century, as opposed to what they were thinking about in relation to the distant past. If, however, historians are to suppose that the 'social and economic character of the intelligentsia rests fundamentally on their membership in the Western-educated community literate in English [. . .]',[93] surely it would remain unnecessary – or inconsequential – for scholars of the colonial period to think about the history of political thought and languages in the *longue durée*? However colonial literacy might have impacted local politics, which it surely did, it was influential to the extent that activists wished to adapt it to complicate and distil older ways of thinking about the past. As Stephen Feierman has shown in his work on Tanzania,

---

[91] Ibid., p. 13.
[92] Emma Hunter, *Political Thought and the Public Sphere in Tanzania: Freedom, Democracy and Citizenship in the Era of Decolonization* (Cambridge: Cambridge University Press, 2015).
[93] Zachernuk, *Colonial Subjects*, p. 13.

colonial intellectuals were defined by their place in unfolding, ongoing processes that reached into the early nineteenth century and beyond.[94] Intellectual life during the colonial period in the Shambaa-speaking regions of Tanzania, for example, derived its political logic from older discourses regarding fertility, production and public healing (*kubani shi* and *kuzifya shi*).[95] By choosing local agents to administer northern Tanganyika, German and British administrators were ultimately subject to discourses of which they had little control.[96] Colonial life was an arena shaped by competing historical visions as individuals and communities struggled to create histories of self-assertion and political mobilisation.[97]

In summary, the activists explored in this study, to whose respective careers I now turn, were not fundamentally unique to the extent to which they belonged to a particular class of Western-educated elites. I use the term *intellectual* more expansively: to describe Baganda who understood themselves at least to some degree as historical thinkers (*–bannabyafaayo*), mediators of distant pasts that could be used to imagine and create new possibilities during a long moment of social and political change. These pasts often presented themselves as a palimpsest, and could be concurrently local, regional, global and mythic. Colonial knowledge was quickly enveloped into powerful and complicated historical debates unfolding in Buganda throughout the nineteenth and twentieth centuries.

Sources and Case Studies

This book highlights four of the historiographical and argumentative tropes that circulated throughout the twentieth century in southern Uganda. The biographies that comprise this book were selected due

---

[94] Steven Feierman, *Peasant Intellectuals: Anthropology and History in Tanzania* (Madison: University of Wisconsin Press, 1990), pp. 17–20.

[95] Ibid., p. 7.

[96] Ibid., pp. 120–2. See also Thomas Spear, 'Neo-Traditionalism and the Limits of Invention in British Colonial Africa', *The Journal of African History*, 44 (2003), 3–27.

[97] My language in this sentence borrows from Paul la Hausse de Lalouvière's excellent study on Zulu intellectuals: *Restless Identities: Signatures of Nationalism, Zulu Ethnicity and History in the Lives of Petros Lamula and Lymon Maling* (Pietermaritzburg: University of Natal Press, 2000), pp. 3–4.

to both the availability of sources and the extent to which they enabled me to complicate Buganda's official and academic historiography. While these case studies were not the only projects moving throughout colonial Buganda, they did constitute four of the most consequential and complicated historical and political visions that developed throughout the interwar and postwar periods.

My approach to the study of private libraries and archives in Buganda builds upon Derek Peterson's work on literacy in colonial Kenya. As Peterson has shown, Kikuyu intellectuals during the twentieth-century often took 'books' characters on themselves, mining the storyline for words, phrases, and ideas that are usable in their own world'.[98] Peterson suggests that texts 'do not belong on library shelves, tucked away from the sweat, blood, emotion, and idealism of human life'.[99] By contrast, '[r]eaders and writers are participants in a much wider body of composition that goes on off the written page'.[100] Tin-trunk archives are useful not only because they illuminate the novelties that accompanied the world of colonial officialdom, as Karin Barber emphasises.[101] They are useful precisely because they help us place colonial activists beyond the mid-twentieth century, into the world of historical imagination. Intellectuals worked to contextualise written sources and conflicting memories about precolonial state formation to imagine alternative political futures.

My book begins by exploring the intellectual project of Ignatius Kangave Musazi (1905–90), Buganda's foremost trade unionist in the 1940s and the founder of Uganda's first political party, the Uganda National Congress. To do so, I use his private library, which I unearthed near Musazi's ancestral burial ground in Bulemeezi, northern Buganda. Near the family cemetery is a house that contains Musazi's remaining library, which is preserved in two stacks. Resting in one corner of the residence sits a bundle of nine books. This small collection is stored with other sources, including a journal that was used in the 1980s and a picture of Musazi in Moscow in the 1950s. On the other side of the room,

---

[98] Derek R. Peterson, *Creative Writing: Translation, Bookkeeping, and the Work of Imagination in Colonial Kenya* (Portsmouth, NH: Heinemann, 2004), p. xi.

[99] Ibid.

[100] Ibid.

[101] Karin Barber, 'Introduction: Hidden Innovators in Africa', in *Africa's Hidden Histories: Everyday Literacy and Making the Self*, ed. by Karin Barber (Bloomington, IN: Indiana University Press, 2006), pp. 1–24.

behind a white cloth, sits a second deposit of around ninety books on a medium-sized bookshelf. Musazi's existent library of one hundred books is the vestige of a collection once far more voluminous.[102] In his 1927 copy of H.M. Gwatkin's *Early Church History, Vol. II*, Musazi stated that the book was the only one that remained out of a personal library of 300 volumes destroyed in 1966.[103]

From his library, one can see that Musazi was an avid reader, actively engaged in reading from the time of his education at King's College, Budo, in the early 1920s (Chapter 1), to at least 1987. Among the eighty-two texts that I have analysed – those he actually autographed – no fewer than 2,156 passages are underlined and 297 annotated.[104] The library indicates that there were two books that Musazi clearly read more than any other: an English Authorized Bible, used from 1924 to at least 1946 and an English Book of Common Prayer, used during the same period.[105] With no fewer than 1,321 underlined passages and 226 annotated texts combined, Musazi's Bible and prayer book constitute roughly 62 per cent of all underscored text and 76 per cent of all annotation in the library. Besides the Bible and the Book of Common Prayer, the most annotated book is Harold Laski's *Reflections on the Revolution of our Time*, which Musazi read alongside Émile François Zola to envision political protest in the 1940s.

By the interwar period, Uganda was Great Britain's second largest supplier of cotton. The expansion of capital economies regulated by Indian middlemen instigated social unrest. In the late 1930s and 1940s, economic grievance translated into open political protest, where communities, organised by Musazi, demanded the right to gin their own

---

[102] Interviews: Edward N. Musazi, 11 December 2009, Timina (Luwero); Elizabeth Musazi, 10 February 2010, Kampala; Mary Mulira, 11 June 2010, Kampala.

[103] Musazi's library contains nine additional books from approximately the same period as Gwatkin's church history and an additional thirty-six books published and/or autographed before 1966. A frequent traveller, Musazi, who moved with books and papers, kept portions of his library in various locations before consolidating the collection after 1966.

[104] In my analysis, one underscored unit constitutes an underlined sentence or cluster of sentences within a single paragraph. In instances of multiple underscoring within a prolonged paragraph or section, numeration is topically interpreted.

[105] Musazi's autograph indicates that the Bible was received in 1924. Two separate annotations are dated in 1946.

cotton. Balemeezi petitioned Buganda's king to defend the economic and political rights of rural farmers, which was part of a much longer struggle over power and authority between communities in northern Buganda and the kingdom's monarchs. Apolo Kaggwa used the past to legitimise Buganda's economy. He adapted *Bassekabaka be Buganda*, in particular, to undermine royalist sympathies in northern Buganda, which consistently threatened to unravel Buganda's colonial order. Kaggwa edited Buganda's history to discredit the generals and kings of Buganda's northern frontier. By underscoring political instability in northern Buganda's past, Kaggwa aimed to delegitimise contemporary dissent. Kaggwa argued that Bulemeezi's military king, Mawanda, had fallen out of favour with the state's heroic king, Kintu, whose priests allegedly criticised Bulemeezi's political activists in the eighteenth century.

To complicate Kaggwa's claim, Musazi organised the Descendants of Kintu, *Abazzukulu ba Kintu*, Buganda's foremost dissenting organisation in the late 1930s. In doing so, Musazi sought to recreate political continuity between his Bulemeezi constituency and Buganda's first king. By the 1940s, *Abazzukulu* became the Uganda African Farmers' Union, whose activists organised a series of protests throughout the mid- to late 1940s. The constituency of *Abazzukulu* was largely Protestant, and to challenge the kingdom's colonial ethos they used their bibles. By mining the Bible's royalist chronicles and the stories of Herod and Pilate, Musazi advocated for the revival of Buganda's strong monarchy, the type of kingship that Kaggwa had worked to restructure around the state's Christian regents. Musazi read his Bible in the 1940s alongside the political writings of Émile Zola, whose letters he had studied as an ordinand in England, and Harold Laski, whose Fabian socialism offered a useful framework to rethink Buganda's economic history. Musazi used colonial literacy to reinforce the legitimacy of Bulemeezi's royalist political historiography. For Musazi and his northern trade unionists, the revival of Buganda's strong monarchy was central to restoring responsible governance in a kingdom torn by colonial rupture.

The political career of Eridadi Mulira (1909–95) preoccupies Chapters 2 and 3. Mulira played a prominent role in securing the return of *Kabaka* Muteesa II from exile in 1955. In the late 1950s, he was Buganda's foremost Protestant constitutional thinker, helping produce Uganda's timeline toward independence. David Apter and Donald Anthony (Tony) Low talked with Eridadi Mulira during the mid-1960s to persuade him to deposit his private papers into a public repository. But Uganda's postcolonial instabilities prompted activists to guard their collections tightly, if not destroy them all together. During the course of my research, I was pleased to find that Mulira's papers were still largely preserved. His collection is comprehensive and contains thousands of documents: letters, pamphlets, private diaries and more. In conversation with Peter Mulira and the Mulira family, it was decided that the collection should be housed in the Cambridge Centre of African Studies, where it has been deposited and catalogued. In 2012, I completed a finding aid, which is now available online.[106] The collection was digitised with the assistance of Emily Rodes during the summer of 2015. Digital copies are accessible through Apollo, the digital repository of the University of Cambridge.[107]

Mulira was from Kooki, a tributary state in western Buganda. His private papers show that he used the writings of the Ghanaian educationalist James Aggrey to adapt Kooki's cosmopolitan history throughout the 1940s and 1950s. In doing so, he laboured to liberalise Buganda's increasingly patriotic landscapes. Mulira was also a linguist and novelist, trained in Ghana and at the School of Oriental and African Studies in London. He used this time to create a Luganda grammar and numerous Luganda plays and novels. Through the classification of local grammar and cultural production, Mulira contested Musazi's royalist historiography. Unlike Musazi, and many others in Buganda's secessionist state, Mulira imagined a kingdom for non-Baganda commoners and women, not powerful ethnic kings. Chapter 3 also gives considerable attention to how Mulira used the British press to shape the high politics of Westminster.

As different as Musazi and Mulira were, their respective projects were both shaped by Protestant sensibilities. And while both Musazi and Mulira sought to push Buganda's monarchy in different directions, they tended to not question Protestant legitimacy – it was taken for granted. Both Musazi and Mulira built upon their respective Protestant pasts; they were not dismissed. To complicate Protestant historiography, Chapter 4 explores the long history of Islamic political thought in central Uganda and the political career

---

[106] Further analysis of the collection and a finding aid are found here: www
.library.african.cam.ac.uk/Collections/archivelist/mulira.

[107] www.repository.cam.ac.uk/handle/1810/257498.

of Abubakar Kakyama Mayanja (1929–2005). It begins by examining the development of Buganda's semi-Islamic state from the 1840s up until the 1890s, when Christian chiefs secured political control of the kingdom through superior weaponry. To legitimise Protestant power in the early 1900s, historians worked diligently to undermine the integrity of Islamic statebuilding under the kingships of Ssuuna, Muteesa I, Kiweewa and Kalema. Hamu Mukasa, Apolo Kaggwa and colonial historians suggested that Buganda's kingdom had been rocked by violence under the leadership of Muslim chiefs. By the 1940s, though, Muslim historians recast official historiography, retelling the nineteenth century as a period when Muslim statebuilders returned calm to the kingdom after an unusually long period of military expansion. In the mid-1900s, these debates focused on the political makeover of *Kabaka* Mukaabya, one who causes tears or suffering, who during the course of the late 1800s assumed the name Muteesa, one who consoles or comforts. Whereas Protestants had argued that this transition was the result of Christian conversion, Muslims argued that this happened during a period when Buganda's kings and Muslim chiefs worked hand-in-hand with communities with different religious convictions to administer equity. When Muslims governed the state, they contended, tolerance was common in Buganda; something that was no longer evident in Buganda's discriminating kingdom.

In the mid-1900s, Abubakar Mayanja was poised to further develop Buganda's Muslim historiography. After studying history at King's College, Cambridge, Mayanja, whose father and family were devout Muslims, became Uganda's most outspoken anti-colonial nationalist. He argued that Buganda's Muslim community had exhibited anti-colonial resistance as early as the 1890s. In the early 1960s, Mayanja, along with additional Muslim activists and historians, was a leading minister in the *kabaka*'s government. Superficially, Mayanja's patriotic activism contradicted his earlier nationalism. In turn, Mayanja's volteface has often been viewed as capricious politics in Uganda's nationalist history writing.[108] I use Muslim-produced sources and histories, however, to show that there was a subtle, yet powerful, logic that

---

[108] Apter, *The Political Kingdom in Uganda*, p. 363; Audrey I. Richards, 'Epilogue', in *The King's Men: Leadership and Status in Buganda on the Eve of Independence*, ed. by Lloyd A. Fallers (London: Oxford University Press, 1964), pp. 357–94 (p. 383).

propelled Mayanja's shifting allegiances. For Mayanja, the prospects of independence brought with it new opportunities for articulating older Muslim conceptions of power.

My understanding of Mayanja's changing politics is shaped by sources provided to me by the Mayanja family and documentary evidence provided by both the titular head of Buganda's Muslim community, *Omulangira* Khassim Nakibinge Kakungulu, and the family of the Muslim historian Sheikh Ali Kulumba, Buganda's foremost Muslim historian during the 1950s. Correspondence and personal journals provided by the former activists Neal Ascherson and George Shepherd also provided new perspectives into Mayanja's activism (and Musazi's).

By the early 1960s, Muslim activists dominated the politics of *Kabaka Yekka*, Buganda's foremost patriotic party. Through a partnership with Milton Obote's Uganda People's Congress, Buganda's Protestant and Muslim government in Mmengo sought to undermine the activism of the predominantly Catholic Democratic Party and the Catholic politician Benedicto Kiwanuka (1922–72), Uganda's first prime minister. Chapter 5 explores the intellectual history of Catholic activism in colonial Buganda. It begins by showing how Apolo Kaggwa used folktales to authenticate Protestant control of Buganda's courts. Protestant control of the state's legal apparatus had translated into self-legitimising ways of explaining colonial jurisprudence to Baganda, where the language of executive authority and hierarchy was reinforced. By the 1940s, though, Catholic historians, whose communities constituted Buganda's largest religious demographic, returned to the past to recall a time when justice was an exercise of discussion and compromise. This conception was given its fullest expression in the motto of the Democratic Party – *amazima n'obwekanya*, truth and justice – the etymology of which implied social inclusivity (not executive authority).

Benedicto Kiwanuka was an austere Catholic, trained in Lesotho and London. But in ways that do not sit comfortably with Europe's intellectual history, as I have already begun to indicate, Kiwanuka read his Catholic missal alongside the works of the Oxford Tractarian Cardinal John H. Newman, John Locke and Jean-Jacques Rousseau to envision a liberal kingdom on the eve of Uganda's independence. Far more than Musazi, Mulira or Mayanja, Kiwanuka was a political theorist. And his private papers and annotated library show that after securing the presidency of the Democratic Party in the late 1950s he diligently studied Catholic tradition in tandem with Europe's revolutionary historiography to propose a state without politically obstructive sovereigns.

Throughout their political careers, Musazi, Mulira and Mayanja had tremendous successes and monumental disappointments. For Kiwanuka, who was murdered by the Idi Amin government, the loss was incalculable. However, the (in)ability to direct political argumentation and create social capital had very little to do with the recasting of international political ideals. It was not intrinsically problematic to urban elites or rural farmers that Musazi used Laski, or that Kiwanuka incorporated the writings of an Oxford don into his Luganda political pamphlets. To engineer social legitimacy in Buganda's colonial kingdom, it was necessary for intellectuals to demonstrate the skill to read and adapt global intellectual histories alongside vernacular historiographies and precolonial traditions of power. In the words of Karl Marx, activists succeeded to the extent that they 'summon[ed] up the spirits of the past'. How these spirits were summoned and into what conversations and histories they were challenged to speak is the subject of this work. The end of empire in colonial Buganda constituted an ideational kaleidoscope: a shifting arena within which activists laboured to put forward dissenting, idyllic pasts and different visions of the future, as they looked toward independence.

Additional Sources and Limits of Study

This book is also shaped by material deposited in twenty-two institutional archives in Rome, Uganda, the United Kingdom and the United States. It also works critically alongside the Luganda press. This includes the private collection of 'Jolly Joe' Kiwanuka, another leading activist during the 1950s. I have also used available English translations of the Luganda press, which are housed in Oxford and Cambridge. To compliment my textual work, I conducted approximately one hundred semi-structured interviews in Uganda between November 2009 and July 2010. The majority of these interviews were conducted in English, with partial Luganda. In instances where Luganda etymologies were referenced, interlocutors were asked to explicate in Luganda. Interlocutors were mostly formal activists during the 1950s and 1960s. Prior to my research, I lived in central and eastern Uganda for two years, where I formally studied Luganda and Ateso. Even then, it was necessary to rely upon the excellent translation work of Ssalongo George Mpanga Lutwama.

As with all sources, private archives have their limits – what they can and cannot say; for whom they can and cannot speak; their overt silences. Just as imperial and African archives constitute spaces of power within which statebuilders regulate the past,[109] private archives are shaped by the similar processes of self-editing and production. My work, therefore, is not exhaustive and it is my hope that the unearthing of additional private archives and oral ethnographies in the future will further enrich our understanding of Buganda's intellectual history in ways that this work could not. Early into this project, for instance, I had hoped to offer a chapter on women's politics in the 1950s. I interviewed postcolonial activists, such as Rhoda Kalema,[110] who played an important role in formalising women's politics in postcolonial Uganda. I also interviewed contemporary women activists, such as the current president of the Young Women's Christian Association, Kiyingi Laetitia.[111] I was regretfully unable to produce the necessary sources to complete a full chapter satisfactorily. I have, however, worked to weave larger debates over gender and generational politics into each of the substantive chapters. For the purpose of focusing the analytic framework of this work, I do not explore the politics of spirit possession or dreams in colonial Buganda, which were explored more fully in my doctoral thesis. The politics of these practices will be explored in future articles.

---

[109] Achille Mbembe, 'The Power of the Archive and Its Limits', in *Refiguring the Archive*, ed. by Carolyn Hamilton, Verne Harris, Michèle Pickover, Graeme Reid, Razia Saleh and Jane Taylor (London: Kluwer Academic Publishers, 2002), pp. 19–26.

[110] Interviews, Rhoda Kalema, 5 and 7 January 2010, Kampala.

[111] Interview, Kinyingi Laetitia, 7 January 2010, Kampala.

1 | Ignatius K. Musazi: Powerful Kings and Colonial Economies, c. 1905–c. 1949

To put it simply and plainly, the Kabaka admitted publicly, and perhaps for the first time in the history of Buganda, that though the head of Buganda Government, the 1900 Agreement left him no power whatsoever to make any changes in his Government however desirable changes may be. In other words, in all matters of administration the Buganda Government carry out orders of the Protectorate Government. What a pathetic state of affairs! Indirect Rule Indeed!!

Ignatius K. Musazi[1]

By 5:45 a.m. on 25 April 1949 over 500 agitated farmers and trade unionists had assembled in front of the *Lubiri*, the compound of Buganda's king. By mid-morning, the crowd had swelled to approximately 4,000. Marching between the *Lubiri* and the *katikkiro*'s office, adjacent to the king's palace, activists' flags depicted a rope placed around the throat of a farmer in bark cloth. The flags' inscriptions waved, 'Buganda asks for independence'.[2] Additional flags showed Ganda women standing side by side with the slogan, 'Kabaka gives us liberty – our cotton may be ginned'.[3] Organisers demanded to meet with Buganda's young king, then in his mid-twenties, and by 10 a.m. *Kabaka* Muteesa II received a delegation of eight farmers. In a pamphlet given to the king, entitled 'Long live the Kabaka. We ask for Freedom', farmers demanded that Muteesa reorganise his cabinet and provide the opportunity for farmers to gin their cotton and to have direct accessibility to global markets.[4] Farmer Kulanima Musoke

---

[1] BNA CO 536/223/4 I.K. Musazi, 'Some Observations on the Kingdon Report' (May 1950), p. 7.
[2] 'Report of the Commission of Inquiry into the Disturbances in Uganda during April, 1949' (Entebbe: Government Printer, 1950), p. 14.
[3] Ibid.
[4] 'Long Live the Kabaka. We Ask for Freedom', 25 April 1949, in 'Report of the Commission of Inquiry into the Disturbances in Uganda during April, 1949', p. 21.

advised, 'Your Highness will not be able to grant peace to the public whilst retaining the present rulers'.[5] Farmers' unionist Erieza Bwete argued that Baganda chiefs and Indian ginners were not 'interested in African farmers'. They contended that ginneries, by regulating labour demands in the state, had become Buganda's newfangled royal palace.[6] To the delegation, Muteesa asserted that he needed to seek the counsel of his advisers before intervening on behalf of Buganda's farmers. And following two hours of deliberation the meeting concluded by Muteesa dictating: 'Go and tell your people to return to their homes.'[7]

Buganda's boisterous farmers, however, were not so easily commanded. After the eight representatives returned to the crowd, which refused to disperse as ordered, *Katikkiro* Kawalya Kaggwa, Apolo Kaggwa's son, was sent by the *kabaka* to deliver a formal reply to the farmers. The riposte indicated that the king was unable to redress many of their concerns due to the stipulations of the 1900 Agreement, which had both reorganised land ownership and codified Buganda's colonial order. Cotton would continue to be ginned by Indian middlemen and sold through the colonial government. Before Kaggwa was able to finish delivering Muteesa's message, though, he was silenced by what one colonial report described as vociferous protest.[8] By the end of the day, the crowd demanded Kaggwa's resignation.

The morning of 25 April was one of several moments of political unrest in Buganda throughout late April and early May. Disturbances resulted in over 1,700 arrests and caused concern among colonial officials. In an inward telegram to the Secretary of State for the Colonies and the governors of Kenya and Tanganyika, Governor John Hathorn Hall recounted the stoning of cars and rioters' roadblocks. The night before, noted Hall, 'houses of chiefs and loyalists were burnt and rioters are still actively engaged on (corrupt group) arson throughout area around Kampala'.[9] Hall informed his colleagues that by the end of the day the African Farmers' Union, a movement organised by Musazi, would be classified as an unlawful society and that Buganda would be

[5] 'Report of the Commission of Inquiry into the Disturbances in Uganda during April, 1949', p. 22.

[6] Ibid., p. 23.

[7] Ibid., p. 25.

[8] Ibid.

[9] BNA CO 536/216/1/29 Governor J. Hathorn Hall to Secretary of State for the Colonies, 27 April 1949.

declared a disturbed area. Governor Hall argued that activists were 'seeking to oppose by violence, intimidation, arson and murderous assault all constituted authority, the authority of H.H. the Kabaka's Government, the authority of the Protectorate Government and of the King's forces of law and order'.[10] Officials maintained that bringing 'pressure to bear upon the Kabaka by sitting down before his palace amounted to planning treason and rebellion'.[11] In the past, colonial officials argued, gatherings of April's magnitude resulted in assassination or driving the *kabaka* away from power.[12]

Parliamentarians in London were also concerned about the unravelling of Ugandan politics and its potential impact on Britain's industrial cotton demands. Labour parliamentarian Frederick Skinnard anxiously asked the Secretary of State for the Colonies to work quickly to halt political protest in Buganda: 'In view of the recent reports that there have been a considerable number of cases of arson and that there is increasing activity of a very serious nature [in Uganda], would it not be advisable to give a directive that a report should be issued as soon as possible?'[13] Parliamentarians such as Skinnard were aware of the impact of the Second World War on local economies. In Uganda, retail prices had increased by 60 per cent by the second year of the war. By the end, Ugandans were paying 13.35 shillings for cotton goods that had cost 4.35 shillings as recently as 1941.[14] Pharmaceuticals, shoes, lamps and bicycles were among many of the products whose prices had drastically risen.[15] Colonial bureaucrats in London and Entebbe did not wish to see local discontent, aggravated by hard-hit economies and shoestring budgeting, translate into armed insurrection.[16]

Muteesa II was also pensive about his waning legitimacy among the kingdom's colonial subjects. Before dismissing the farmers' delegation,

---

[10] CCAS 676.1/320 'Message from Governor', 27 April 1949.
[11] 'Report of the Commission of Inquiry into the Disturbances in Uganda during April, 1949', p. 17.
[12] Ibid.
[13] Frederick Skinnard, Parliamentary Debates (Hansard), House of Commons, 29 June 1949, Vol. 466, cc1273.
[14] Gardner Thompson, *Governing Uganda: British Colonial Rule and Its Legacy* (Kampala: Foundation Publishers, 2003), pp. 256–7.
[15] Ibid., p. 257.
[16] Sara Berry, 'Hegemony on a Shoestring: Indirect Rule and Access to Agricultural Land', *Africa* 62 (1992), 327–55.

concerned that rumour would further undermine his credibility,[17] Muteesa implored the group to carefully consider the manner in which they reported their private meeting to demonstrators.[18] Muteesa sent the kingdom's prime minister to address the crowd on his behalf. Drowned by ridicule and threat, he was forced to return to the palace. By the nineteenth century, ridicule directed against a messenger of the *kabaka* was intolerable and often suggested the possibility of intrigue. One proverb recalled: 'Where a messenger of the king is beaten, there will not be peace.'[19] With farmers unwilling to listen to his *katikkiro*, Muteesa issued a public decree to 'the Chiefs and all the people of Buganda' on 28 April. His aim was to galvanise support:

The happenings of the last few days have horrified and disgusted me. I would never have thought it possible that there should be in Buganda traitors capable of the acts of arson and of wanton destruction which have been committed at the instigation of certain political parties now proscribed. Slowly but surely these people are being brought to book, and I agree that the forceful measures that are being taken to deal with the situation are necessary. But it is not enough to leave all this to the Protectorate Government. It is the bounden duty of every one of my citizens to fight these pests and I require that duty from every person whom I rule, for I know that most of you are loyal to me and deprecate these actions. He who hesitates to use his every endeavour towards bringing these people to justice is being unfaithful to me; he who fails loyally to support and defend his Chief is likewise failing in loyalty to me.[20]

Muteesa advocated for a hierarchy within which subjects unquestionably obeyed their king. His message reflected a monarch's political vision, a place in which subjects fight for their ruler and where traitors are powerless to organise arson and resistance. What Buganda's colonial monarch did not realise was that, behind the veneer of public

---

[17] Luise White, *Speaking with Vampires: Rumor and History in Colonial Africa* (Berkeley, CA: University of California Press, 2000), pp. 242–68.

[18] 'Report of the Commission of Inquiry into the Disturbances in Uganda during April, 1949', p. 24.

[19] Ferdinand Walser, *Luganda Proverbs* (Berlin: Reimer, 1982), no. 5202.

[20] 'Message from H.H. the Kabaka to the Chiefs and all the people of Buganda', 28 April 1949, in 'Report of the Commission of Inquiry into the Disturbances in Uganda during April, 1949', p. 50.

protest, farmers sought to resurrect older beliefs about powerful and competent kingship.

During the riots of 1949, farmers were comprised mostly of rowdy royalists, dissenters who sought to recreate distinctly monarchical pasts to regulate Buganda's colonial economy and order. Farmers imagined a time in Buganda's deep past when courageous kings ruled with equity. There were advantages to the autocratic kingships that Apolo Kaggwa and Hamu Mukasa had worked so hard to discredit (Introduction). On the eve of the 1949 riots, the vice-president of the Uganda Farmers' Union, Petero Sonko, published a letter to the *kabaka* in the Luganda press. He argued that moral and economic order in the colonial state was contingent upon the revivification of Buganda's powerful kingship. 'The Growers', Sonko continued, 'are earnestly looking forward to seeing what His Highness [*kabaka*] is going to do for them'.[21] The president of the Union, Ignatius K. Musazi (1905–90), argued similarly. He recounted a time when the 'power of life and death' rested with Buganda's kings.[22] Unlike Muteesa II, Buganda's precolonial kings exhibited political power; they were simultaneously generals, judges, legislators, administrators and 'the reservoir of Kiganda custom, and everything that was regarded Kiganda'.[23] In Buganda's *ancien régime*, admirable kings 'appointed and dismissed [. . .] chiefs at will',[24] a demand now placed before a lesser king. By the late 1800s, argued Musazi, 'the Kabaka was the recognised and acknowledged supreme ruler of what is now known as Uganda Protectorate'.[25] Musazi called upon the Uganda African Farmers' Union to save Uganda,[26] to resuscitate Buganda's kingship in order to produce 'the type of Government the African must have'.[27] Following the 1949 riots, Muteesa II demanded the unwavering loyalty of his subjects. But loyalty was never guaranteed in the past; obeisance was

---

[21] *Uganda Star*, 22 March 1949, in 'Report of the Commission of Inquiry into the Disturbances in Uganda during April, 1949', p. 50.
[22] Musazi, 'Some Observations on the Kingdon Report', p. 5.
[23] Ibid.
[24] Ibid.
[25] Ibid., p. 3.
[26] I.K. Musazi, 'Uganda Farmer Calling. All Members of the Uganda African Farmers Union', Uganda Star, 7 December 1948, in 'Report of the Commission of Inquiry into the Disturbances in Uganda during April, 1949', p. 77.
[27] Musazi, 'Some Observations on the Kingdon Report', p. 26.

contingent upon safeguarding the interests of Buganda's farming villages. As one proverb suggested: 'The king's palace is not reached at once: one who is going to eat [power], reaches first the banana leaves [the weakest subjects].'[28]

This chapter explores the early political thought of Ignatius K. Musazi, Buganda's foremost trade unionist during the 1930s and 1940s. In the early 1900s, Apolo Kaggwa created histories to undermine royalist sympathies in northern Buganda, where Musazi's father collaborated with *Kabaka* Mwanga, the Protectorate's renegade king. Ignatius Musazi and Bulemeezi's cotton farmers were challenged to complicate Kaggwa's historical vision, which argued that there had been a falling out between the founding king of Buganda, Kintu, and Bulemeezi's ancestors. Musazi and his group complicated this claim by branding themselves as the Descendants of Kintu, *Abazzukulu ba Kintu*. For reasons that are explained in this chapter, *Abazzukulu* sanctified their political platform by using bibles to draft letters and critique the social impact of colonial economies. In particular, Musazi's library shows that he explored the administrative careers of Rome's indirect rulers in the Bible, Herod and Pilate, to understand the causes and consequences of monarchical ineptitude in colonial society. During this same period, Musazi contextualised the Fabian socialism of Harold Laski to reflect upon the possibility of replacing Buganda's own king, Muteesa II, with a more competent ruler. Musazi and his Ganda trade unionists argued that the solution to ruptures caused by colonial modernity rested in the revival of their state's powerful precolonial monarchy. Whereas previous studies have interpreted the history of dissent in 1920s and 1940s Buganda by underscoring the importance of clanship,[29] or the arenas within which Bataka activists organised dissent in the 1920s and 1940s by soliciting older ideas about kinship and reciprocal obligations, Musazi's early career shows that conceptions of authoritative kingship also propelled interwar dissent and the ways in which unionists thought about power.

---

[28] Walser, *Luganda Proverbs*, no. 3469. '*Obusiro tebutuukirwako: ajja okulya, atuukira ku ndaggala*'.

[29] Holly E. Hanson, *Landed Obligation: The Practice of Power in Buganda* (Portsmouth, NH: Heinemann, 2003), pp. 203–32; Carol Summers, 'Radical Rudeness: Ugandan Social Critiques in the 1940s', *Journal of Social History*, 39 (2006), 741–70.

Abazzukulu ba Kintu and the Fabrications of Kingship

To contest Buganda's monarchy in the late 1930s, Ignatius K. Musazi and a cadre of farmers established *Abazzukulu ba Kintu*, the Descendants of Kintu, an organisation named after Buganda's proto-mythical king.[30] Members initially organised under the auspice of Uganda's first registered trade union, the Uganda Motor Drivers' Association, which was created to challenge the government's restriction of African-owned public transportation between rural cotton farms and urban distribution posts. *Abazzukulu* appealed to Buganda's government to discipline Ganda chiefs, who by 1909 had begun appointing assistants to travel throughout their respective districts to enforce cotton regulations.[31] The manner in which Baganda cotton inspectors dealt with rural farmers caused considerable alarm among colonial officials. The superintendent of the cotton department noted: 'These men often deal with peasants in a most high-handed way, calculated to make cotton culture distasteful rather than attractive to the natives.'[32]

Uganda's cotton production brought increasing revenues to the country. By 1930, Uganda was Great Britain's largest producer of African cotton, exporting approximately 23,428 metric tons of cotton lint annually and generating revenues of 31,107,000/-.[33] Throughout the 1930s and 1940s, cotton yield produced increasing state revenues. Participation in global markets, however, resulted in frustration among rural communities. In 1938, global prices significantly decreased due to a production surfeit in the United States.[34] Price deflation resulted in lower earnings for farmers. Whereas farmers were paid on average 14.80 shillings per 100 lb of seed cotton in 1930, by 1938 earnings

---

[30] ICS 29/1/5/3 'Who's Who of Buganda's Troubles', n.d. According to David Apter, *Abazzukulu* organised on 28 May 1938 (David E. Apter, *The Political Kingdom in Uganda: A Study of Bureaucratic Nationalism*, 2nd edn (Princeton, NJ: Princeton University Press, 1967), p. 203).

[31] UNA SMP A45/422 Acting Superintendent, Cotton Department, to Chief Secretary to the Government, 30 December 1909.

[32] Ibid.

[33] Jan Jelmert Jørgensen, *Uganda: A Modern History* (New York: St Martin's Press, 1981), p. 349.

[34] UNA SMP A46/1054/210-213 'Notes on the Cotton Situation in Uganda', June 1938. In 1938, America produced a record yield of 19,000,000 bales.

were a little over 8 shillings for the same quantity.[35] The Second World War caused further inflation.

Throughout the late 1930s, *Abazzukulu* implored Buganda's king to defend the economic interests of the kingdom's farmers. On 19 September 1938, Musazi and *Abazzukulu* forwarded a nineteen-page missive to *Kabaka* Daudi Chwa, who governed Buganda from the mid-1910s until his death in 1939. They accused Buganda's regents of intimidating members of the *Lukiiko* and misappropriating cotton revenues. *Abazzukulu* argued that chiefs no longer cared for the 'interests of the people in general and their business enterprises in particular'.[36] Out of fear of compromising potential promotion, chiefs no longer represented their constituencies. As the descendants and sons of Kintu, farmers admonished their king to intervene politically to dismiss avaricious chiefs who implemented detrimental colonial policies. *Kabaka* Chwa, they maintained, was endowed by God to protect the agricultural production of citizens within the state: 'We suffer injustice; we dread the future; will your Highness then now turn a deaf ear to our miseries? It is the duty of our Protector to guard us against any evil.'[37]

Musazi's plea for the intervention of Buganda's king was not philosophical abstraction distanced from the hullaballoo of state formation in central Uganda. It built upon a particular historical interpretation of the emergence of Buganda from the eighteenth century onward, which was firmly grounded in the royalist traditions of Buganda's second most populated *ssaza*, Bulemeezi.[38] Musazi was a son of Bulemeezi, an epicentre of Protestant dissent and the political seedbed from which *Abazzukulu* grew. Bulemeezi's principal chief, *Kangaawo* Samwiri Mukasa, and his son, Shem Spire Mukasa, Daudi Chwa's personal secretary,[39] were executive leaders in Musazi's movement of predominantly Bulemeezi farmers.[40] Another important organiser of *Abazzukulu* was Revd Reuben Spartas Mukasa, whose Orthodox

---

[35] 'Report of the Cotton Commission, 1938' (Entebbe: Government Printer, 1939), in Apter, *The Political Kingdom in Uganda*, p. 189.

[36] BNA CO 536/197/16/1 Descendants of Kintu to Daudi Chwa, 19 September 1938.

[37] Ibid.

[38] By 1908, colonial reports recorded Bulemeezi's population at 78,881. Comprised of 1,442 square miles, Bulemeezi was Buganda's fifth largest *ssaza* (UNA SMP A44/255 'Report of the Kingdom of Buganda', 1907–8).

[39] Hanson, *Landed Obligation*, p. 217.

[40] ARP 7/4/62–63 Audrey Richards, Field Notes, 24 January 1956; Apter, *The Political Kingdom in Uganda*, p. 203; Hanson, *Landed Obligation*, pp. 206–20.

devotees in Buganda were mostly Balemeezi. By the mid-1940s, Spartas recorded that the Orthodox Church had approximately 4,924 adherents in Buganda, 74 per cent of which were Balemeezi.[41]

In the past, citizens in northern Buganda used royalist narratives to inform political activism. Histories produced at healers' shrines were not the only narratives from which rural Baganda renegotiated power,[42] or capitals the only space from which the myths of royalism were conjured. By the late nineteenth century, activists in Bulemeezi saw themselves as royalists, tenacious servants of Buganda's military kings. At the time of Musazi's birth, 1905, Bulemeezi was described as an outpost for Buganda in her perennial military struggles with Bunyoro, the kingdom's northern rival.[43] Richard Reid suggests that by 1875 the *ssaza* chieftaincy of Bulemeezi, the *kangaawo*ship, was considered a military command post.[44] When the *ssaza* chiefs of Ssingo and Bulemeezi were described to Henry Morton Stanley, who first observed the use of bronze cast spears in Uganda in Bulemeezi,[45] they were portrayed as 'military commanders in charge of certain stretches of frontier'.[46] Life in Buganda's military outpost was uncharacteristically difficult. Nyoro campaigns into northern Buganda resulted in the seizure of slaves from Ssingo and Bulemeezi.[47] As a result of constant military activity and forced migration, Bulemeezi experienced frequent plantation abandonment, resulting in the decline of agricultural productivity.[48] One Ganda proverb reflected the adversity of life in Bulemeezi: 'The Balemeezi are similar to banana stalks left in the cooking pot.'[49] In consequence, Balemeezi were characterised by tenacity, as those who did not

---

[41] MUA Revd Reuben Spartas Mukasa, *History*, 1946.

[42] In his excellent book on precolonial clanship, Neil Kodesh uses clan histories to challenge Buganda's royalist historiographies. While I do not challenge Kodesh's central argument, I wish to suggest that royalist discourses could also be used to critique Buganda's monarchies. See Neil Kodesh, *Beyond the Royal Gaze Clanship and Public Healing in Uganda* (Charlottesville, VA: University of Virginia Press, 2010).

[43] Richard J. Reid, *Political Power in Pre-Colonial Buganda: Economy, Society and Welfare in the Nineteenth Century* (Oxford: James Currey, 2002), p. 183.

[44] Ibid., p. 209.

[45] Ibid., p. 85.

[46] Ibid., p. 209.

[47] Ibid., p. 117.

[48] Ibid., p. 37.

[49] Walser, *Luganda Proverbs*, no. 30. *Abalemeezi nkolo: ziremedde mu ntamu*. Stocks of the banana were typically eaten only during famine and not highly valued.

possess *obuntubulamu*, Buganda's highest virtue in public morality.[50] *Obuntubulamu* was aspired to in speech and social etiquette. Deference toward elders and clansmen characterised social interaction.[51] By contrast, Balemeezi were renowned for shrewd manners. One proverb stated: '*Bulemeezi teva muto: eva musisiirwa*', 'There comes no simple child from Bulemeezi, only someone fully grown.'[52] The task of creating and defending military borders not only fostered obstinacy, it instilled the importance of political hierarchy, where the chain of command in military conflict was crucial. A dynamic relationship between Buganda's military chiefs and her monarchs enabled geopolitical expansion. In Bulemeezi's military culture, kingship was a vested interest that created intense feelings of monarchical loyalty.

Conceptions of monarchical loyalty in the early twentieth century were central to much older ways of remembering the birth of modern Buganda from her northern outpost, where courageous military kings were revered and kings were expected to guarantee security and stability. In the 1890s, I.K. Musazi's father, Nakyama Kangave, was a *ggombolola* chief in Bulemeezi, posted to the Buganda–Bunyoro border. As chief, he was referred to as '*omulinda buzibu*', one who waits for trouble.[53] Following the religious wars, *Kabaka* Mwanga was apprehended after he fled into Acholiland.[54] Shortly before he was deported to the Seychelles, Mwanga was detained in Nakyama's village in Bulemeezi.[55]

---

[50] Interview, Fred Guwedeko, 25 February 2010, Makerere University. See also Mikael Karlström, 'Imagining Democracy: Political Culture and Democratisation in Buganda', *Africa: Journal of the International African Institute*, 66 (1996), 485–505 (p. 486). The term received considerable treatment in *Munno* in the early twentieth century and was generally thought of as 'implying the possession of courtesy, compassion, good breeding, culture, etc.' (Murphy, *Luganda-English Dictionary*, p. 44). Commenting on *obuntubulamu*, E.M.K. Mulira wrote: 'Good manners and kindness were the chief virtues and manners were inspired by the idea of "Obuntu" – a difficult word which has no proper equivalent in English, but according to one writer it is the spirit of humanity or humaneness' (E.M.K. Mulira, *Troubled Uganda* (London: Fabian Publications, 1950), p. 7).

[51] Summers, 'Radical Rudeness', 741–70.

[52] Walser, *Luganda Proverbs*, no. 1013.

[53] Interview, Hugo Barlow, 11 November 2010, Munyonyo (Kampala).

[54] Interview, Sallie S. Kayunga, 25 November 2010, Makerere University. For Nakyama's account, see George Shepherd, *The Early Struggle for Freedom and Unity in Uganda: I K Musazi and the Farmer's Cooperative Movement* (New York: The John Day Company, 1955), pp. 36–8.

[55] Interview, Hugo Barlow, 11 November 2010, Munyonyo (Kampala).

During the incarceration, Nakyama demonstrated loyalty through prepared banquets and prostration, gestures that infuriated Buganda's aspiring prime minister, Apolo Kaggwa.[56] During a period when the 1900 Agreement was being created, Kaggwa was concerned that Nakyama was orchestrating the military reorganisation of Mwanga's kingship in Bulemeezi, which threatened the premier's political ambition. Kaggwa, therefore, had good reason to stamp out vestigial power in Bulemeezi. He did this by blemishing the history of kingship and good governance in the region.

For Buganda's official history writer, the birth of Bulemeezi was cast to underscore the proliferation of monarchical violence in precolonial Buganda, an account that he used to legitimise the state's newfound colonial hierarchy. In particular, Kaggwa focused on the mid-eighteenth century, a time when *Kabaka* Mawanda incorporated Bulemeezi into Buganda's expanding polity. Protestant historians like Kaggwa saw Mawanda as the father of violent statebuilding in Buganda.[57] Kaggwa argued that, after securing the throne following a period of intense violence,[58] Mawanda 'was appointed that all the people might bow down before his honor'.[59] Mawanda was problematically 'fierce, brave and tyrannical', a king who dismissed his leading chiefs without discretion or deliberation. In consequence, he noted, the name 'Mawanda' became a formal title bestowed upon each of Buganda's subsequent kings. Kaggwa's analysis was inimical. As Semakula Kiwanuka argues, 'Kaggwa's judgement of Mawanda's character may of course have been coloured by the fact that Mawanda dismissed many important traditional chiefs.'[60] Kaggwa could not afford to be governed or restricted by Mawanda's sort of kingship: autonomy was paramount.

To undercut royalist sensibilities among farmers and dissenters in northern Buganda, though, it was not enough to argue that Mawanda

---

[56] Ibid.

[57] Semakula Kiwanuka, *A History of Buganda: From the Foundation of the Kingdom to 1900* (London: Longman, 1971), p. 72.

[58] Christopher Wrigley, *Kingship and State: The Buganda Dynasty* (Cambridge: Cambridge University Press, 1996), pp. 207–20.

[59] Apolo Kaggwa, *Ekitabo Kye Mpisa Za Baganda*, ed. by May M. Edel, trans. by Ernest B. Kalibala (New York: Columbia University Press, 1934), p. 33.

[60] Semakula Kiwanuka, in *Apolo Kaggwa, Bassekabaka be Buganda*, trans. by Semakula Kiwanuka (Nairobi, Dar Es Salaam, Kampala: East African Publishing House, 1971), p. 76.

had simply dismissed chiefs without consultation. To unravel royalism, it was vital for Kaggwa to argue that Mawanda had broken faith with Buganda's earliest heroic king, Kintu. *Kabaka* Mawanda was one of only two kings to have sought an audience with the spirit of Buganda's first king.[61] According to Kaggwa's account, one of Kintu's mediators had approached Mawanda and provided instructions for him to visit Kintu, whose shrine was in Magonga, Busujju. Mawanda was ordered by Kintu's priests to travel to the shrine with only his sister: 'Go and tell King Mawanda that if he wants to see me [Kintu], he must come only with his queen sister, Ndege. On no account must he come with any other person.'[62] The king travelled to Kintu's palace with his sister. But when the meeting with the spirit-king began, an uninvited man appeared, whom Kintu believed to have travelled with Mawanda. Kintu interpreted this as an act of defiance: 'Did I not strictly warn you that you must come alone? Now who are these people following you?'[63] After Mawanda turned to see the unwelcomed guest, Kintu disappeared. Having failed to hold audience with Kintu, Mawanda returned to his capital in Bulemeezi 'full of grief'.[64] While still despairing the outcome of his ineptitude, Mawanda was informed that his deceased predecessor, *Kabaka* Kagulu, had risen from the dead and was mobilising an army to reclaim the throne. In response, Mawanda sent General Matumpaggwa, Bulemeezi's first *kangaawo*, to assemble an army. But while organising his forces, Kaggwa suggested, Matumpaggwa was betrayed by Mawanda, resulting in the general's death on the battlefield. While dying, argued Kaggwa, Bulemeezi's *kangaawo* stated: 'The king must never send a messenger to my headquarters because he betrayed me.'[65] Kaggwa's chronicle is a story about carelessness and betrayal. It began by recounting a negligent king who was unable to maintain an audience with Kintu. It concluded by pitting Bulemeezi's military chief against Buganda's centralising and tyrannical monarch, a capricious king incapable of moving Buganda beyond perennial violence.

---

[61] Wrigley, *Kingship and State*, p. 211; Kodesh, *Beyond the Royal Gaze*, pp. 138–43.
[62] Kaggwa, *Bassekabaka be Buganda*, p. 72.
[63] Ibid., p. 73.
[64] Ibid.
[65] Ibid., p. 74.

But among Bulemeezi's farmers, there were other ways to remember the frontier's distant past. In the eighteenth century, Mawanda invented a new class of military chiefs, *batongole*, who answered directly to him.[66] In their earliest capacity, *batongole* worked hand-in-hand with Buganda's kings to geographically expand the state's political and economic interests in the region. *Omutongole* Matumpaggwa's name, after all, meant 'one with big ears', a trustee who listened to Mawanda.[67] For restoring social and economic stability in the kingdom following an extensive period of monarchical violence, one Kilemeezi historian argues that '[e]veryone admired the new king, who was brave and fearless.'[68] He was a 'popular hero', one with 'qualities which endeared him to the people'.[69] Mawanda frequently travelled throughout Buganda,[70] indiscriminately dismissing chiefs who disrupted state stability through self-aggrandisement. The summary dismissal of Buganda's chiefs was to be appreciated, not snubbed. It was a certain type of king that Balemeezi appreciated: monarchs who demonstrated responsibility and courage in protecting the subjects of their kingdom, an ideal for which many of their ancestors had died defending on the northern frontier.

This understanding of the role of kingship did not cease with colonial conquest. Throughout the twentieth century, Balemeezi farmers and chiefs valued the history of their peculiar relationship with Buganda's monarchy and their first military general,[71] Matumpaggwa, one who listened to Buganda's state-building king. Oral histories from northern Buganda suggested that Balemeezi saw themselves as royalists who were responsible for ensuring stability and military protection during times of conflict. One commentator in *Munno* observed that when '*kangaawo*'s were appointed they had to announce the spirit of the first dead *kangaawo*, Matumpaggwa, who reigned in the times of the King

[66] Wrigley, *Kingship and State*, p. 209; Hanson, *Landed Obligation*, pp. 82–7.
[67] Wrigley, *Kingship and State*, p. 208.
[68] Kiwanuka, *A History of Buganda*, p. 72.
[69] Ibid., p. 73.
[70] John Roscoe, *The Baganda: An Account of Their Native Customs and Beliefs*, 2nd edn (London: Frank Cass and Co. Ltd, 1965), p. 222.
[71] Michael B. Nsimbi, *Amannya Amaganda N'ennomo Zaago* (Kampala: Published for the Uganda Society by the East African Literature Bureau, 1956), pp. 75–6.

Mawanda'.[72] During initiation, guests and chiefs signified their allegiance to the welfare of the state by eating the liver of a sacrificed cow,[73] whose mythology was traceable to earlier Kintu narratives. By the 1910s, this became one way to reconnect the performance of power in northern Buganda with Kintu, whom Kaggwa had distanced from the frontier.

When I interviewed Buganda's current *kangaawo*, Gideon Kisitu, he too talked about the loyalty of Bulemeezi's earliest military chiefs. Contrasting Kaggwa, he argued that Matumpaggwa and Mawanda were competent rulers who maintained a cherished relationship throughout their lives. He underscored Matumpaggwa's allegiance to Mawanda, and Mawanda's protection of the kingdom. 'The largest part of Bulemeezi was under the Bunyoro Empire,' he explained.[74] He continued:

From Nakaseke, the next hill over was where Buganda ended. It is a very long hill and wherever it goes, it has different names. At that [exact] spot we call it *Migganvule*. There was once a *kangaawo* [sent] to fight and expand Buganda. His name was Matumpaggwa of the Mmamba clan. He went with Ssempala of the Ffumbe clan and Namuguzi of the Empologoma clan. Wherever they defeated the Banyoro they came and gave reports. One time they gave a report that 'we have fought and the enemies are running away from us. We are at the river Kafu now. Should we cross the river'? The Kabaka said, 'No. Halt. Stop there for a time.' When the Banyoro heard this, they translated it into Runyoro as *kangaawo* which means 'stop there' [one who listens when commanded].

For Kisitu, Bulemeezi's kings and chiefs exhibited discretion; they listened to each other. With his northern general, Mawanda worked to both expand and stabilise the state. Kaggwa, on the contrary, had sought to undermine royalism in northern Buganda by painting intrigue onto the political canvas of Buganda's eighteenth-century monarchy. After failing to secure an audience with Kintu, it was suggested that Mawanda, unable to follow instructions, failed to stabilise Buganda from his capital in Bulemeezi.

In summary, in the 1890s one of Bulemeezi's leading outpost chiefs, Musazi's father, Nakyama Kangave, remained committed to the tradition of audacious kingship in northern Buganda. When Musazi's

---

[72] RCMS 126/IV/S1/318–25 'The Ancient Acts of the Rulers of Bulemezi', *Munno*, n.d.
[73] Ibid.
[74] Interview, *Kangaawo* Gideon Kisitu, 14 January 2010, Nakulabye.

rural farmers organised in Bulemeezi during the late 1930s, they did so as the heirs and descendants of Kintu. In so doing, activists were actively rewriting Kaggwa's history. Royalists remembered a time when Buganda was governed by strong kings who were not afraid to dismiss chiefs who undermined the development of the state. Kaggwa attempted to distance northern royalists from the mythologies of Kintu. But by declaring themselves the Descendants of Kintu, Musazi's Kilemeezi cohort emphatically reclaimed the legitimacy of Mawanda's – and in turn, Bulemeezi's – authoritative approach to statebuilding. Throughout his political career, I.K. Musazi remained emotionally close to his father and the movers and shakers of Bulemeezi politics. Musazi's heir, Edward N. Musazi, recalled that his father had an unusually close relationship with Nakyama.[75] Musazi's political project was often associated with his Bulemeezi heritage.[76] Bulemeezi owned Musazi as a son and her political constituency throughout his long political career publicly and consistently offered support.[77] Like Matumpaggwa, Musazi saw himself as a general of Bulemeezi, devoted to strengthening Buganda's monarchical control of regional economies and politics.

Biblical Rulers and Corrupt Sovereigns

Bulemeezi's military history constituted one discursive register from which Musazi developed his emerging politics. As communities converted to Christianity in the early 1900s, they learned different types of literacy through missionary education. More than any other text, converts mined their bibles to inform larger historical and political arguments that pertained to Buganda's monarchy. Building upon his Kilemeezi heritage, Musazi read biblical accounts of kingship to compare and contrast legitimate forms of governance in the 1940s with the corruptibility of imperial-backed kings.

By the early 1900s, Buganda's largest Protestant county was Bulemeezi, where church membership statistics indicated religious fervour. The Church Missionary Society reported that by 1908 Bulemeezi

---

[75] Interview, Edward N. Musazi, 11 December 2009, Timina (Luwero).
[76] Interview, Nick Ssali, 17 November 2009, Radio One (Kampala).
[77] *Musazi ye President: Ab'e Bulemezi Bwe Batyo Bwe Bagamye, Uganda Eyogera,* 9 October 1956, p. 1. Interviews: Nick Ssali, 17 November 2009, Kampala; *Kangaawo* Gideon Kisitu, 14 January 2010, Nakulabye.

and its neighbouring county, Buruli, had 181 churches combined, with an average weekly attendance of 9,260.[78] In Buganda, this accounted for 26 per cent of all churches and 28 per cent of total Protestant membership.[79] By 1939, *Lukiiko* reports estimated that there were 81,019 Protestants in Bulemeezi and Buruli, with 69,160 of these being Balemeezi.[80] For Bulemeezi and Buruli, this constituted a 775 per cent increase over a period of approximately 30 years.

Complementing Protestant congregations, Bulemeezi appointed prominent Protestant chiefs. In 1892, Zakariya Kizito Kisingiri was appointed *kangaawo*. Kisingiri was an early convert from Islam to Protestantism and was admired in the Native Anglican Church (NAC) for his role in the religious wars during the 1890s. Kisingiri was known as one who had 'fought in many wars in Buganda where he exhibited [. . .] courage and strength'.[81] In 1900, Kisingiri was appointed *omuwanika* (treasurer) in Buganda's central government and served as one of *Kabaka* Chwa's regents.[82] Revd Samwiri Mukasa was Bulemeezi's next *kangaawo*. Mukasa had been an assistant translator for Henry Wright Duta and George Pilkington in their work to translate the Bible into Luganda.[83] Musazi and his father were no exception to Bulemeezi's Protestant fervour (Figure 1.1). In the 1950s, when Nakyama Kangave recounted the religious wars to George Shepherd, an American economist working with Musazi's Farmers' Union, he talked about 'God's glory' and 'God's wrath'.[84] In 1939, just as *Abazzukulu* was being organised, Balemeezi church leaders and *ggombolola* chiefs developed a consolidation fund for the purpose of simultaneously funding priests and local leaders. The stated intent of the fund was to further peace and stability in the county.[85]

---

[78] UNA SMP A44/255 'Report of the Kingdom of Buganda', 1907–8.

[79] Ibid.

[80] RDA 99.2 *Bulange-Enju-Y'Olukiko Mmengo; Emitwe Egy'omwaka*, 1939.

[81] Apolo Kaggwa, *'Ebyobulamu bwa Z.K. Kisingiri', Ebifa mu Buganda* (1917), 228–32 (p. 229).

[82] Ibid., p. 230.

[83] J.D. Mullins and Ham Mukasa, *The Wonderful Story of Uganda* (London: Church Missionary Society, 1904), p. 82; Samwiri Mukasa, 'The Record of My Service to the Kingdom of Buganda and the Important Government of Britain, the Protector of this Nation Buganda,' in *The Mind of Buganda*, pp. 57–61 (p. 58).

[84] Shepherd, *The Early Struggle for Freedom and Unity in Uganda*, p. 37.

[85] UCU BA 1/41.12 Rev. Canon Kezekiya Kaggwa to Bishop of Uganda, C.E. Stuart, 8 August 1938.

Figure 1.1 Nakyama Kangave and I.K. Musazi with family Bible, n.d.
Source: Courtesy of Edward N. Musazi

Protestant and biblical literature provided an archive from which Baganda drew to dispute the past. The Bataka historian James Miti used his Bible to talk about Buganda's precolonial society. He opened his 300,000-word history by arguing that God had a special relationship with Buganda's pre-monarchical rulers (clan heads), not unlike God's blessing upon Israel's patriarchs prior to the Davidic monarchy.[86] In February 1922, Miti, with no fewer than 320 signatories, reminded Kabaka Daudi Chwa that the 1900 Agreement contradicted biblical

---

[86] James Kibuka Miti Kabazzi, *Buganda, 1875–1900: A Centenary Contribution*, trans. by G.K. Rock, 2 vols (London: United Society for Christian Literature, n.d.), vol. I, p. 3.

teaching: '[W]hen we read through the Holy Bible, in [Ezekiel 46:18–19,[87] Leviticus 25:23–25,[88] I Kings 21:2–4,[89]] and in [Deuteronomy 27:17][90] [w]e find out that God as well is defending hereditary lands from being alienated permanantly [*sic*] from the legal owners of the same.'[91] Not to be outwitted, Buganda's landed regents responded by forwarding Chwa an eighteen-page commentary where they criticised Miti's exegesis:

As regards the reference to the quotation in the Bible that 'no man should take his neighbour's butaka land', this does not in the least affect the matters now before you, more especially as we have already explained that it was the usual custom for the Kabaka to change about people's butaka land and give it to other people; following this custom the Regents in the name of the Kabaka distributed all estates among the chiefs and people either butaka or not.[92]

In 1939, Revd Bartolomayo Zimbe published his extensive history, *Buganda ne Kabaka*. Like Miti, he used the Bible to complicate

[87] 'Moreover the prince shall not take of the people's inheritance by oppression, to thrust them out of their possession; but he shall give his sons inheritance out of his own possession: that my people be not scattered every man from his possession. After he brought me through the entry, which was at the side of the gate, into the holy chambers of the priests, which looked toward the north: and, behold, there was a place on the two sides westward' (Authorised translation).

[88] 'The land shall not be sold for ever: for the land is mine, for ye are strangers and sojourners with me. And in all the land of your possession ye shall grant a redemption for the land. If thy brother be waxen poor, and hath sold away some of his possession, and if any of his kin come to redeem it, then shall he redeem that which his brother sold' (Authorised translation).

[89] 'And Ahab spake unto Naboth, saying, Give me thy vineyard, that I may have it for a garden of herbs, because it is near unto my house: and I will give thee for it a better vineyard than it; or, if it seem good to thee, I will give thee the worth of it in money. And Naboth said to Ahab, The LORD forbid it me, that I should give the inheritance of my fathers unto thee. And Ahab came into his house heavy and displeased because of the word which Naboth the Jezreelite had spoken to him: for he had said, I will not give thee the inheritance of my fathers. And he laid him down upon his bed, and turned away his face, and would eat no bread' (Authorised translation).

[90] 'Cursed be he that removeth his neighbour's landmark. And all the people shall say, Amen' (Authorised translation).

[91] BNA CO 537/4667, James Miti et al., to Daudi Chwa, February 1922, 'Bataka Land Commission', p. 550.

[92] BNA CO 537/4667, Apolo Kaggwa, Stanislas Mugwanya, Andereya Kiwanuka and Yakobo L. Musajalumbwa to Daudi Chwa, 18 March 1922, 'Bataka Land Commission', p. 576.

Kaggwa's earlier histories, *Bassekabaka be Buganda* (1901) and *Ekitabo Kye Mpisa Za Baganda* (1905). In the introduction, Zimbe argued that his history was written to explore 'things which you cannot find in those books [*Bassekabaka* and *Empisa*], and I have attempted to correct those I found untrue'.[93] His history offered a way to explore how Christianity might empower Buganda's living kings. '[T]he most important things which makes the nation and its crown great', argued Zimbe, 'is to believe in the Gospel of Christ. A Muganda youth, whoever he may be, must always bear in his mind those things.'[94] Like *Abazzukulu*, Zimbe imagined a politically empowered monarch – *Buganda ne Kabaka*, Buganda and [the living] King. Drawing from the language of Christianity, he used his history to talk about a politically active monarch in stark contrast to a history of dead kings (*Bassekabaka*),[95] the latter of which purposely ignored the kingships of Mwanga, Kiweewa and Kalema.

During this same period, Musazi and *Abazzukulu* activists combed their bibles to engage Ganda politics. In a letter to *Kabaka* Chwa, the heirs of Kintu talked about the 'right hand' of God to compel Buganda's king to intervene on behalf of their organisation's rural farmers. *Abazzukulu* argued that 'we are the only people on the earth whom the Good God has placed under your protection and governance'. They asserted that 'in your lifetime your right hand will ever stretch out to defend us'.[96] Chwa was reminded that God's political intention was for kings to 'work and live for the welfare and protection of their fellow men'.[97] God aimed to fashion strong kings like Mawanda, Bulemeezi's founding monarch, who protected the interests of rural producers in the state.

Musazi's missionary education had prepared him to work critically with biblical texts. In the early 1920s, Musazi's father arranged for

[93] B. Musoke Zimbe, *Buganda and the King*, trans. by F. Kamoga (Mengo, 1978), p. 1.
[94] Ibid., p. 4.
[95] *Enkuluze y'Oluganda ey'e Makerere*, ed. by K.B. Kiingi, Deo Kasiriivu, Douglas K. Nkonge, Deo Kawalya, Ibrahim Ssentongo and Anatole Kiriggwajjo (Kampala: Foundation Publishers, 2007), p. 844.
[96] BNA CO 536/197/16/1 Descendants of Kintu to Daudi Chwa, 19 September 1938.
[97] Ibid.

his son to pursue ministerial studies in England.[98] In 1925, Musazi matriculated at Trent College, Nottingham, after which he transferred to St Augustine's College, Canterbury, no later than October 1927.[99] Earlier at Trent, Musazi testified to a calling to missions.[100] In a five-page letter to Bishop Willis, the leader of Buganda's Protestant church, Musazi shared that at the age of nine he felt God's calling upon his life to missionary service while in his father's village, a calling that 'kept on knocking within'.[101] After Musazi's village experience, he enrolled in the kingdom's foremost Protestant school, Mengo High School (later King's College, Budo), where he was allegedly surprised to find two classmates with similar callings. The three prayed regularly, specifically asking God to make them 'perfect to do His will'.[102] Musazi wrote: 'We wanted to take up missionary work before we could accomplish, our education, [and] we went to Mr. Holden who was our school master that time, he advised us not to until we finish our training.'[103] Undeterred in their zeal, Musazi and his classmates continued to pursue ministry:

Few months later we were again in wish of going, we went to Archdeacon Baskerville, who with an affectionate face offered us a prayer, smilingly but courageously he told us to keep, and obey our call with a determination minds, but [stick] to our education until we have good and a better training. With unsatisfactory minds we troded back to our enclosure. But still having the same idea of going, our last effort was to go to Archdeacon Blackledge, who advised us the same. Unknowingly we thought them as great boulders which blocked our way to respond to our call. [O]nly afterwards we confessed our sudden rush, that it was rather foolish of us to had given up our education.[104]

---

[98] ARP 7/4/71 Audrey Richards, Field Notes, 24 January 1956. Due to the financial and political advancement the post offered, the chieftainship of *kangaawo* was a highly coveted position in Ganda politics by the late nineteenth century (Reid, *Political Power in Pre-Colonial Buganda*, p. 209).

[99] UCU BA 1/66.2 Knight, St Augustine's Warden, to Bishop Willis, 15 October 1927. For additional discussion on St Augustine's College, see Hillary M. Carey, *God's Empire: Religion and Colonialism in the British World, c. 1801–1908* (Cambridge: Cambridge University Press, 2011), pp. 271–86.

[100] UCU BA 1/66.2 I.K. Musazi to Bishop Willis, 16 March 1927.

[101] Ibid.

[102] Ibid.

[103] Ibid.

[104] Ibid.

During his training for ordination, Musazi interacted extensively with texts, especially the Bible. Examination for Orders required demanding assignments on numerous biblical passages. Musazi exegeted Isaiah and translated Greek texts, such as portions from Mark's gospel and Acts. Many of the passages studied by Musazi contained political implication.[105] Students were asked to translate Acts 3²¹ from Greek to English: 'ὃν δεῖοὐρανὸν μὲν δέξασθαι ἄχρι χρόνων ἀποκαταστάσεως πάντων ὧν ἐλάλησεν ὁ Θεὸς διὰ στόματος τῶν ἁγίων ἀπ' αἰῶνος αὐτοῦ προφητῶ'. The text explored the social and political unification of heaven and earth, restitution 'which God has spoken by his holy prophets since the world began'. In his personal Bible, Musazi specifically commented upon this theme, noting the 'new world' that God aimed to create.[106]

Musazi was required to apply his study of the Bible to a broader curriculum. He drafted essays on Christology, pneumatology, pastoral theology, religious education and the question of race in relation to Christianity.[107] In her study on St Augustine's College, Hilary M. Carey shows that first-year students studied the history of the Bible, the Greek gospels, Latin and apologetics. In the second year, students studied Bishop John Jewell's *Apology of the Church of England* (1562), Christopher Wordsworth's *Theophilus Anglicanus*, the Thirty-Nine Articles, as well as Hebrew and additional Greek. In their final year, students continued to study language, the history of Christian mission and Joseph Butler's *Analogy of Religion, Natural and Revealed* (1736), which influenced the intellectual history of eighteenth-century Great Britain.

Musazi completed requirements for ordination at St Augustine's, but was not permitted to remain in England for his curacy. He was instructed to return to Uganda for six months of local parish ministry, a decision that 'annoyed Musazi greatly'.[108] Musazi later expressed to George Shepherd that 'he could not accept ordination because of discrimination against Africans in the Church of England'.[109] Musazi's frustration was exacerbated by circumstances surrounding

---

[105] UCU BA 1/66.2 'Examination for Priests' Orders', 1929.
[106] IKML English Bible/Revelation 21:1–8, annotation.
[107] UCU BA 1/66.2 'Examination for Priests' Orders', 1929.
[108] Interview, Hugo Barlow, 11 November 2010, Munyonyo (Kampala).
[109] JLEP George Shepherd to Jonathon L. Earle, 24 January 2010.

an engagement with an English woman, what some have suggested was the actual cause of his precipitous return to Uganda.[110] After returning, Musazi continued pursuing ordination. As an instructor at King's College, Budo, where he worked from 1928 to 1933, Musazi read additional books required by the Church. These books, no fewer than nine, covered the topics of biblical study, prayer and sacraments, doctrine and Church history.[111] Formal ministerial pursuits ceased after the Bishop of Uganda expressed strong disapproval toward a homily that Musazi preached.[112] By the early 1930s there was evident tension between Musazi and the Church of Uganda – compounded by the inability of Musazi and Budo's headmaster, Canon Grace, to 'get on' with one another.[113] In 1934, Musazi left Budo to assume a position as educational inspector in the colonial department of education, an experience that incited his growing concern over the relationship between colonial economies and social inequality.[114] After protesting low housing standards for Ugandan inspectors on assignment, Musazi refused to travel to Fort Portal and resigned shortly thereafter.[115] He then transitioned into full-time politics.

[110] ARP 7/4/71 Audrey Richards, Field Notes, 24 January 1956. Richards suggested that the woman in question was English; family members recalled Musazi identifying her as a daughter of a British parliamentarian (Interviews: Hugo Barlow, 11 November 2010, Munyonyo (Kampala); Edward N. Musazi, 11 December 2009, Timina (Luwero)).

[111] UCU BA 1/66.2 E.S.D., CMS, to Bishop of Uganda, n.d. Musazi was asked to read two works by John Paterson Smyth: *The Bible in the Making in the Light of Modern Research* (1914) and *A People's Life of Christ* (1920). Additional readings included: on biblical studies, commentaries on St Matthew's gospel and I Corinthians; on prayer, Charles Neil and J.M. Willoughby (eds.), *The Tutorial Prayer Book: For the Teacher, the Student, and the General Reader* (1912/13); on doctrine, Griffith Thomas, *The Catholic Faith: A Manual of Instruction for Members of the Church of England* (1920); on Church history, Henry Melvill Gwatkin, *Early Church History to A.D. 313, Vol II* and Edward L. Cutts, *Turning Points of General Church History*. In mid-January 1930, Musazi asked the Bishop of Uganda to bring the required books to him at Budo (UCU BA 1/66.2 I.K. Musazi to Bishop of Uganda, 13 January 1930).

[112] ARP 7/4/71 Audrey Richards, Field Notes, 24 January 1956. The content of Musazi's homily is unknown.

[113] Ibid.

[114] Interview, Hugo Barlow, 11 November 2010, Munyonyo (Kampala).

[115] ARP 7/4/71 Audrey Richards, Field Notes, 24 January 1956. See also BNA CO 536/197/16/1 Descendants of Kintu to Daudi Chwa, 19 September 1938.

Figure 1.2 'Ginning Cotton, Kampala', early twentieth century
Source: EEPA 2000-005-0033. Uganda Photographs, 1897–1903, Eliot
Elisofon Photographic Archives, National Museum of African Art,
Smithsonian Institution.

After helping manage *Abazzukulu* in the late 1930s, Musazi organised the Uganda African Farmers' Union in the early 1940s. Much of
the Union's activism was directed against Indian ginners and Buganda's
chiefs, who oversaw the production and collection of cotton from
rural farmers. Indeed, Bulemeezi was Buganda's largest supplier of
cotton (Figure 1.2).[116] Here and elsewhere, farmers complained regularly of cut earnings at the hand of Indian ginners, who became a focal
point of political resistance between 1945 and 1949. In a letter sent to
the Secretary of State for the Colonies, Arthur Creech Jones, Musazi,
Erieza Bwete and Petero Sonko, complained that farmers had failed
to receive 'amelioration and removal of an oppression which brinks to
sheer robbery and [have not received] any redress from the Police
who are responsible to see that any violation of the cotton ordinances
be brought to book'.[117] The triumvirate spoke of 'open robbery' and

---

[116] UNA SMP A43/200/1 Leakey to Deputy Commissioner, 27 August 1907.
[117] BNA CO 536/216/1/11 Musazi, Bwete and Sonko to A. Creech Jones, 6
May 1948.

ginners who had 'accumulated enormous wealth at the expense of the illiterate cotton growers'.[118] Musazi, Bwete and Sonko used biblical language to argue that the only purpose served by colonial ginners was 'to grab the tax from the pockets of the peasant seller as soon as he receives in some cases his widow's mite'.[119] In an additional letter sent to the Secretary of State, Musazi reflected: 'The Uganda Government makes the Africans a prey for Indians. On the ground of "malpractices" in the cotton industry by Indians, the Africans are justified in seeking understanding and arbitration from you.'[120]

In January 1945, tensions erupted in protest, first in Entebbe, then throughout the kingdom.[121] On 15 January, noted one report, 'groups of intimidators were at work bringing pressure to bear and assaulting those who remained at work'.[122] The inquiry into the disturbances summarised: 'They [protesters] were armed with sticks and stones and attacked Indian property as well as their servants. They invaded private dwellings including those of Europeans. Their object clearly was to force every African to stop work.'[123] The following day, riots climaxed when after 110 European and 48 Asian Special Constables were deployed, a demonstrator shot and killed a police officer.[124] Following the outbreak, Muteesa II returned from safari and organised an investigation committee that focused its attention on Musazi, who was deported to northern Uganda following a formal Commission of Enquiry.[125] Accused of going away on a hunting expedition while colonial police shot his subjects, Muteesa II was allegedly slapped by an unidentified Ganda activist.[126] Amid threats of burning down the king's palace, Muteesa II yielded to populist demands to force the resignation of Buganda's treasurer, Serwano Kulubya, whom farmers had

---

[118] Ibid.

[119] Ibid. See Mark 12:41–44 and Luke 21:1–4.

[120] BNA CO 536/216/1/66 Musazi to Creech Jones, 11 February 1949.

[121] 'Report of the Commission of Inquiry into the Disturbances which Occurred in Uganda During January, 1945' (Entebbe: Government Printer), p. 14.

[122] Ibid.

[123] Ibid., p. 15.

[124] Ibid.

[125] Apter, *The Political Kingdom in Uganda*, p. 228.

[126] I.K. Musazi, Interview by S.S. Kayunga, June 1988, Tinda (Kampala), in Sallie S. Kayunga, 'Uganda National Congress and the Struggle for Democracy: 1952–1962' (Working Paper No. 14, Centre for Basic Research Publications, Kampala, 1995), pp. 14–15.

accused of embezzling agricultural funds.[127] In September, following public accusations of corruption, *Katikkiro* Martin Luther Nsibirwa was assassinated at St Paul's Cathedral, Namirembe.[128] For Musazi, the disturbances of 1945 largely defined the political timbre of the second half of the decade, including the eventual 1949 disturbances.[129]

Musazi's remaining library shows that he scrutinised the Bible to inform his understanding of good governance and monarchical politics throughout this period of rioting. Musazi's Bible shows that in July 1946, during his exile, he believed that God 'revealed' to him the meaning of Isaiah's 'trust fast' (Figure 1.3), a prophet narrative that accentuated the themes of economic equality and political emancipation:[130]

Is not this the fast that I have chosen? to loose the bands of wickedness, to undo the heavy burdens, and to let the oppressed go free, and that ye break every yoke? Is it not to deal thy bread to the hungry, and that thou bring the poor that are cast out to thy house? when thou seest the naked, that thou cover him; and that thou hide not thyself from thine own flesh?[131]

In the same year, Musazi read Amos, a book in the Hebrew Bible that explored a shepherd's prophecy in the eighth-century kingdoms of Judah and Israel (BCE). Amos castigated Israel's elites, those '[t]hat pant after the dust of the earth on the head of the poor, and turn aside the way of the meek'.[132] For Amos, opulence at the expense of the poor resulted in 'a famine in the land, not a famine of bread, nor a thirst for water, but of hearing the words of the Lord', or what Musazi simply called 'A Hungry World'.[133] Throughout Musazi's Bible, these dated themes are consistently annotated. It is apparent that Musazi focused his reading on the interdependence of social justice and the necessity of strong kingship.

The biblical language of fasting and famine resonated with earlier critiques that had been directed against Buganda's kings, while it

---

[127] Apter, *The Political Kingdom in Uganda*, p. 228.
[128] MUA Ssejjemba Ssewagaba, '*Lwaki Katikkiro; Martin L. Nsibirwa Yatemulwa nga 5/9/1945*' (Printed Pamphlet, n.d.).
[129] Musazi, 'Some Observations on the Kingdon Report'.
[130] IKML Common Book of Prayer/Isaiah 58, annotation. In his Bible, Musazi recorded, 'Revealed to me on 30/7/46 Kitgum Deportation'.
[131] IKML English Bible/Isaiah 58:6–7, underscore.
[132] IKML English Bible/Amos 2:7.
[133] IKML English Bible/Amos 8:11–12, annotation.

Figure 1.3 Musazi's Annotated Bible, Isaiah 56:7–59:8

Annotation 1: 'Peace, peace . . . that is near'.

Annotation 2: 'Revealed to me on 30/7/46 Kitgum Deportation'

Annotation 3: 'Lord's inflow'

Annotation 4: 'This Ch. Example of a nation departing from the Lord'.

Annotation 5: 'Shall not know peace'.

Source: IKML English Bible (190 mm × 260 mm)

also helped explain social disruption in the colonial state. In the past, Buganda's kings could be criticised for declaring fasts of which they did not take part. One proverb castigated state fasts under the kingship of Muteesa I: 'The king sent Kakoloboto to proclaim a fast: yet he ate himself.'[134] Kakoloboto was a position that Buganda's nineteenth-century monarchs invented to regulate religious practice.[135] In Musazi's reading of the Bible, God used kings and fasts to rectify social injustice and reform corrupt societies. The Bible provided Musazi with a theological archive from he could legitimise dissent and critique weak

---

[134] Walser, *Luganda Proverbs*, no. 2088.

[135] A.B.K. Kasozi, 'The Impact of Islam on Ganda Culture, 1844–1894', *Journal of Religion in Africa*, 12 (1981), 127–35.

monarchs, such as Muteesa II, who failed to administer justice during periods of economic uncertainty.

Musazi's annotations also correlated the theme of kingship with political justice in Daniel and the gospels, whose writers argued that kings were obliged to protect the rights of the poor and economically oppressed. In God's moral economy, political kingdoms developed or regressed according to their ability or unwillingness to ensure rectitude during periods of social rupture. In Daniel, Musazi focused mostly on Chapters 2, 4 and 7, which recorded a series of dreams experienced by the Babylonian emperor Nebuchadnezzar and the prophet Daniel. The story accentuated Daniel's political interpretation of these dreams. In Daniel 2:44, Musazi noted Daniel's claim that political kings were mandated to serve God's kingdom. In Daniel 4:3, 34 and 17:13–14, 27, Musazi annotated 'Everlasting Kingdom', 'His Kingdom from generation to generation', 'His Kingdom not to be destroyed' and 'Whose Kingdom is an everlasting Kingdom'.[136] God's kingdom was compared with the Exodus narrative recounted in Daniel 9, where in Israel's deliverance from bondage, Musazi observed a 'Righteous God' and political template for Buganda.[137] Similarly, in II Chronicles 18:1–3 and 19:2 Musazi observed divine judgment exhibited toward corrupt monarchs and rulers.[138] In Isaiah, again, he specifically noted that God removed royalty from power for refusing to care for the poor and oppressed.[139] Failure to care for the disenfranchised was intrinsically linked to the 'perishing of kingdoms and nations'.[140] For Musazi, God's work on Earth – and in consequence, the function of political monarchy – was to facilitate a 'habitation of justice'.[141]

In the New Testament, Musazi noted how imperial-backed sovereigns interacted with John the Baptist and his cousin, Jesus. In the Markan narrative, a corrupt sovereign in the royal palace executed John the Baptist, who had been arrested for speaking against conjugal infidelity between Herod and his brother's wife. Initially, John was protected from Herod's lover's desire to have him executed. As Musazi

---

[136] IKML English Bible/Daniel, varied annotations.
[137] IKML English Bible/Daniel 9:14, annotation.
[138] IKML English Bible/II Chronicles, underscore.
[139] IKML English Bible/Isaiah 3:13–16, annotation.
[140] IKML English Bible/Isaiah 60, annotation.
[141] IKML English Bible/Jeremiah 31:23, annotation.

noted, Herod feared John because he was a 'just man'.[142] However, through a rather bizarre sequence of promises, Herod eventually executed John. For Musazi, this reflected a struggle between just peasants and corrupt royals. John and Herod's confrontation was considered a 'moral battle',[143] and having defined this narrative as moral, Musazi applied the story to mid-twentieth century Buganda, annotating: 'live as it was 1,900 years ago'.[144]

Matthew 27 recounts the story of Judas' suicide and Jesus' trial and crucifixion. In Matthew's narrative, the governor who tried Jesus' civil case, Pilate, is portrayed as someone who knew with some degree of certainty that Jesus was innocent before his accusers. In this regard, the story is like Herod and John the Baptist. Regardless of Jesus' innocence, though, Pilate capitulated to the demand of the masses due to 'fear'.[145] More specifically, Judea's provincial prefect was afraid of being removed from power by the Roman emperor, Tiberius, who backed his controversial rule. In Musazi's words, Pilate 'fear[ed] to do justice'.[146] Whereas Pilate refused to administer justice due to political expediency and fear, Musazi underscored Jesus' willingness to confront a corrupt and bribed Judas. In Matthew 26, Jesus exemplified for Musazi the 'courage of a true man'.[147]

In conclusion, just monarchs were obliged to care for their subjects, protecting them from ill-informed masses and royal politics. Musazi believed that Pilate and Herod were corrupt for having failed to do either. Comparable to Muteesa II, and dissimilar to Mawanda, Pilate and Herod were misguided and ineffectual kings whose authority derived primarily from the imperial metropole. Both stories underscored overconfident sovereigns and the adverse consequences of imperial pressure: the death of agrarian subjects. The setting in both stories is a royal palace. Herod both feared and admired the Baptist, who was to be released in due course. But Herod, publicly at a dinner party, extended his wife the opportunity to receive a gift within his power: the prophet's head was paraded on a platter. Pilate's role in the crucifixion of Jesus is similar. Canonical literature suggested that

---

[142] IKML English Bible/Mark 6:20, underscore.
[143] IKML English Bible/Mark 6:21–28, annotation.
[144] Ibid.
[145] IKML English Bible/Matthew 27:24, annotation.
[146] Ibid.
[147] IKML English Bible/Matthew 26:15, 23, 25, annotations.

Pilate was given the opportunity to pardon Jesus during his trial. For Musazi, Pilate was mandated by God to protect Galilee's rural messiah. But like Herod, Pilate was misinformed; the outcome was unscrupulous. Like Pilate, Muteesa governed according to imperial pressure, not farmers' interests.

Reading Revolution and Intrigue[148]

When Uganda's colonial government invested Muteesa II in 1942, they believed that they had backed the reign of 'the undoubted Kabaka' of Buganda. The logic of colonial rule necessitated predictable power and social stability guaranteed by sure-fire sovereigns. Prior to colonialism, though, political fluidity and the frequent transition of monarchical power best described the contingencies of sovereignty in Buganda. Regicide and usurpation were common. In the mid-1940s, Musazi, like many others, did not believe that Muteesa was skilled enough to govern Buganda effectively. For many farmers, Muteesa's sovereignty was not sacrosanct. 'Old thatch' was not enough to legitimise monarchical authority in Ganda politics.[149] Kings were expected to ensure political health and economic stability among their subjects. 'The kinyomo-ant which takes the flying ants, guards them', recounted one Luganda proverb about kingship.[150] In the 1700s and 1800s, farmers supported intrigue to remove incompetent royals during periods of ecological crises to realign local economies and the practice of power.[151] Bulemeezi's Mawanda had, after all, secured his kingship during a period of considerable rivalry.

Archived interviews with rioters in the 1940s suggest that organisation was under way to remove Muteesa II from Buganda's throne. One colonial report indicated that, with the support of Musazi and leading farmers' activists, aspiring princes sought to eat Buganda's

---

[148] Some of the material in this section was reproduced earlier in Jonathon L. Earle, 'Reading Revolution in Late Colonial Buganda', *Journal of Eastern African Studies*, 6 (2012), 507–26.

[149] Walser, *Luganda Proverbs*, no. 1149.

[150] Ibid., no. 4925.

[151] David L. Schoenbrun, 'We Are What We Eat: Ancient Agriculture between the Great Lakes', *Journal of African History*, 34 (1993), 1–31.

kingship – '*okulya Bwakabaka*'.[152] Reports following the 1945 riots showed that 'many rumours' circulated among communities about the poor health of Buganda's king, a youth 'subject to fits'.[153] It was concluded that rioting had been the result of the 'youth and inexperience of the Kabaka and the general belief that he was unduly subject to European influence'.[154] After the 1945 riots, Entebbe investigators conducted interviews with leading antagonists, many of whom were deported to northern Uganda. One dissenter, anonymously identified as a 'Protestant Preacher', argued that effort was being made to 'get rid of the Kabaka' because he refused to remove self-serving chiefs from their positions of power.[155]

Interviews from the period also indicated that one of the leading conspirators who aimed to usurp Buganda's throne was Prince Ssuuna, the son of Buganda's deposed monarch, Mwanga. By the early 1940s, Ssuuna had begun organising intrigue. As one colonial analysis remarked, Ssuuna 'thought that with a young Kabaka on the throne the time was ripe for him to try and assert his own authority'.[156] As early as 1943, one year after Muteesa's coronation, Ssuuna worked toward removing Muteesa from power. Buganda's conspiring prince did not believe that the kingdom's young monarch was able to govern their state effectively. With the support of Musazi and Buganda's northern trade unionists, *Omulangira* Ssuuna marketed himself as an aspirant king who would rule the state with power and equity. Meetings occurred throughout the kingdom to organise Ssuuna's bid. In 1943, Ssuuna, Musazi and a cohort of other political activists gathered in Butambala, Buganda's Muslim capital, to strategise removing Muteesa from power (Chapter 4).[157] With his cohort of

---

[152] 'Report of the Commission of Inquiry into the Disturbances which occurred in Uganda during January, 1945', p. 10.
[153] BNA CO 536/215/10 'Pointers', Director of Security Intelligence, 5 April 1945.
[154] BNA CO 536/215/10 Government House, Uganda, to Secretary of State for the Colonies, 7 March 1945.
[155] BNA CO 536/215/11 'Commission of Inquiry into Civil Disturbances in Uganda: Supplementary Secret Report, A Protestant Preacher', January 1945, pp. 70–1.
[156] BNA CO 536/215/10 'Analysis of the Strike' [early 1945], p. 2.
[157] BNA CO 536/215/11 'Commission of Inquiry into Civil Disturbances in Uganda: Supplementary Secret Report, A Responsible Ssaza Chief', January 1945, p. 25.

usurpers, Prince Ssuuna summoned a meeting around what had been advertised as 'a big feast'.[158] To a chief in Butambala, Ssuuna wrote: 'I write to tell you to get ready for we are coming to you to put things to rights and to prepare them [. . .] These are to help us in drafting our affairs which we want to prepare together, and we ask you to get your matters ready on that day. We will continue working until our plan is complete.'[159] Musazi's father had been loyal to Ssuuna's. And if need be, the prospect of investing a new king to govern Buganda was both appropriate and historically unsurprising.

Ssuuna and Musazi corresponded extensively throughout 1944. In letters written between May and June 1944, Ssuuna referred to his Ffumbe clansman, Musazi, as a 'parent'.[160] 'I am your child,' Ssuuna wrote in one letter to Musazi.[161] In 1945, the two were principal organisers of the riots.[162] With the help of the Uganda African Farmers' Union and the Motor Drivers' Union, Ssuuna circulated rumours, planned meetings and directed the distribution of food. In a letter to the director of the Motor Drivers' Union, Ssuuna asserted: 'What I ask is this: that you allow food stuffs to be brought in and bought by local Baganda for their food but don't let it be taken into the Township.'[163] He continued: 'Now, my men, I ask you to listen to what I say and give consideration to my request that I have put before you.'[164] Ssuuna's public performance was reminiscent of the past, a time when pretender kings assumed the etiquette of kingship. As recently as the sovereignty of Ssuuna's namesake (*Kabaka* Ssuuna), the organisation of feasts and food blockades had

---

[158] BNA CO 536/215/11 'Commission of Inquiry into Civil Disturbances in Uganda: Supplementary Secret Report, A Muganda in a Responsible Position', January 1945, p. 15.

[159] BNA CO 536/215/11 *Omulangira* Y. Ssuuna to *Omwami* Alamanzane Ganya, 17 September 1943.

[160] BNA CO 536/215/10 Dispatch to the Secretary of State on the Strikes and Disturbances, 'Notes on Political Background to Recent Events in Buganda', Appendix B to Annexure A, 10 February 1945.

[161] Ibid.

[162] BNA CO 536/215/10 Dispatch to the Secretary of State on the Strikes and Disturbances, 'Notes on Political Background to Recent Events in Buganda', Annexure A, January 1945.

[163] BNA CO 536/215/10 *Omulangira* Y. Ssuuna to J.M. Kivu, Uganda African Motor Drivers Trade Union, 19 January 1945.

[164] Ibid.

been used to centralise political power.[165] The consumption and distribution of food was central to how reciprocal obligations were forged in the past;[166] and its preparation and distribution were used to organise and end periods of political violence.[167] In 1945, Ssuuna hoped that food politicking would translate into popular support for his coronation.

During a private meeting following the riots, Muteesa II confronted Ssuuna, who confessed that the ultimate intention of the 1945 disturbance was to 'dethrone the Kabaka and usurp the position'.[168] This alarmed colonial officials. 'It should be remembered in connection with these rumours', noted one report, 'that in the old days it was customary for the death of the Kabaka to be accompanied by disputes extending frequently to civil wars between the surviving princes who contended for the succession'.[169] In response, with the support of Uganda's colonial government, Ssuuna was deported to the Ssese Islands on charges of political intrigue.[170]

The Bible and the long history of usurpation in Buganda were not the only ideological archives from which Musazi imagined upheaval. Like many activists in the 1940s, Musazi used global intellectual history to reflect on the possibilities of regime change.[171] In addition to teaching him to read texts, Musazi's training in England had exposed him to international politics. From its founding in the nineteenth century, St Augustine's was a training ground for colonial diocesan clergy

---

[165] Reid, *Political Power in Precolonial Buganda*. For further discussion on the politics of etiquette and food in the history of modern Africa, see John Iliffe, *Honour in African History* (Cambridge: Cambridge University Press, 2005), p. 62; Derek R. Peterson, *Ethnic Patriotism and the East African Revival: A History of Dissent*, c. 1935–1972 (Cambridge: Cambridge University Press, 2012), pp. 141–3; Summers, 'Radical Rudeness', 741–70.

[166] Walser, *Luganda Proverbs*, nos. 904 & 1205; Hanson, *Landed Obligation*, pp. 173–5.

[167] Mukasa, 'The Rule of the Kings of Buganda', p. 138.

[168] BNA CO 536/215/10 'Record of an Interview at Government House of the Kabaka and Prince Ssuuna, with His Excellency, in the presence of the Chief Secretary and the Resident, Buganda', [early 1945].

[169] BNA CO 536/215/10 Annexure A, Dispatch to the Secretary of State on the Strikes and Disturbances, 'Notes on Political Background to Recent Events in Buganda', January 1945.

[170] BNA CO 536/215/10 BNA CO 536/215/10 'Analysis of the Strike: Sequel', [early 1945].

[171] LFP 30/12 D.S.K. Musoke, '*Buganda Nyaffe*, Part I: A Descriptive Booklet about Land and its Users', Mss., [c. June 1944], pp. 33–6. Musoke used the global history of Atlantic slavery to critique British colonial policy.

and 'native' ministers,[172] a tradition the school upheld at least until the mid-twentieth century. In 1953, students from no fewer than thirteen countries from around the world constituted St Augustine's student body.[173] It is reasonable to suggest that the student body was comparably diverse during Musazi's coursework.[174] International students, moreover, attended a college that exhibited political sensibilities. The English Church inspired the political nationalism of Edward Coleridge (1800–83), the College's founder. Edward Coleridge had also been influenced by the writings of his forebear, Samuel Taylor Coleridge (1772–1834), a Romantic poet whose shade of nationalism and dissent was influenced by notions of social equality and environmental sustainability.[175]

Musazi's stay in England coincided with the General Strike of May 1926, which gave shape to his developing sense of social justice.[176] Organised by the Trade Union Congress over low wages and poor working conditions among coal miners, the strike demonstrated to Musazi the importance of organised mass protest. Hoping to recreate the strikes in postwar Uganda, Musazi incorporated the strategies of the General Strike in 1945, a connection that colonial officials specifically noted in one report.[177] The General Strike also fuelled Musazi's interest in the history of peasant struggle in nineteenth-century France. When he returned to Uganda, Émile François Zola was arguably his favourite writer and activist.[178] Musazi's deep appreciation for Zola resulted in an effort to persuade his sister to name her son Émile. After failing to convince his sister, Musazi successfully lobbied for the name

---

[172] Carey, *God's Empire*, pp. 275–6.
[173] UCU BA 1/179.9 K. Sansbury to Anglican Archbishops and Bishops, December 1953. Students attended from the following regions: East, West and Central Africa, Canada, Ceylon, England, India, Hong Kong, Japan, Mauritius, New Zealand, Pakistan and the United States.
[174] Carey, *God's Empire*, p. 285.
[175] Ibid., pp. 272–3. For further discussion on Coleridge's social and environmental vision, see Richard Holmes, *Coleridge: Early Visions, 1772–1804* (London: Pantheon, 1989), pp. 59–88.
[176] Interview, Hugo Barlow, 11 November 2010, Munyonyo (Kampala). See also 'Report of the Commission of Inquiry into the Disturbances which occurred in Uganda during January, 1945', pp. 9 & 11.
[177] 'Report of the Commission of Inquiry into the Disturbances which occurred in Uganda during January, 1945', p. 9.
[178] Interview, Hugo Barlow, 11 November 2010, Munyonyo (Kampala).

of Victor Hugo, his second favourite French writer.[179] Musazi studied French,[180] and read Zola's *J'Accuse!*, the central literary document of the Dreyfus Affair.[181] Printed in *L'Aurore* on 13 January 1898, Zola appealed to France's president on behalf of Alfred Dreyfus, a Jewish officer who had been removed from the military without trial:

Since they have dared, I myself shall also dare. I shall speak the truth, because I promised to do so if the normal channels of justice did not proclaim it fully and completely. My duty is to speak [. . .] My night would be haunted by the specter of the innocent man who, far away, is suffering the most atrocious of tortures for a crime he did not commit. I cry out this truth to you, *monsieur le Président*, with all the force of my outrage as an upright and decent man. In deference to your own honor, I am convinced that you do not know the truth. And to whom else shall I denounce the maleficent crowd of true criminals, if not to you, the chief magistrate of the land.[182]

Three decades later, when Musazi organised *Abazzukulu*, the letters of the movement echoed the nuances of Zola's argument. In the 1930s, the British government had dismissed without trial two members of Buganda's *Lukiiko*. The dismissal reminded Musazi of Dreyfus' controversial sentence. And to chide British policy, Musazi argued similarly to Zola:

[I]f anyone lying under the flag of the British Justice can be dismissed without having his case first tried by the Lukiiko, and if this becomes a custom, many people are liable to suffer a doom when those People in authority know very well that they can do whatever they like without being checked.[183]

By reading Zola alongside the history of Buganda's kingship, Musazi engaged in the creative practice of imagining alternative political futures. In the mid-1940s, Musazi's reading of Zola was radicalised further. Working with Prince Ssuuna, and mindful of both the long

---

[179] Ibid.
[180] UCU BA 1/66.2 Knight, St Augustine's, to Bishop of Uganda, 15 October 1927.
[181] Mark K. Jensen, *Emile Zola's J'Accuse!: A New Translation with a Critical Introduction* (Soquel, C.A.: Bay Side Press, 1992), p. 5.
[182] Ibid., p. 15.
[183] BNA CO 536/202/4/6 The Kintu Descendants to Governor of Uganda, 30 August 1939.

history of intrigue in central Uganda and the critique of monarchical corruption in the Bible, Musazi used Harold Laski to rethink the
mutability of power in colonial Buganda.

On the evening of the 1945 riots,[184] Musazi was closely reading
the political theory of the Fabian intellectual Harold Laski (1893–
1950), Labour parliamentarian and lecturer at the London School
of Economics.[185] Next to the Bible and the Book of Common Prayer,
Musazi's most-read book in his library is Laski's *Reflections on the
Revolution of our Time* (1943). Published in 1943, *Reflections* is
one of only two books dated to the 1940s that remained in Musazi's
library.[186] Musazi's copy contains twelve annotated passages and no
fewer than fifty-three underscored sections. Buganda's political landscape is specifically referenced five times throughout the book.[187] The
first four read:

LASKI TEXT: The challenge to our system of values is, if this argument be correct, the outcome of our failure to maintain the right to hope; and that failure, in its turn, is
born of the fact that our relations of production do not
enable us to exploit with sufficient adequacy the forces
of production at our disposal.

ANNOTATION: Yes So it is in Buganda now.[188]

LASKI TEXT: And we are entitled to conclude that where, to-day,
that development is not organized it is because those
who refuse to attempt it have vested interests enlightenment would weaken.

ANNOTATION: True with Buganda of today.[189]

---

[184] IKML Harold Laski, *Reflections on the Revolution of Our Time*, pastedown,
annotation.

[185] Isaac Kramnick and Barry Sheerman, *Harold Laski: A Life on the Left*
(London: Hamish Hamilton, 1993); Jeanne Morefield, 'States Are Not People:
Harold Laski on Unsettling Sovereignty, Rediscovering Democracy', *Political
Research Quarterly*, 58 (2005), 659–69.

[186] Musazi's library contains a copy of P.A. Wadia and K.T. Merchant's *Our
Economic Problem* (Bombay: New York Company, 1945), which he
autographed in 1948.

[187] Musazi also referenced 'Uganda' in relation to the Atlantic Charter (IKML
Laski *Reflections*, p. 190, annotation).

[188] IKML Laski *Reflections*, p. 179, annotation.

[189] IKML Laski *Reflections*, p. 185, annotation.

LASKI TEXT: For any society in which the few are so wealthy and the many so poor that their minds are driven to perpetual consideration of their wealth and poverty is, in fact, a society at war, whether the fight be open or concealed. It is a society, once its power to expand is arrested, which cannot think in terms of a common interest because whatever is taken from one class is given thereby to another.

ANNOTATION: Is Buganda not challenged![190]

LASKI TEXT: The public opinion of this country is ready for fundamental change. Its traditional habits have been profoundly disturbed.

ANNOTATION: Buganda too[191]

For Musazi, Laski's analysis illuminated Buganda's political topography. Musazi and his colleagues believed that corrupt chiefs, Indian ginners and colonial bureaucrats were economically and politically undercutting the interests of their kingdom. But Buganda's young king was politically impotent. Marginalia emphasised economic impartiality and political liberation. Buganda was a kingdom adversely impacted by 'relations of production', a polity ruled by leaders whose 'interests Enlightenment would weaken'. Consequently, Musazi concluded that Buganda was a 'society at war', a kingdom 'ready for fundamental change'.

Musazi was able to draw from Laski what he needed; it was not necessary to subscribe to Laski's or Marx's revolutionary call for the abrogation of feudal monarchs. Unlike other labour or socialist organisers throughout the 1800s and 1900s, including Nkrumah, Nyerere and Obote, the revivification of kingship was central to addressing colonial crises for Musazi. Republican revolution did not drive his public activism in ways that followed the logic or predicated outcomes of Vulgar Marxism. In Laski's *Revolution*, Musazi reflected on the collapse of over 400 years of monarchical rule in Russia's agrarian empire:

LASKI TEXT: It is expressed again in the French Revolution by the *Enragés*, and by those who, with Babeuf, made the last despairing effort to recapture the fraternity for which

---

[190] IKML Laski *Reflections*, p. 186, annotation.
[191] IKML Laski *Reflections*, p. 190, annotation.

men hoped in the great days of 1789 when those 'petty lawyers and stewards of manors' whom Burke regarded with such contempt, legislated a new world into being. We catch again the same accent in the spacious dreams of 1848 and, above all, in that supreme optimism which enabled Marx and Engels, in a hundred pages, to trace the whole pattern, past and future, of human evolution. It is present, again, in that sudden sense of emancipation felt by the whole world when the Russian people struck off the chains of Czarist despotism.

After reading the text, Musazi annotated: 'True[;] May it come in Buganda of today?'[192] Musazi offered an interrogative, not political proposition. The alleged necessity of the Bolshevik's revolution did not clearly translate in central Uganda in 1945. Lenin's critique of imperialism, that it represented the highest stage of capitalism, and Laski's analysis, aptly explained social rupture in rural Buganda. But political prognosis was more complicated. Evidence suggests that Musazi supported the removal of Buganda's weak king prior to the 1945 riots, not the abrogation of the institution of kingship. The hope of Bulemeezi's heir of Kintu was to restore Buganda's monarchy to a time when strong kings protected the state's citizens from political and economic exploitation.

Conclusion: Textual Annotations

Musazi's annotations offer no fewer than three insights into the intellectual history of colonial Buganda. First, his marginalia muddle the supposed boundaries of colonial knowledge. While the Bible was the most annotated text in Musazi's remaining library, it was certainly not the only literature that he used to explore Buganda's colonial monarchy. Musazi's connection with Buganda's northern frontier provided him with a strong sense of authoritative kingship, which he advocated for throughout the late 1930s and 1940s. Building upon this intellectual and political tradition, Musazi comfortably adapted varying texts. The themes of his annotations are largely consistent across both the Bible and Laski. These notations indicate that his exegetical practice

---

[192] IKML Laski *Reflections*, p. 184, annotation.

was not compartmentalised into two separate fields of literary production: one 'religious', the other 'secular'. Second, Musazi's notations show the extent to which the expected outcomes of European intellectual history were largely problematic in Buganda. Musazi used Laski to formalise social critique, not to formalise systematic solutions. Orthodox European interpretations of religion or revolution did not overly concern Musazi; colonial literary practices were far more creative. Finally, Musazi's use of literacy highlights some of the various discursive registers from which activists drew in the 1940s to imagine political alternatives. This chapter has suggested that royalist discourse constituted a particular trope; there were many others. Activists such as Apolo Kaggwa and Musazi had different interpretations of Buganda's eighteenth-century kingship, and from these competing pasts they sought to regulate power and economic production in the colonial state. Reading practices and historical interpretations, though, did not only raise concerns about the fictions of kingship. They raised a larger set of questions about citizenship and political representation in Buganda, especially following the Second World War. It is these concerns that preoccupy the next chapter.

2 | *Eridadi M.K. Mulira: Cosmopolitanism and Citizenship, c. 1909–c. 1949*

Musazi had founded Bazzakulu ba Kintu [. . .] and incurred immediate opposition from Mengo [. . .] Mulira was less forceful – quiet, very truthful, and always refusing to make rash promises. He was very inclusive – always trying to heal divisions and bring people together.

Ernest K.K. Sempebwa[1]

There is no nation on earth that can progress when one part is enjoying freedom while the rest are slaves. But the Bakopi in Buganda cannot claim freedom [. . .] We long for a government with peoples' representation. We want all the parts to be with representation in all the councils of this nation. It sounds a distant cry from where we now are, but when you look at it critically, you find that it is the only type of government that can satisfy everyone's soul.

Eridadi M.K. Mulira[2]

Eridadi M.K. Mulira (1909–95) was the foremost Protestant statesman in Buganda by the late 1950s. As a member of Buganda's parliament, he lobbied for the federal integration of Buganda during a moment of intense secessionist politicking on the eve of independence. In the mid-1950s, he helped secure the return of *Kabaka* Muteesa II from exile in London (Chapter 3). Earlier, during the late 1940s, Mulira was an international commentator on Buganda's postwar politics.[3] Less than four months before the 1945 riots, Ignatius K. Musazi

---

[1] Interview, Gordon P. McGregor with Ernest Sempebwa, March 2002, Makerere, in Gordon P. McGregor, *King's College Budo: A Centenary History, 1906–2006* (Kampala: Fountain Publishers, 2006), p. 138.

[2] E.M.K. Mulira, *Government Gyennonya: Abakopi Okuba N'eddobozi mu Buganda* (Kampala: Uganda Bookshop Press, 1944), p. 5.

[3] BNA CO 537/4677/87 E.M.K. Mulira to Joseph Sheridan, 'Background to the Troubles in Buganda: Being a Contribution to His Honour Sir Joseph Sheridan's Enquiry', n.d. See also E.M.K. Mulira, *Thoughts of a Young African* (London: Lutterworth Press for the United Society for Christian Literature, 1945); E.M.K. Mulira, *The Vernacular in African Education* (London: Longmans, Green & Co., 1951), pp. 30–2.

visited Mulira, his former colleague at King's College, Budo.[4] Now
at Bishop Tucker's School, Mukono, Musazi handed Mulira a memorandum that he was preparing to send to the *kabaka* and the colonial government. Musazi asked Mulira to think through the document
during the evening, so that its contents might be discussed the following morning. In the evening, Mulira read Musazi's draft with care.
Musazi argued for Buganda's parliament (*Lukiiko*) to be dismissed
and reconstituted with a new order of chiefs, uncorrupted by bribery,
who would champion the economic and political rights of the kingdom's rural farmers.[5] For Musazi, a powerful monarchy would be well
positioned to ensure this. After he finished reading the draft, Mulira
rejected Musazi's central argument, summarising: '[U]nfortunately,
I was not satisfied, in fact to be truthful I was very disappointed. I did
not feel the Memorandum had tackled the problem at issue; in the
main it was very vague.'[6] Mulira remarked further: 'I wondered very
much whether, if that was the best that could be expected, we would
give the new leadership we were clamouring after. I went to bed very
disturbed.'[7] At 3:00 am, Mulira awoke with what he described as a
crystal-clear proposal for the reform of Buganda's monarchy; he began
editing Musazi's proposal. The result of Mulira's revision was the publication of his first political treatise, *Gavumenti Ey'abantu: Abakopi
Okuba N'eddobozi Mu Buganda* (*Government of the People: The
Commoners to Have a Voice in Buganda*).

In *Gavumenti Ey'abantu*, a sixteen-page essay, Mulira provided
a detailed administrative model for the kingdom of Buganda. Like
Musazi, Mulira believed that Mmengo was a government operating 'in
darkness'.[8] In contrast, though, he argued that Mmengo was ethically

---

[4] CCAS MP E.M.K. Mulira, ['Autobiography'], Mss., n.d., p. 84 (hereafter 'Autobiography'). Mulira dated the visit to an unidentified Saturday in
September 1944. Concerning the autobiography, Peter Mulira, E.M.K. Mulira's
heir, suggests that it was written largely while his father was in exile in the late
1950s as a means of passing time. To Peter's knowledge, E.M.K. did attempt
to publish the autobiography (JLEP Peter Mulira to Jonathon L. Earle, 22
December 2011).

[5] CMS ACC 549/z6 E.M.K. Mulira, 'The Legacy of Two Schools: Being a
Historical Background to the Causes of Trouble in Uganda, in 1945', Mss., [c.]
1945, p. 8.

[6] 'Autobiography', p. 84.

[7] Ibid.

[8] Mulira, *Government Gyennonya*, p. 2.

obliged to provide equal parliamentary representation from among Buganda's peasantry. Until the 1950s, Buganda's parliament was comprised mostly of appointed chiefs, which Musazi's memorandum did not address. For Mulira, Mmengo's political 'darkness' was the result of its failure to legislatively incorporate *bakopi*, rural and urban commoners of no particular royal or chiefly distinction. Development in the state required the political incorporation of commoners.[9] It was not sufficient for strong kings to simply guard the economic and social welfare of farmers, as Musazi had argued. Commoners in the state were to possess the same political power as chiefs or Musazi's courageous kings.

Disagreements about representation and the protection of economic interests were part of a larger conversation about citizenship and authenticity in postwar Uganda. Musazi and his Balemeezi farmers had reclaimed older traditions about powerful kingship to legitimise their group's interests. Other organisations, however, looked elsewhere to invent useful pasts and public legitimacy. The Bataka Union, for example, was a prominent movement throughout the late 1940s. Their leaders argued that they represented the interests of Buganda's clans and clan heads. The principal activist of the association was the Catholic dissenter Semakula Mulumba, who used the language of authenticity and clanship to petition Buganda's leadership for political concessions. According to Mulumba, the priority of the Bataka was to 'see that the indigenous customs and traditions, rights and powers of the Bataka of Uganda are most carefully preserved in their purity and integrity for the perpetuation of the national culture of Uganda'.[10] Mulumba used copious letter-writing in the late 1940s to support his interests. To *Kabaka* Muteesa II, Mulumba noted that 'the Protectorate Government ought to be proud of the "Bataka Uganda" (BU), because it is the only indigenous institution truly representative of our unadulterated Uganda culture'.[11] To colonial officials, Mulumba advocated for a society where citizens were obliged to present their concerns

---

[9] Ibid., p. 5.
[10] BNA CO 537/3593 'The Bataka of Uganda (BU)', n.d. See also BNA CO 537/3593 Semakula Mulumba to Grandfathers and Sirs, the Chiefs and all Ankole people, 17 May 1948; BNA CO 537/4666 For and on behalf of the Christians of Uganda [21 signatures] to Semakulu Mulumba 14 February 1949.
[11] BNA CO 537/4666/24 Semakula Mulumba to Muteesa II, 21 February 1949.

before 'the Bataka for public discussion'.[12] And to the Anglican bishop of Uganda, Mulumba accused the Protestant church of raping the country of her cultural virtues and resources: 'The Church of England and the British Government are the mother and the father of their daughter, Uganda. Indeed, it makes one feel most uncomfortable to think of a mother who screens her husband while he rapes their own charming little daughter of 6!'[13]

This chapter contrasts E.M.K. Mulira's early political thought with Musazi's and Mulumba's. It begins by placing Mulira's activism within the long history of social mobility in Kooki, a tributary kingdom in western Buganda. Mulira recast the political history of Kooki with Christian overtones and the social philosophy of the Ghanaian intellectual James Aggrey to author plays and novels throughout the 1940s. During a period when Musazi and Mulumba were advocating for their respective brands of nativism, I argue that Mulira used literary production to advocate for types of social progress that were not contingent upon the historical fabrication of either powerful kingships or clans. Mulira's intellectual project focused on the life and movement of ordinary citizens (*bakopi*). To explore alternative citizenship, Mulira fixated on gender hierarchies and the importance of cosmopolitan states. In doing so, his project shows that communities in Buganda had very different ideas about what it actually meant to be *Baganda* in the mid-1900s. What exactly did one have to do or believe to be an upright Muganda or command political authority in the late 1940s? What sort of citizen or subject was worthy of emulation in the public sphere? Mulira's early intellectual biography shows that these questions were highly contentious.

Inclusive States and Christian Centrism

During the 1940s, Mulira's political sensibilities were moderate. As Musazi and Mulumba organised radical politics, Mulira offered measured responses that underscored a centrist's approach to social reform. Mulira's political leaning was shaped both by his upbringing

---

[12] BNA CO 537/4666 Semakula Mulumba to Boyd, British Resident in Buganda, 31 March 1949.
[13] BNA CO 537/3593 Semakula Mulumba to Bishop C.E. Stuart, 26 July 1948.

in Kooki and by the impact of Christian experience and discipleship. Throughout the postwar period, he adapted a particular interpretation of Kooki society and Christian community that modelled ethnic inclusivity and social impartiality.

Eridadi Medadi Kasirye Mulira was born on 28 February 1909 in Kamesi, Kooki. E.M.K.'s father, Rwamahwa Nasanaeri Ndawula Kiwomamagaaya [Mulira] (c. 1873–1953), was the paternal grandson of *Omukama* (King) Ndaula I, whom E.M.K. believed to have ruled the kingdom of Kooki from approximately 1810 to 1835.[14] At the time of Nasanaeri's birth, Kooki was a tributary state of her much larger neighbour to the east, Buganda.[15] If nineteenth-century Bulemeezi is best described as a platform for tenacious and royalist politics (Chapter 1), Kooki may equally be designated as an arena of arbitration, a place where statebuilders were constantly challenged to mediate competing regional claims. By the nineteenth century, Kooki's *kibiito* kings had taken formal steps to sever their royal ties with Bunyoro, the land of their origin.[16] According to Mulira, as early as the late eighteenth century, Kooki's third king, Mujwiga, sent emissaries to Buganda's king, *Kabaka* Jjunju, to reinforce dissociation from Bunyoro.[17] Michael Twaddle suggests that by the nineteenth century, Kooki 'depended upon playing off one powerful neighbour against another while keeping its own agricultural clans and slaves under careful control'.[18] With Buganda to the east, Bunyoro to the north, Ankole to the west and Rwanda to the south, Kooki relied increasingly upon 'controlling an appropriate

---

[14] CCAS MP E.M.K. Mulira, 'The Kingdom of Kooki during the 19th Century', Mss., 1972, p. 13. Rwamahwa was the childhood name of Ndaula. Following captivity, he was given the names Katezi and Kiwomamagaaya ('Autobiography', pp. vii–viii).

[15] Michael Twaddle, *Kakungulu and the Creation of Uganda, 1868–1928* (London: James Currey, 1993), p. 2.

[16] Ibid., p. 1.

[17] CCAS MP E.M.K. Mulira, 'The Kingdom of Kooki', pp. 11 & 37. E.M.K.'s sources included his recollection of oral traditions, his father's narration, Apolo Kaggwa's published histories and traditions reprinted in *Munno* and *Ebifa*.

[18] Twaddle, *Kakungulu and the Creation of Uganda*, p. 1. For further discussion on the history of Kooki, see 'Ebyafaayo bya Koki', *Munno*, 1929, pp. 99 and 193; Nasanaeli Ndawula Mulira, 'Engoma ye Koki', *Munno*, November 1921, pp. 171–2.

percentage of the manufactures imported into the East African interior during the second half of the nineteenth century, firearms especially'.[19]

During the effort to consolidate armaments and mediate competing regional claims,[20] *Kabaka* Muteesa I authorised a plundering expedition into Kooki in 1875.[21] Muteesa's raid resulted in the loss of approximately 4,000 Kooki cows, and an unidentified number of women and children were taken into servitude.[22] Nasanaeri and members of the royal family were taken to Buganda's capital (*kibuga*) by Tebukozza Kyambalango, who was the general spearheading the operation.[23] Muteesa I distributed the Kooki royals and Nasanaeri was placed under the family of Kisawuzi, a Ganda chief living near Mmengo.[24] During the struggle for converts in late nineteenth-century Buganda, Nasanaeri – like his newfound chief – converted to Islam.[25] However, following Christian efforts to secure Buganda's throne from *Kabaka* Kalema in October 1889 (Chapter 4),[26] Nasanaeri converted to Protestantism under the teaching of the Christian chief Danieri Mulyagonja, from whom Nasanaeri received the name 'Mulira'. The name 'Mulira' was taken from the saying, *mulira mu ngalo* (one who eats from the fingers).[27] For Mulyagonja, it reflected the seriousness with which Mulira took his Protestantism.

Mulira participated in the religious wars of Mmengo, during which he met George Baskerville, who worked with the Church Missionary Society (CMS). Following the religious wars, Nasanaeri became Baskerville's *omuweereza* (labourer), before accompanying him in January 1893 to

---

[19] Twaddle, *Kakungulu and the Creation of Uganda*, p. 1.
[20] For further analysis, see John Beattie, *The Nyoro State* (Oxford: Clarendon Press, 1971), pp. 33–94; Shane Doyle, *Crisis and Decline in Bunyoro: Population and Environment in Western Uganda 1860–1955* (Oxford: James Currey, 2006), pp. 42–93.
[21] Twaddle, *Kakungulu and the Creation of Uganda*, p. 4.
[22] Ibid.
[23] CMS ACC 265 z6/1 A.B.K. Mulira, '*Ebisarira okumpi ebyo bulamu bwa Nasanaeri Ndaula Mulira*', Mss., 1956.
[24] CCAS MP E.M.K. Mulira, 'In Search of My Origin: Being an Attempt to Trace the Origin of the Hamite Rulers of Uganda', Mss., n.d., p. 43.
[25] 'Autobiography', p. viii.
[26] For further discussion see John A. Rowe, 'The Baganda Revolutionaries', *Tarikh*, 3 (1970), 34–46.
[27] 'Autobiography', p. viii.

Figure 2.1 'George Baskerville and his household at Ziba, 1894'

Back Row (left to right): Ibulayima Kyagulanyi; Kezekiya Disasi; Musa Kabusemere, herdsman; Yusito Bakisula, the new herdsman; Yakobo Mulira; Nasanaeri Mulira, assistant cook, later promoted steward; Yusito Gwavu, valet and laundryman

Centre Row: Aloni Muyinda, the head boy; the Revd George Baskerville; Esiteri Bakyerabidde, daughter of Tebuta, later wife of Gwavu

Front Row: Musa Tabula, herdsman; Enoka Kategere; Agiri, wife of Disasi; Zipola Tebuta, assistant cook; Enoka Kinywa, head cook
Source: Taylor, *The Growth of the Church in Buganda*

establish a mission outpost in Ziba, Kyaggwe (Figure 2.1).[28] In the same month Nasanaeri was baptised, and in September 1894 he was commissioned by Baskerville to evangelise and teach near Ngogwe, Kyaggwe.[29] In May 1896, Nasanaeri married Esiteri Nnambirya (c. 1877–?).[30]

---

[28] CMS ACC 265 z6/1 Mulira, *'Bulamu bwa Ndaula Mulira'*. For further discussion on the Baskerville Mission and the life and ministry of Nasanaeri, see John V. Taylor, *The Growth of the Church in Buganda: An Attempt at Understanding* (London: SCM Press, 1958), pp. 73–84; W.S. Musoke, 'Reverend George Baskerville's Work at Ngogwe and the Rest of Kyaggwe County' (unpublished Bachelor of Arts thesis, Makerere University, 1970).
[29] 'Autobiography', p. ix.
[30] CMS ACC 265 z6/1 Mulira, *'Bulamu bwa Ndaula Mulira'*.

Like Nasanaeri, Esiteri had converted from Islam to Protestantism, and after she was baptised at Namirembe in 1893, Nnambirya became an ardent worker with her husband at the CMS mission in Kyaggwe.[31]

Nasanaeri, with his family, returned to Kooki for the first time after his captivity in late 1898.[32] Over the following decades, the family spent significant periods of time in Kooki, alternating between church and government responsibilities. Following the 1900 Agreement, *Kamuswaga* (King) Edward Ndaula II apportioned Nasanaeri – his cousin – two square miles. Nasanaeri's return to Kooki was part of a larger development in the early 1900s to renegotiate power between Buganda's tributary state and Mmengo. Protestant chiefs who were sympathetic toward colonial statebuilding were appointed to work in politically sensitive areas, such as southern Buddu and Kooki. Apolo Kaggwa and Ganda powerbrokers worked with colonial backing to manage cattle herding practices and regulate the production of salt and iron in Kooki, whose chiefs, it was argued, obstructed the region's economic and political assimilation into Buganda. In 1911, Kaggwa informed colonial officials that the *Lukiiko* was sending a Muganda chief and clerk to 'help show him [*kamuswaga*] what he must do' to demonstrate cooperation with Ganda chiefs.[33] Equally concerned, in a letter to the colonial government, Kooki's provincial commissioner noted: 'The work of the Kooki Chiefs has been very unsatisfactory for some time past, and Captain O'Neill informed me that the repeated warnings they have received had no effect.'[34] The commissioner continued: 'With such incapable Sub-chiefs no doubt Kamuswaga, the Saza Chief, is handicapped, but as soon as they are weeded out and replaced by capable men, there is no reason why Kooki should not go ahead and keep pace with the other Sazas of this district.' Nasanaeri was appointed to the *Lukiiko* in late 1910 as a representative of Kooki, before being appointed the *kabaka*'s representative in Buddu in 1911, where he worked with the county's district surveyor.[35] In 1914, Nasanaeri and two chiefs supervised the partitioning of southeastern Buddu.[36]

[31] 'Autobiography', pp. xiii–xiv.
[32] CMS ACC 265 z6/1 Mulira, '*Bulamu bwa Ndaula Mulira*'.
[33] UNA SMP A46/663/3 A. Kaggwa and Z. Kisingiri to Buganda Provincial Commissioner, 2 June 1911.
[34] UNA SMP A46/668/13 Provincial Commissioner to Government Chief Secretary, 5 February 1913.
[35] CMS ACC 265 z6/1 Mulira, '*Bulamu bwa Ndaula Mulira*'.
[36] 'Autobiography', p. 7.

Eridadi Mulira's political sensibilities were influenced by Kooki's social landscapes. As a youth, he spent time in the *ekikaali* (palace) of Rakai, Kooki, listening to extensive discussions concerning Apolo Kaggwa, Stanislaus Mugwanya, Zakariya Kisingiri, Hamu Mukasa and Revd Henry Duta Kitakule.[37] Mulira recalled: '[R]akai was my first real eye-opener. At the palace I saw splendour that I had not imagined [. . .] There was court everyday and I loved to go and listen to the [courtiers] wrangle public affairs.'[38] The high discourse of palace politics complemented Mulira's growing interest in rural society and western Uganda's environs, where the allure of rural topography and simple farming and herding provided a point of reference to address urban rioting in the mid-1940s. In his later political career, Mulira recalled social practice in rural Kooki with nostalgia:

Most of our relatives: uncles, aunts, grand uncles and grand aunts etc. lived in [the kraal] with their cattle. We paid many happy visits to them and stayed with their cattle. Thus we learnt to look after the cattle and to milk the cows. I loved these visits very much; I loved the smell of burnt cow dung; which kept the fire going all the time; I loved the fresh milk drunk immediately after milking – it was hot – I loved the roasted meat eaten at Olusaka (Olusaka simply meant a bush) [. . .] In the Kraal we slept together on one large bed called Ekitabu. I loved the stories told at night.[39]

Mulira's lifelong interest in Kooki's past resulted in two unpublished histories: *In Search of My Origin: Being an Attempt to Trace the Origin of the Hamite Rulers of Uganda* (forty-nine pages, n.d.),[40] and *The Kingdom of Kooki during the 19th Century* (thirty-eight pages, 1972).[41] By the late 1940s, Mulira employed the political and environmental landscapes of Kooki to imagine a place for rural bakopi to live lives of rewarding labour in a cosmopolitan kingdom, a theme most readily observed in the novel *Teefe*, which I analyse below.[42] Mulira also used Kooki's ecological landscapes in the mid-1950s to critique

---

[37] 'Autobiography', p. 10.
[38] Ibid., p. 9.
[39] Ibid., p. 5.
[40] CCAS MP Mss.
[41] CCAS MP Mss.
[42] E.M.K. Mulira, *Teefe* (Kampala: Uganda Publishing House, 1968).

patriotic politics in Buganda, which is seen in his novel *Aligaweesa: Omuvubuka wa Uganda Empya* (Chapter 3).[43]

Mulira's dispassion toward patriotic politics in the 1940s, though, was also shaped by Christian experience. Mulira's parents were ardent Protestants. His father read the Bible every day, prayed in the morning and evening (which included praying for each Mulira child by name), and led compulsory family prayers twice daily.[44] E.M.K. exhibited his parents' spiritual fervour. By the 1930s, he studied the Bible and Christian literature regularly. Parables from the gospels permeated his literary corpus in the 1940s, and Mulira defined his later political nationalism in the 1950s as a distinctly Christian nationalism.[45] Mulira's Christianity was also characterised by frequent spiritual revelations, which he used to envision cosmopolitan space in colonial Buganda.

Mulira first experienced a Christian revelation shortly before his matriculation at King's College, Budo, in 1927.[46] By 1930, he had begun interpreting his dreams alongside Christian literacy to explore the politics of ethnicity in Buganda's capital. Mulira's private diaries contain sections that detailed his mysterious encounters, including the map of a geographical area that he traversed in a dream on 5 May 1930, while a student at Makerere College (Figure 2.2). To decipher the dream, Mulira adapted John Bunyan's *Pilgrim's Progress*, which Hamu Mukasa had helped reproduce in Luganda a few years earlier.[47] In the dream, Mulira found himself standing on the campus of Makerere College, Kampala's cosmopolitan university, where

---

[43] E.M.K. Mulira, *Aligaweesa: Omuvubuka wa Uganda Empya* (Kampala: Uganda Bookshop Press, [1955]). For further comparison, see E.M.K. Mulira, *Kiribedda ne Balizzakiwa: Abavubuka Ababiri Ab'omulembe* (Nairobi: East African Printers Kenya Ltd, 1963).

[44] 'Autobiography', p. xi.

[45] UCU BA 1/136.5 E.M.K. Mulira to H.M. Grace, [c.] 4 October 1959; ICS PP.UG.PP/1 E.M.K. Mulira, 'Self-Government for Uganda, An African State: Manifesto by the Progressive Party', Mss., n.d.

[46] 'Autobiography', p. 35. Material in this section is reproduced in Jonathon L. Earle, 'Dreams and Political Imagination in Colonial Buganda', *Journal of African History*, 58 (2017), 85–105.

[47] Isabel Hofmeyr indicates that *Pilgrim's Progress* was first published in Luganda in 1896 (Isabel Hofmeyr, *The Portable Bunyan: A Transnational History of The Pilgrim's Progress* (Princeton, NJ: Princeton University Press, 2004), p. 240). A third edition was printed in 1927, within which Hamu Mukasa is pictured in two of the prominent illustrations (John Bunyan, *Omutambuze*, trans. by E.C. Gordon, 3rd edn (Kampala: Uganda Bookshop, 1927)).

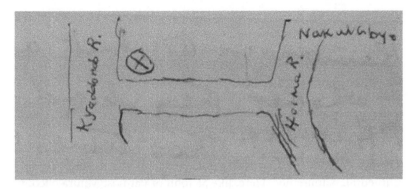

Figure 2.2 E.M.K. Mulira's Dream Map, n.d.
Source: CCAS MP E.M.K. Mulira, [Journal], Mss.

God showed him that 'the Baganda had chosen the broad way that led to destruction [. . .] going to perdition, and [. . .] completely lost.'[48] Mulira recounted:

In my dream I saw the students [Makerere students] in a crowd in the street (Hoima Road as it was called then) just where Kyaddondo Road joins with that Hoima Road. They were heading in the direction of Nakulabye. Then I heard a voice say 'All the Baganda have taken to the broad road including K . . . [*Kabaka* Chwa (?)], only the two students from Zanzibar have not joined them.' When I turned I saw the two Zanzibar students standing behind me motionless, Then I found myself turning to the right and taking a very faint path hardly noticeable.[49]

As the dream unfolded, Mulira was guided past Kyaddondo Road, where he soon encountered an 'old Kiganda hut', dirty and full of smoke. Outside of the home sat a group of inebriated elders, who refused to offer direction:

They [Ganda elders] paid no attention to me. I asked them a second time and they paid no attention either. Then I decided to turn to the left at almost right angles with the Kyaddondo Road. When I turned that way I saw a footpath. I walked on it a few [yards] until I came to a very filthy pit, so

---

[48] CCAS MP E.M.K. Mulira, [Journal], Mss., 8 April 1983.
[49] CCAS MP E.M.K. Mulira, [Journal], Mss., 'God's Uttermost Love for Me[:] The Dream', n.d.

filthy that I had never seen anything like it in all my life – I was aghast and turned back and went back to the dirty hut. I asked the gentlemen in the hut again whether they had seen my friends. This time, they rebuked me and shouted at me rude words and threatened that if I disturbed them again they would beat me. Meanwhile I saw my friends passing me in a crowd along the road from the Hoima Road. When they hit the Kyddondo Road they just walked across it in a crowd. After they had passed me I walked following in their trail but I could not cope with their speed.[50]

The dream concluded with Mulira hiking upward toward St Paul's Cathedral, Namirembe. Here, like St John of Patmos, Mulira encountered twenty-four elders who wore noticeably clean robes. He also observed a number of fantastic creatures before hearing Jesus, who now hovered above him, declare, 'Mulira, I will make you my servant among the people and I will grant to you whatever you will need'.[51]

Mulira's recounting of the dream borrowed from the symbolism used in Bunyan's text. In the dream, a young Mulira approached a cadre of Baganda sitting alongside a road that penetrated into the heart of Buganda's capital, Kyaddondo. Here, he found drunkenness, hostility and an absence of wisdom among Ganda elders, similar to those in Bunyan's 'certain place' and Vanity Fair. The compound on which the elders were found was strikingly dirty, as is the adjacent ground, where Mulira observed 'a very filthy pit, so filthy that I had never seen anything like it in all my life'. Mulira's picture paralleled Bunyan's 'Slough of Dispond [sic]', where pilgrims were 'grievously bedaubed with the dirt'.[52] In Bunyan's dream, 'miry Slough' symbolised the conviction of sinners, a place where the unconverted lived due to 'many fears and doubts, and discouraging apprehensions'.[53] The story's protagonist, Christian, is informed that the king does not take pleasure 'that this place should remain so bad'.[54] In consequence, virtuous labourers and surveyors, 'from all places of the King's dominions',[55] attempted to

---

[50] Ibid.
[51] '*Mulira, ndikufuula omuweereza wange mu bantu na buli ky'onoyagalanga nnaakikuko beranga*' (Ibid.).
[52] John Bunyan, *Pilgrim's Progress* (New York: P.F. Collier & Son, 1909), pp. 1 and 19.
[53] Ibid., p. 20.
[54] Ibid.
[55] Ibid.

cultivate the ground.[56] Like Bunyan's account, Mulira's vision pointed his audience to see the importance of citizens in the state who were not originally from the area. Running parallel to Mulira's road to destruction is Hoima Road, the 'narrow way',[57] which leads to and from the capital of Bunyoro. It is from those travelling to Bunyoro, Buganda's precolonial rival, that Mulira discovers his bearings. He is not guided by inept Ganda elders, but by non-Baganda youth.

In Mulira's retelling of the dream, he approached an interpreter after waking up:[58] the chaplain of Makerere College, Revd Nasanaeri Zake. To Zake Mulira critiqued Buganda's ineffectual gatekeepers, kings and chiefs, who, having built their homes near the Slough, enabled doubt and apprehension throughout society. In Bunyan's dream, Christian's monarch took definitive steps to unify different communities for common purpose and labour. For Buganda's elders, no such king is evident. Buganda's king is aloof, removed from Buganda's dirty politics. In Bunyan's model kingdom, society is inclusive, actors of 'all places' serve God's purposes. For Mulira, the luminaries in his dreams are not Baganda; they are commoners from Zanzibar and Bunyoro. Like Christian's Interpreter, Zake advised Mulira to keep his vision, 'a very important dream', near to his heart.

By using Christian literacy to recount his dream, Mulira creatively conjoined multiple forms of knowledge production in interwar Buganda. Contrary to what has been argued by scholars such as Jack Goody and Michael Ong,[59] communities and elites throughout eastern Africa were not simply preoccupied with written texts. As rural activists and urban elites engaged in new types of textual practice, they were participating in far-reaching conversations off the written page, where dreams and literary practice mutually shaped each other. In Mulira's case, this relationship allowed him to begin to reflect upon the question of ethnic mobility in the kingdom.

Mulira's Kooki sensibilities and Christian centrism were also impacted by the teaching and mentorship of Revd Canon Harold Myers Grace (1888–1967), with whom Mulira studied and worked at King's

---

[56] Ibid.
[57] Ibid., p. 32.
[58] Ibid., pp. 32–41.
[59] Jack Goody, *The Logic of Writing and the Organization of Society* (Cambridge: Cambridge University Press, 1986); Walter J. Ong, *Orality and Literacy*, 2nd edn (London: Routledge, 2002).

College, Budo. As I show in the following section, it was also under Grace's mentorship that Mulira studied James Aggrey's philosophy of co-education. Grace served with the CMS in Uganda from 1914 to 1934, and served as the headmaster at Budo from 1926 to 1934.[60] At Budo, Mulira and Grace forged a mutually influential relationship that characterised their friendship until the latter's passing toward the end of the 1960s.[61] According to Mulira, his evangelical conversion at Budo had estranged him from a number of his Ugandan peers.[62] Mulira found solace in his friendship with Grace, who opened his library and home to Mulira:

The Rev. Grace had [. . .] given me permission to borrow any book from his study [. . .] Because I could drop in at the Grace's house any time especially at the week-ends, I managed to meet important people who visited the school either at 10.00 o'clock tea or at afternoon tea.[63]

Following a period of study at Makerere in the early 1930s, Mulira returned to teach at King's College in 1932, where for the next few years he worked closely with Grace. Under Grace's guidance, Mulira further developed a particular centrism that would typify much of his activism throughout the 1950s. This approach was often formulated by blending local and European political traditions, which Mulira had been encouraged to do by Grace:

All of us loved and respected him [Grace] and we would do anything to support his cause, and it was a very noble cause he had at Budo. His chief aim was to give to the African the best in the Western culture at the same time helping him to develop the best in his own culture.[64]

Indeed, as early as the mid-1940s, in *Government Gyennonya*, Mulira had advocated for the integration of European and Ganda political

---

[60] For further discussion see McGregor, *King's College Budo*, pp. 52–86.

[61] Interview, Peter Mulira, 3 November 2009, Kampala.

[62] 'Autobiography', p. 42.

[63] Ibid.

[64] Ibid., p. 63. For further discussion see CCAS MP E.M.K. Mulira, 'Memorial Service to the Late Rev. H.M. Grace Talk to King's College, Budo, Chapel Service', Mss., 11 June 1967; CCAS MP E.M.K. Mulira, 'Obituary: One of Africa's Best Friends, H.M. Grace, Dies', Mss., [1967].

culture. He contended that Baganda should not superficially dismiss the political traditions of Great Britain. For Mulira, Ganda rulers were well positioned to contextualise political traditions from throughout eastern Africa and Europe.[65] As I explore more fully in Chapter 3, Mulira repurposed European constitutional traditions throughout the 1950s. To persuade Buganda's conservatives to moderate their austere royalism, Mulira argued that Buganda's nineteenth-century kingship had begun the process of remodelling state power by adapting English political practices: 'Salvation is not in going back to the old ways as some misleaders of the people allege. Muteesa I saw this more than 80 years ago. Nor is it in merely anglicising everything and destroying the old. Political salvation, therefore, is in enlightened integration of the new and the old.'[66]

By the mid-1940s Mulira had begun to build upon his social and religious background to complicate the respective political visions of Musazi and Mulumba, who had marketed their projects as representing autochthonous interests and ambitions. The remaining two sections will now show how Mulira used drama and a novel to produce a cosmopolitan vision for communities in late colonial Buganda. As these sections show, Mulira sought to pluralise the state's gendered and ethnic landscapes in ways that Musazi and Mulumba did not.

'Is it a crime to have been a woman?': Dramatising Domesticity and Difference

Throughout the 1940s, communities in Buganda debated the status of women in society and the politics of reproduction. As missionary hospitals and colonial health policies became more common, women and men were concerned that government regulations would overly restrict

---

[65] Mulira, *Government Gyennonya*, p. 5. Mulira's syntax is ambiguous, but it seems to suggest that activists in Buganda should assimilate European political traditions when appropriate: '*Tetugenderera kukoppa bukoppi Gavumenti ya Bungereza nga abatalaba* [We are not going to blindly copy Britain's government], *naye kyetugenderera kwe kugezako okutandika ennono ya Gavumenti zonna ennungi mu nsi yaffe* [. . .] [but we are going to set up cultures (traditions) of all good Governments in our country].'

[66] RHOP 514/4 E.M.K. Mulira to Secretary of State for the Colonies, 'The African Revolution: Being the Letter by the Progressive Party to the Secretary of State for the Colonies on the Question of the Legislative Council', Mss., 18 March 1958, p. 6.

sexual and reproductive practices. During the 1945 riots, for instance, activists had argued that women admitted to Mulago hospital were given injections that prevented pregnancy.[67] These claims coincided with larger debates about co-education and the implementation of Christian monogamy. Related to this was considerable public scandal over the remarriage of Buganda's Queen Mother in the early 1940s and the marriage of Muteesa II in 1948,[68] both of which were not conducted in accordance with royal custom and populist demands.[69] Within this context, Mulira used theatrical production to recast Ganda home life in the 1940s. By the 1920s, educators and political activists in Buganda had begun to debate the co-educational ideals of the Ghanaian intellectual James Aggrey, which Mulira studied under Canon Grace at King's College, Budo, and in Ghana. In 1946, Mulira produced *Omw. N'Omuk. Yokana Kaye: Omuzanyo Ogulaga Obufumbo Obwada Obuggya* (Mr and Mrs Yokana Kaye: A Play Showing a Marriage Made Anew). In this three-act play, he recycled Aggrey's philosophy of co-education to discuss gender equality in Buganda's patriarchal hierarchy. Mulira's play shows how debates over the regulation and practice of gender norms in colonial Uganda were not shaped only by local ideologies and the invention of patriotic pasts. Mulira drew from discussions across the Black Atlantic to create space for ordinary citizens, including women, to participate in postwar society.

At the request of the western African educator Alek G. Fraser,[70] Canon Grace left King's College in the mid-1930s to assume the position of principal at the Prince of Wales' College in Achimota, a suburb of Accra. Fraser, James Aggrey and Gordon Guggisberg, a colonial officer in the Gold Coast, had established the Prince of Wales' College in 1924. Grace assumed the post, among other reasons, to secure further education for Budo's African teaching staff.[71] And in January 1936, Mulira and Amos

---

[67] 'Report of the Commission of Inquiry into the Disturbances which occurred in Uganda during January, 1945', p. 7.

[68] Nakanyike B. Musisi, 'Women, "Elite Polygyny," and Buganda State Formation', *Signs*, 16 (1991), 757–86.

[69] Ernest Z. Kibuuka, *Omulembe gwa Muteesa II* (Kampala: Crane Books, 2004), p. 32; Laurence D. Schiller, 'The Royal Women of Buganda', *The International Journal of African Historical Studies*, 23 (1990), 455–73 (p. 459).

[70] CCAS MP E.M.K. Mulira, 'H.M. Grace at Achimota', 25 June 1967. Cf., McGregor, *King's College Budo*, pp. 80–3; W.E.F. Ward, *Fraser of Trinity and Achimota* (Accra: Ghana Universities Press, 1965), pp. 263–4.

[71] ARP 6/20/T2 E.M.K. Mulira, 'My Life Since 1930', Mss., n.d., p. 1.

K. Sempa set out on a fifty-six-day journey to Accra.[72] The two studied in Ghana for two years. Grace had intended for Sempa to be appointed King's College's first African headmaster,[73] while Mulira studied for the Cambridge School Certificate and the London University Intermediate Course,[74] which would qualify him for educational administration in Uganda or graduate school in Great Britain.

By the time Mulira arrived in the Gold Coast, educators and activists in Buganda had already begun to grapple with Aggrey's articulation of co-education. In March 1924, James Aggrey visited B/Uganda as a member of the Phelps-Stokes Commission, which concerned 'Native education' throughout eastern Africa.[75] The Commission's emphasis on home life resulted in the formation of the Buganda Welfare Association, whose organisation followed a meeting between Aggrey, Canon Grace and a cadre of influential Baganda (Figure 2.3).[76] During the Phelps-Stokes Commission, Grace spent considerable time with Aggrey. For two to three weeks he accompanied Aggrey to no fewer than forty meetings.[77] In the 1970s, Mollie Grace, Canon Grace's wife, told Mulira that Aggrey's philosophy of culture and co-education had deeply impacted her husband:

Aggrey's thoughts and ideals and theories made a profound impression on H.M.G. I should say that [Aggrey] influenced him almost more than anything else in his attitude to and thinking about education in East Africa[,] and naturally one of his subjects that was influential as much as any was the education of girls: the question of co-education.[78]

Following Aggrey's visit to Uganda, the Graces visited Aggrey in the United States. Mollie recalled that the highlight of the trip was a visit to the Tuskegee and Hampton Institutes, where the two were moved by the practice of co-education:

[T]he schools were co-educational and we were profoundly impressed by the obvious complete lack of sex discrimination and the equality of

[72] 'Autobiography', pp. 70, 74.
[73] CCAS MP E.M.K. Mulira, 'Memorial Service to the Late Rev. H.M. Grace'.
[74] ARP 6/20/T2 Mulira, 'My Life Since 1930', p.1.
[75] 'The Phelps Stokes Commission', *Uganda Herald*, 29 February 1924, p. 25.
[76] 'Buganda Welfare Association', *Uganda Herald*, 18 April 1924, p. 12.
[77] CCAS MP H.M. Grace to W. Kingsley, 3 January 1962.
[78] CCAS MP Mollie Grace to E.M.K. Mulira, 28 April 197[5(?)].

Figure 2.3 Phelps-Stokes Commission, 1924
James Aggrey (Row 1, first left); Canon Grace (Row 1, second left);
Serwano Kulubya (Row 2, second left)
Source: Courtesy of Michael and Rae Grace

boys & girls, completely different from what we were used to in Uganda. I should say that this visit was one of the most informative contributions to H.M.G.'s future attitude to Education in E.A.[79]

Motivated by Aggrey and the practice of female education at Tuskegee and Hampton, Grace implemented co-education at King's College, Budo, in the early 1930s.[80]

Aggrey's ideals on co-education had begun to shape political discussions in Buganda by the 1940s. Shortly after Aggrey's visit to Buganda,

---

[79] Ibid.
[80] For further discussion see McGregor, *King's College Budo*, pp. 53, 66, 84.

Figure 2.4 King's College, Budo, Staff, c. 1933

Usher Wilson (Row 1, fifth left); Bisase Kisosonkole (Row 2, first left); Mollie Grace (Row 2, second left); I.K. Musazi (Row 2, sixth left); Canon Grace (Row 2, seventh left); E.M.K. Mulira (Row 2, eighth left)
Source: Courtesy of Michael and Rae Grace

Ignatius Musazi and Kupuliano Bisase Kisosonkole, then teachers at King's College (Figure 2.4), argued that 'to neglect Female Education is to neglect the home; [and] the system of Education that does not take home-life in its account is worthless'.[81] They indicated that there 'is no hope for any country to advance if its women are left behind'.[82] In the same year, Musazi and Kisosonkole initiated the Young People's Organisation (YPO), a society that built on the momentum of the Phelps-Stokes Commission to bring men and women together to 'discuss problems of common interest'.[83]

---

[81] I.K. Musazi and K.B. Kisosonkole, 'Education in Uganda', *Uganda Church Review* 18 (April 1930), 50–5 (p. 52).
[82] Ibid.
[83] 'Autobiography', p. 51. The Luganda press indicates that there was widespread interest throughout Buganda in the co-education policies of Achimota. See 'The Prince of Wales College and School Achimota. Gold Coast', *Ebifa mu Uganda*, June 1931, pp. 125–8; '*Okuyigirizibwa kwe Achimota* [Education at Achimota]', *Ebifa mu Uganda*, August 1932, pp. 184–91; '*Okulengera ku Nkigiriza mu Gold Coast ne Uganda* [Looking at Education in the Gold Coast and Uganda]', *Ebifa mu Uganda*, January 1933, pp. 66–7.

Hamu Mukasa was also deeply impacted by Aggrey's ideals. During the Phelps-Stokes Commission, Mukasa met Aggrey.[84] And when Mulira began his research for 'Aggrey, *Muganda Waffe*' (Aggrey, Our Brother), he designated Mukasa, his father-in-law, to be a key interlocutor.[85] Mukasa's remaining personal library shows that the prominent chief began reading Edwin W. Smith's *Aggrey of Africa* on 13 June 1929, annotating sixty-four passages and underscoring an additional 104.[86] Mukasa specifically considered a speech that Aggrey delivered on the practice of gender equality in black communities during the American Civil War.[87] For Mukasa, gender equality within African American communities during the bellum period demonstrated the type of progress for which he advocated in Buganda. In the first volume of *Simuda Nyuma*, Mukasa adapted Aggrey to question the practice of gender violence in Buganda: 'Have the violent ways of treating wives in Buganda, which was prevalent in the past, changed?'[88] 'Now', concluded Mukasa, 'progress is killing it slowly.'[89] By gazing toward Aggrey and diasporic communities in the United States, Mukasa recast Ganda social practice in the language of Christian progress, a political path from which there was no turning back (*simuda nyuma*).

After attending Achimota, Mulira returned to Uganda in 1938 as the headmaster at Mengo Junior Secondary School.[90] He then taught at King's College from 1941 until late 1942.[91] Mulira worked at Bishop Tucker's College, Mukono, from January 1943 until 1947, during which he spent considerable time writing plays and essays to engage politics and gender in Buganda.[92] In his 1945 book, *Thoughts of a Young African*, Mulira examined the question of women and co-education in his

---

[84] W.J.W. Roome, 'Visit of the Phelps-Stokes Commission', *Uganda Herald*, 28 March 1924, p. 13.

[85] CCAS E.M.K. Mulira, 'Aggrey, *Muganda Waffe*', Mss., n.d.

[86] HML Edwin W. Smith, *Aggrey of Africa: A Study in Black and White*, 2nd edn (London: Student Christian Movement Press, 1929), annotations.

[87] HML Smith, *Aggrey of Africa*, p. 130, annotation.

[88] MUA HMP AR/BUG/78/1 Ham Mukasa, *Simuda Nyuma I: Ebiro bya Mutesa*, Mss., 1938, p. 10.

[89] Ibid., p. 4. *Okugenda mu maso kugenda kubita.*

[90] 'Autobiography', p. 82.

[91] For discussion on Mulira's departure see Carol Summers, '"Subterranean Evil" and "Tumultuous Riot" in Buganda: Authority and Alienation at King's College, Budo, 1942', *The Journal of African History*, 47 (2006), 93–113.

[92] 'Autobiography', pp. 82b–83b.

chapter on Achimota and in an additional chapter entitled 'Advantages of Co-Education'.[93] Following the 1945 riots, Mulira dramatised Aggrey's social philosophy in *Omw. N'Omuk. Yokana Kaye: Omuzanyo Ogulaga Obufumbo Obwada Obuggya*, as mentioned above.

Omw. N'Omuk. Yokana Kaye was first performed on 25 March 1946 at the residence of the Bishop of Namirembe,[94] and was reproduced in *Ebifa mu Uganda* during the same year.[95] Mulira's play focused on the marriage of a Mr and Mrs Yokana Kaye, whose marriage, as indicated by the title of the first scene, *Obufumbo Obutabusse* (A Marriage Gone Wrong), had fallen on hard times. The story begins with Mrs Kaye and a group of children sitting in the living room of the Kaye home as the time for tea approaches. One child, Nasimbwa (a niece), arranges teacups while another, Yakobo (a nephew), enters the room with a kettle of hot water.[96] As tea is being prepared, Mrs Kaye expresses her frustration at constantly taking tea without milk and sugar: 'Endless tea without milk and sugar is somewhat tiresome.'[97] Upon hearing his aunt's lament, though, Yakobo recalls that his uncle had accidentally left at home the keys to the cupboard, where the household supply of sugar is securely stored. After Yakobo announces the good news, Mrs Kaye responds:

Bring them so that we too can have some sugar. In fact, the sugar is dying in there! He [Mr Kaye] comes home having already drunk his alcohol; he doesn't take tea and yet for those of us who take it he is forever not giving us any sugar! Go and bring them.[98]

---

[93] Mulira, *Thoughts of a Young African*, pp. 20–3, 29–33.

[94] E.M.K. Mulira 'Omw. N'Omuk. Yokana Kaye: Omuzanyo Ogulaga Obufumbo Obwada Obuggya: Scene 1, Obufumbo Obutabusse', *Ebifa mu Uganda*, May 1946, pp. 80–1 (p. 80) [hereafter 'Scene 1, Obufumbo Obutabusse'].

[95] 'Scene 1, Obufumbo Obutabusse', pp. 80–1; 'Omw. N'Omuk. Yokana Kaye: Omuzanyo Ogulaga Obufumbo Obwada Obuggya: Scene 2, Ewa Muliranwa', *Ebifa mu Uganda*, June 1946, pp. 99–100 [hereafter 'Scene 2, Ewa Muliranwa']; 'Omw. N'Omuk. Yokana Kaye: Omuzanyo Ogulaga Obufumbo Obwada Obuggya: Scene 3, Mu Maka ga Kaye Nate', *Ebifa mu Uganda*, July 1946, pp. 120–3 [hereafter 'Scene 3, Mu Maka ga Kaye Nate']. Copies of the *Ebifa* reproductions and Mulira's English translations are deposited in the Cambridge collection. My citations draw from Mulira's English translations.

[96] 'Scene 1, Obufumbo Obutabusse', p. 80.

[97] Ibid.

[98] Ibid.

Following a heated discussion about what could happen if Mr Kaye learns about the sugar's depletion, the family cautiously removes some of the sugar from the cupboard. During the process, however, Mrs Kaye, unintentionally and unnoticed, spills granules on the floor. And once the sugar is in their possession, Mrs Kaye and the children decide to use an exorbitant amount. Mrs Kaye and Nasimbwa next enter into a discussion regarding the ill-mannered Mr Kaye. They ask: what kind of man buys sugar, only to refuse sharing it with his family? Who would entertain guests without offering them sugar? Nasimbwa complains: 'And even when there's a visitor we have to fight to give him some sugar.'[99]

Shortly after the family begins to drink their tea, Mr Kaye is heard outside. The family then quickly removes the cups from the room before Mr Kaye enters and passes his wife. Mr Kaye, however, notices the spilt sugar near the cupboard:

MR KAYE: Where did this sugar come from?
MRS KAYE: Where [What sugar?]?
MR KAYE: This [Here].
MRS KAYE: I don't know.
MR KAYE: Why do you lie on such a small matter? Do you think it came here by itself?
MRS KAYE: Hmm! (She makes [a] rude gesture [. . .]) Are you so sure that I'm the one who put it there! Do you think we know where you drink *your* sugar? I'm a poor frustrated lady who doesn't drink sugar.[100]

Yokana then opens the cupboard and discovers the depleted canister, confirming his suspicion. The two then enter into a heated verbal exchange; Mrs Kaye is physically abused. While quarrelling, she laments, 'How can I keep quiet when you are constantly picking on me whenever you are drunk! Is it a crime to have been a woman?' Conversely, Mr Kaye voices, 'Poor old me! Quarrelling! Quarrelling! Won't I ever get any peace!'[101] The scene concludes with the two in separate rooms loathing the status of their marriage.

Scene 2, *Ewa Muliranwa* (At the Neighbours), takes place on the following day. Mrs Kaye and two women, Mrs Lutta and Zirimu,

[99] Ibid.
[100] Ibid.
[101] Ibid.

are found discussing their husbands' alcoholism. As the conversation unfolds, the audience is informed that Mr and Mrs Kaye's marriage is further strained by Mrs Kaye's affair with Omuseveni, a soldier in the King's African Rifles.[102] Mrs Kaye remarks: 'My friend, for my husband it is not only *waragi*. (She talks somewhat gleefully.) It is my serviceman boyfriend who is worrying him.'[103] Mrs Kaye's affection toward the unidentified serviceman is based upon aesthetics and manners, which Mulira illustrated by scripting Mrs Kaye bursting into song:

> I love him, I love him
> He who walks smartly, truly speaking;
> In his Khaki Uniform, he surpasses
> I love that 'darle' so much.
> I love that boy, I love him
> He is far better than all of them that I have
> I love that boy, I love him,
> He is better than all I knew.[104]

After Mrs Kaye concludes, the ladies hear a bicycle approaching. Contrasting yesterday's unwanted arrival of Mr Kaye, the serviceman appears. Mrs Lutta invites him to sit and talk, but he is unable to do so due to other commitments. However, he offers a gift of an expensive dress to Mrs Kaye before then saluting her and departing.[105] Mrs Kaye's lover is not only aesthetically attractive, he is well mannered and a bearer of gifts, unlike the tight-fisted Yokana Kaye.

The play's final scene, *Mu Maka ga Kaye Nate* (In Kaye's Home Again), takes place six months after the second scene.[106] It begins with Mrs Kaye in her residence meticulously cleaning and beautifying the home with flowers. Mrs Kaye calls for Nasimbwa and then asks her to prepare a glass of orange juice for the soon to arrive Mr Kaye. Yakobo is once again asked to prepare tea. As the home is being cleaned,

---

[102] *'Scene 2, Ewa Muliranwa'*, p. 100. The term *omuseveni* referred to a war veteran. The word is used here to reference a veteran of the Second World War, a member of the 7th Battalion of the King's African Rifles (John D. Murphy, *Luganda–English Dictionary* (Washington, DC: Consortium Press for Catholic University of America Press, 1972), p. 380).

[103] *'Scene 2, Ewa Muliranwa'*, p. 99.

[104] Ibid.

[105] Ibid., p. 100.

[106] *'Scene 3, Mu Maka ga Kaye Nate'*, p. 120.

Mrs Lutta and Zirimu once again appear. They are puzzled by what they find:

MRS LUTTA: You appear to be busy; are you expecting visitors?

MRS KAYE: My friend, these days I am like this all the time, even when I am not expecting visitors.

... ...

MRS LUTTA: What kind of reviving is this?

MRS KAYE: These days we are in a new 'life'. My husband had a change of heart suddenly and he really became someone new. He even buys meat and sugar now.

... ...

MRS LUTTA: By the way, what changed you?

MRS KAYE: God's grace.[107]

Mr Kaye then returns home and the play concludes with an extended conversation between Mr and Mrs Kaye, written to contrast with Scene 1:

MRS KAYE: Welcome home.

MR KAYE: (Still very cheerful) Yes! (To Yakobo) My child, undo what I have brought for your Auntie on the bicycle.

MRS KAYE: What have you brought for me?

MR KAYE: You will see. (Addressing himself to the ladies) I am very pleased to see you.

THE LADIES: We are, too.

MR KAYE: How are you?

MRS KAYE: What would you like, orange juice? You see I had pre-pared it at lunchtime but you didn't come home. Or would you prefer some tea?

MR KAYE: Not to trouble you too much, I think I will have some of the orange juice.

(His wife brings the orange juice on a tray. At the same time Yakobo brings in the package he has taken from the bicycle. Mrs Kaye puts the tray in front of Mr Kaye. She turns to look at what Yakobo has brought in.)

MRS KAYE: Oh! My dear! (Looking into the basket.) Goat's meat which I love! And a cake, too! Thank you very much, dear.[108]

---

[107] Ibid.
[108] Ibid., p. 121.

The play resolves with the two discussing God's transformative work in their marriage before they walk into a single bedroom to kneel and pray together.

As Mulira's play begins, the Kayes disembody reciprocal manners and fidelity. Mr Kaye is cast as one who does not provide his family with basic provisions, such as sugar. In consequence, Mrs Kaye describes herself as 'a poor frustrated lady who doesn't drink sugar'.[109] Even guests know about Mr Kaye's stinginess, which was generally frowned upon in Ganda society and resulted in family stress. One Ganda proverb, for example, embodied the frustration that wives felt due to inhospitable husbands: 'My husband, you despise me: give me at least a hoe and a working garment (that I can offer food to my relations, when they come to visit me).'[110] The generosity of Mrs Kaye's lover, Omuseveni, underscored Mr Kaye's lack thereof. While Mr Kaye refused to provide something as basic as sugar, Omuseveni is portrayed as a generous gift bearer, one who is gladly received.[111]

In the second scene of the play, Mrs Kaye is portrayed as obstinate, gossipy and sexually promiscuous – a wife who fails to demonstrate faithful reciprocity toward her husband. Her sexual relationship with a member of the King's African Rifles is evocative and embodied what Mulira saw as the disintegration of local social values during the interwar period. In the late 1930s, Mulira had joined the 7th Battalion of the King's African Rifles,[112] during which he wrote about sexual practices in military culture across eastern Africa.[113] And while Mrs Kaye's relationship with her serviceman embodied partial reciprocity, Mulira intentionally framed the affair as unsustainable. Upon being invited to sit and visit, Omuseveni can *only* present gifts. He is unable to enter into normative expectation and exchange. Illicit sex and alluring gifts are used to circumvent mutual obligation. In turn, Mulira

---

[109] 'Scene 1, Obufumbo Obutabusse', p. 81.

[110] Walser, Luganda Proverbs, no. 0935.

[111] For further discussion on the politics of manners in colonial Buganda see Carol Summers, 'Radical Rudeness: Ugandan Social Critiques in the 1940s', Journal of Social History, 39 (2006), 741–70.

[112] Mulira, Thoughts of a Young African, pp. 10–17; 'Autobiography', p. 87. For further insight into the 7th Battalion see Timothy Parsons, The African Rank-and-File: Social Implications of Colonial Military Service in the King's African Rifles, 1902–1964 (Portsmouth, NH: Heinemann, 1999), p. 24.

[113] Mulira, Thoughts of a Young African, p. 17. For further discussion on the relationship between sexual practices and military culture in colonial eastern Africa, see Parsons, The African Rank-and-File, pp. 145–59.

used Christian language and Aggrey's beliefs about gender equality to create a space where actors, following Christian conversion, sacrificially provided for each other's needs and committed to mutual prayer in the bedroom, not unrestrained sexual impulse. Mulira's ideal marriage modelled a relationship in which 'everyone [is] considerate of everyone else',[114] no longer tight-fisted, argumentative or unrestrained.

The dramatisation of gender in the mid-1940s helped set the stage for Mulira's political performance throughout decolonisation. During the height of Farmers' Union and Bataka activisms, he argued that Buganda's laws should be constructed by a female-inclusive legislature.[115] Nearly ten years later, when he developed a memorandum for the Progressive Party, Mulira sought to 'raise the status of women'.[116] During the Party's early branch elections, his wife, Rebecca Mulira, was elected as Kampala's branch chair,[117] a position she maintained until 1958.[118] During the same year, as Baganda debated the prospect of constitutional integration into Uganda, Mulira argued for the participation of women in national politics.[119] Drama, though, did not simply provide Mulira with space to imagine gender equality following the Second World War. The political participation of female citizens in public affairs was part of Mulira's broader attempt to create a commoners' kingdom, a place of unhindered equality during a period of considerable debate over the importance and function of social hierarchy and authentic citizenship.

Sons of the Soil: Rewriting Land and Belonging

To recreate Buganda's hierarchy in the 1940s, dissenting activists imagined pasts uncorrupted by colonial power and collaborating chiefs. Bataka and Farmers' activists, respectively, incorporated the

---

[114] Mulira, *Thoughts of a Young African*, p. 49.
[115] Mulira, *Government Gyennonya*, p. 7.
[116] BNA CO 822/852 'Extract from Uganda Monthly Intelligence Appreciation', 31 January 1955.
[117] CCAS MP Mary Stuart, 'Rebecca Mulira: A Great Lady of Uganda', Mss., n.d., p. 15.
[118] Rebecca Mulira, 'Curriculum Vitae', [c. 2001]. I wish to thank Ham M. Mulira for providing me with a copy of Rebecca Mulira's *curriculum vitae*.
[119] MUA AF UC UZ.67 Extra Mural/CCE/164c John Colman, 'Weekend Conference on "The Christian in Politics"', 28 January 1958.

rhetoric of nativism and rural land (*–ttaka*, soil, arable) to generate critique. As early as the 1920s, Bataka activists protested the loss and abuse of *their* land. In the 1924 Bataka trials, Shem Spire Mukasa argued: '[T]his Commission will do a great deal towards restoring our good native customs which had been spoilt by the Respondents [Buganda's Regents].'[120] Plaintiffs would 'give evidence as to how the Respondents seized the estates which belonged to the Bataka and how they drove the Bataka away from these estates'[.]'[121] Adapting older discourses, Bataka in the 1940s sought to preserve and reclaim Buganda's land, what was argued to be *–ttaka* land.[122] Similarly, Farmers' activists praised the land that God had given to them. Reflecting upon dissenting songs in the 1940s, Erieza Bwete recalled: 'The farmers' songs carried different tunes and meanings. The songs were nice to listen to and praised the fertility of the soil and the blessings that God gave to both the farmers and to the people in general.'[123] The invention of supposedly legitimate political cultures coincided with the authentication of authority in colonial Buganda.

In the late 1940s, Mulira produced the novel *Teefe*, in which Kooki and theological narration were used to critique the political dissent of Bataka and Farmers' Unionists, activists who had legitimised riot and protest by claiming to be Buganda's trustworthy sons: sons of the soil, or sons of Kintu. Mulira, by contrast, used the imagery of soil to cultivate a place to build virtuous, inclusive societies governed by communal principles – communities not dominated by any one claimant, Baganda, *bakungu*, *bataka* or otherwise. Mulira argued that rural commoners and urban youth were virtuous or authentic (truly Ganda, *Ganda ddala*) to the extent that they devoted themselves to rewarding labour and the making of inclusive communities.

Mulira produced a first draft of his thirty-nine-page novel as early as 1948,[124] before publishing a first edition in 1950.[125] The book was titled after the story's protagonist, Mensusera William Besweri Teefe,

---

[120] BNA CO 536/133 Shem Spire Mukasa, 'Bataka Land Commission Minutes', 'Evidence, Written Statements, etc.', 11 April 1924.

[121] Ibid.

[122] LFP 30/12 D.S.K. Musoke, '*Buganda Nyaffe*, Part I: A Descriptive Booklet about Land and its Users', [c. June 1944], p. 1.

[123] EBP Erieza Bwete, [Memoirs], Mss., n.d.

[124] CCAS MP Uganda Bookshop to E.M.K. Mulira, 17 August 1948.

[125] CCAS MP E.M.K. Mulira, 'Curriculum Vitae', Mss., n.d.

whose name derived from the Luganda proverb, *Eteefe etuusa mugenyi.*
Literally, the proverb states, 'The chicken that is not going to die shall
bring a visitor'. More loosely it means, 'Visitors often save people from
harm'.[126] The book's opening chapters are set in Kampala in the early
1940s,[127] and Teefe is portrayed as a young Muganda originally from
Kooki. Young and dislocated,[128] Teefe devoted his time to living loosely
in Uganda's urban landscapes, spending his days drinking: 'Teefe and his
friend Paatiriisi were known drunkards who set off to look for drink in the
morning until late at night.'[129] One morning, a long-lost friend, Matiya,
visited Teefe. Matiya brought with him an article taken from *Ebifa mu
Uganda*, *Atakola n'okulya talyanga* (S/he who does not work shall not
eat),[130] which used II Thessalonians 3:10 to argue that excessive drinking
among youths caused poverty and political discontent. The confiscation
of Bataka land, corrupt chiefs or colonial policy were not to blame for
rampant poverty. Matiya and *Ebifa* showed Teefe that the accumulation
of wealth was possible, but only through a life of diligent labour in the village, where Baganda commoners and non-Baganda (Banyankole, Bakiga
and Banyarwanda) lived and worked together in community.

Matiya's *Ebifa* article emphasised the ideals of James Aggrey and
the New Testament. Aggrey was presented as a brilliant African who
argued that Africa's greatest resource was in the soil, being walked
upon unknowingly.[131] In addition to II Thessalonians, the article used
the story of the temptation of Jesus in the wilderness to advocate
for the virtue of rural labour: '*Anti oli Mwana wa Katonda, gamba
amayinja gano gafuuke emmere*', 'If you are the Son of God, tell these
stones to change into food.'[132] Refusing to succumb to temptation,
though, Jesus resisted Satan by committing himself to a life of hard
work: walking while preaching, diligent thinking, wearing a crown
of thorns, bearing the cross and undergoing physical abuse. The article suggested that God called his followers to a life of difficult but

---

[126] Walser, *Luganda Proverbs*, no. 5010.
[127] Mulira, *Teefe*, p. 7.
[128] While it is not clear in the novel, Mulira likely cast Teefe as an urban 'house boy'.
In *Thoughts of a Young African*, Mulira wrote in detail about the sociological
challenges that confronted young migrant labourers in Kampala (pp. 60–1).
[129] Mulira, *Teefe*, p. 7.
[130] Ibid., pp. 10–11.
[131] Ibid., p. 11.
[132] Ibid., p. 12.

rewarding labour. After listening to Matiya and *Ebifa*, Teefe decided that he, like Jesus, must work in the kingdom's rural communities and that he must return to his father's land in Kooki. Teefe now believed that his father might warmly welcome him, like the prodigal son's father in St Luke's gospel. He then set out on a pilgrimage that offered the promise of a cosmopolitan community and gratifying labour.

As he began his journey, though, Teefe found it difficult to deviate from what was considered Satan's scheme to keep him in urban circumstances.[133] But as he confronted constant opposition, Teefe imagined a new social identity, where being virtuous was more important than being Baganda or Bataka. Into his journey, Teefe's bicycle is damaged and he is forced to approach someone who is purposely cast as a Muganda. Teefe asks his fellow Muganda to assist him by virtue of being a Muganda: 'Please help me, I am your fellow Muganda.'[134] To his dismay, Teefe's fellow Muganda is not swayed by ethnic solidarity: 'You are a Muganda? And where did we meet to decide that I would help you simply because I am a Muganda?'[135] Teefe's fellow Muganda is willing to help, but only on the condition of exorbitant compensation. Bewildered, Teefe soon finds a man whom Mulira casts as an Omunyarwanda, a citizen of the colonial kingdom of Rwanda. Contrasting his fellow Muganda, the Rwandan man happily aids Teefe and adamantly refuses compensation.[136] The newfound Rwandan companion then invites Teefe into his home, where he is generously fed and offered lodging for the evening. But determined to reach Kooki, Teefe refuses and ventures out. Following his departure, Teefe is nearly killed by a lion before finding a tall tree to rest in safely for the night. The following morning, he is found and consoled by a non-Baganda woman, Kooga, a Muhima. The two come to love each other and marry and settle in Kooki. Teefe's journey is complete.

In time, Teefe becomes one of Kooki's exemplary farmers.[137] He employs thirty workers, cultivates 180 acres and possesses forty head

---

[133] '*Mu Kulowooza ennyo n'ategeera nti Ssetaani y'ayagala okumunyweza, naye asana omulundi guno amuwangule, naye ne Ssetaani n'agaana*', 'Thinking deeply, he realized that Satan wanted to fully own him, but this time he had to come out victoriously, and yet Satan persisted' (Ibid., p. 17).

[134] Ibid., p. 22.

[135] Ibid.

[136] Ibid.

[137] '*Teefe afuuka ekyokulabirako ky'abalimi*' (Ibid., p. 32).

of cattle.[138] Teefe and his Muhima wife become renowned in the area for exhibiting kindness toward their neighbours and workers, embodying many of the conjugal virtues that Mulira explored four years earlier in *Mr and Mrs Kaye*. Once an urban youth, Teefe is transformed into an agrarian contemplative – virtuous, sociable and given to a life of productive farming and constant reading and prayer:

His fame spread in many places [. . .] The agricultural officer always cited him as an example to the farmers and included him in many reports. Teefe experienced a new life through hard work. The words of our Lord are very relevant to Teefe, when he said, 'Whoever loses his life shall regain it.'[139]

Mulira concluded the novel by having Teefe present a speech to the farming community, during which six insights are offered to his Luganda readers:

1. In the past, I wanted everything to be done for me. But now, I ask: 'What have I done for Buganda?'
2. In my garden, I contemplate two particular issues: plants and my manners (or behaviour). A farmer who is not trustworthy loses out.
3. All we can do is plant, but it is God who causes growth. It is for this reason that I never stop asking God to bless my work.
4. I have dedicated my entire life to my garden. It is by being in one's garden that one becomes a man.
5. Plants are like children, they need feeding. I use the insights I gain from my [non-Baganda] workers to feed the plants.
6. The stomachs of the labourers are the theme of the garden. I try hard to provide them with food and shelter. When I pay them well, they work hard and are full of happiness. When you do this, you will not be short of workers.[140]

The speech climaxes as Teefe contrasts his newfound agrarian philosophy with the dissenting ethos of Musazi's and Mulumba's rioters:

I who had died have been resurrected by agriculture. When I lay on my bed, I reflect on the life of ignorance I once lived – the years spent looking for joy

[138] Ibid., p. 34.
[139] Ibid., p. 36.
[140] Ibid., p. 38.

were wasted! I remember that one day we rioted to add but one mere shilling to our salary. When I remember all that, I can't stop thinking about how God has opened my eyes.[141]

After Mulira castigated B/Uganda's rioters, he admonished his readers to replicate Teefe's politics: '*Kale bannaffe olugero lwa Teefe lukomye awo. Ggwe obulamu obubwo buli butya?*', 'My friends, the story of Teefe ends here. How have you spent your life?'[142]

Mulira used his novel to recast Ganda social life in the 1940s. Whereas Bataka and Farmers' activists incorporated the metaphor of rural land (*–ttaka*) to bolster social criticism and to create a place for *Abazzukulu ba Kintu* or Bataka, Mulira employed land to imagine a public space where 'there is no Muganda, Munyoro, Musoga, Mukedi, Munjunja, or Muzungu'.[143] For Mulira, Buganda's sons of the soil were those 'resurrected through agriculture', activists who lived in diverse communities characterised by ethical virtue and shared labour. In Mulira's kingdom, it was pointless to unquestionably advocate for the rights of Bataka and 'fellow' Baganda. By creating space for urban Baganda to participate in rural community, Mulira returned to a past characterised by ethnic integration within Ganda political life. He directed Teefe away from Buganda's monarchical and hereditary traditions, reminding his readers about Buganda's long tradition of assimilation.[144] By casting Teefe's social redemption in an ethnically diverse Kooki,[145] Mulira moved his idyllic kingdom away from the

---

[141] Ibid.
[142] Ibid., p. 39.
[143] SOAS MS 380474 E.M.K. Mulira, 'Mackay the Dauntless: A Play in Three Acts', Mss., c. 1944, p. 7.
[144] P.G. Powesland, 'History of the Migration in Uganda', in *Economic Development and Tribal Change: A Study of Immigrant Labour in Buganda*, ed. by Audrey I. Richards, 2nd edn (Nairobi: Oxford University Press, 1973), pp. 17–51; Audrey I. Richards, 'The Assimilation of the Immigrants', in *Economic Development and Tribal Change: A Study of Immigrant Labour in Buganda*, ed. by Audrey I. Richards, 2nd edn (Nairobi: Oxford University Press, 1973), pp. 161–93.
[145] Audrey Richards' study does not indicate that Kooki had a particularly high percentage of migrant labourers in the early twentieth century. For further analysis see J.M. Fortt, 'The Distribution of the Immigrant and Ganda Population within Buganda', in *Economic Development and Tribal Change: A Study of Immigrant Labour in Buganda*, ed. by Audrey I. Richards, 2nd edn (Nairobi: Oxford University Press, 1973), pp. 77–118.

spaces of Buganda's precolonial powerbrokers – kings, chiefs or clan heads – thereby advocating for ethnic cosmopolitanism during a period of growing patriotism.

Conclusion: Decolonisation and Global Discourse

E.M.K. Mulira spent the closing years of the 1940s in the United Kingdom, where he developed a standardised Luganda orthography at the School of Oriental and African Studies (Chapter 3). After Mulira returned to Uganda, he was elected to the *Lukiiko* in late 1950.[146] In 1951, Mulira and a small coterie organised a society that advocated for political unity between Buganda and the remaining Protectorate.[147] During this same time, Musazi launched the formation of the Uganda National Congress on 2 March 1952.[148] Mulira attended the meeting but felt that Musazi's policies were convoluted, as he had concluded earlier in Mukono in 1944.[149] In Mulira's words, Musazi's meeting 'was a flop'.[150]

One year later, though, Mulira and Musazi boarded a plane in Entebbe bound for Rangoon to attend the first Asian Socialist Conference.[151] Musazi, who was delayed in Egypt due to a ticketing mistake,[152] failed to reach the Conference by the time he was scheduled to address a plenary session.[153] In his place, Mulira was asked to speak. Mulira's speech was similar to Teefe's; it communicated the importance of solidarity and cosmopolitan communities: 'Africa with her philosophy of love and brotherhood which is universal in scope, beckons the western world to the fact that the battle is one – a battle against man's inhumanity to man – which can be fought victoriously if we will plan to treat others the way we wish them to treat us.'[154]

---

[146] 'Autobiography', pp. 204–6.
[147] Ibid., p. 207.
[148] Ibid., p. 208. Cf., BNA CO 822/849/2 'Uganda National Congress', Mss., n.d.
[149] 'Autobiography', p. 209.
[150] Ibid., p. 208.
[151] For Mulira's account see 'Autobiography', pp. 212–18. For press coverage see 'First Asian Socialist Conference', *New Times of Burma*, 7 January 1953, p. 1.
[152] 'Autobiography', p. 214.
[153] Ibid., p. 216.
[154] 'Speech by I.K. Musazi President of the Uganda National Congress and Representative of Kenya African Union', *New Times of Burma*, 15 January 1953, p. 6. Mulira expressed frustration that his speech was printed under Musazi's

Mulira's address illuminated the translation of local political thought into the language of international decolonisation. Mulira was not only challenged to speak to Ganda farmers; the nearness of independence attracted a larger audience. Following the exile and return of *Kabaka* Muteesa II, political gravitas shifted in Buganda. Activists in Uganda were presented with a largely unanticipated set of political questions that had not been formalised: What would a constitutional monarchy look like in Buganda? When will Uganda secure independence? What will Buganda's legal and political relationship with Uganda look like after independence? Should Buganda secede from the Protectorate? Such questions were not only debated in the homes and administrative halls of Buganda; activists, such as Mulira in Rangoon, were challenged to engage in an increasingly wider sphere of debate that characterised decolonisation throughout Africa and Asia. In Chapter 3, I explore how debates over citizenship and political virtue in Buganda shifted following the deportation and return of Muteesa II. The constitutional arrangement that guaranteed Muteesa's return in 1955 propelled Buganda and Uganda toward independence. This forced Mulira and others to address the question of Buganda's autonomy in postcolonial Uganda.

---

name, which had been written in the original programme ('Autobiography', p. 216). Mulira indicated that his speech was reproduced on the following morning, 9 January, in the *Rangoon Times*. However, the *Rangoon Times* had ceased circulation by 1942 ('Chronology of the Press in Burma', *The Irrawaddy* (May 1, 2004) www.irrawaddy.org/research_show.php?art_id=3533). After examining the Burmese press for January 1953, I suggest that Mulira intended to reference the *New Times of Burma*, which did not reproduce the speech until 15 January, not 9 January. At the conference, discussions led by Musazi and Mulira were well received. In the *Daily Herald*, Prime Minister Clement Attlee recalled: 'There were also a number of fraternal delegates from Africa. Of these, the Egyptian and Tunisian delegates seemed to be rather more Nationalists than Socialists, but the two representatives from Uganda made an impression by their good sense' (Clement R. Attlee, 'Socialist Leaders of the East', *Daily Herald* (London), 23 January 1953, p. 4).

3 | *Eridadi M.K. Mulira: Buganda's Status in Uganda, c. 1953–c. 1959*

We had struggled long and hard to retain our integrity during the life of the Protectorate Government. Now the situation was to be different and we looked ahead to see if there were different dangers. Where would we stand in an independent Uganda?

Kabaka Edward Muteesa II[1]

When the Kabaka, Sir Edward Muteesa, was allowed to come back from exile in 1955, there was a new Constitution, a Buganda Constitution [. . .] In that Constitution there was a time frame, a provision [. . .] for political development not only in Buganda but in the entire Uganda set-up. That time frame was that there [should] be no major changes [. . .] for six years from the time the new Constitution of 1955 started. [. . .] All the politicians in Buganda – in the *Lukiiko* and the political parties – [. . .] were preparing themselves [for] the major changes that would take place after six years. [. . .] The *Lukiiko* was very watchful. In that generation there was a lot of debate.

Omulamuzi A.D. Lubowa[2]

As soon as the recommendations of the Namirembe Conference were published the traditionalists seized the opportunity to get into power. It was easy. What they had to do was to accuse the Committee of having betrayed the country and of having robbed the Kabaka of his power. This was in objection to the Kabaka being a Constitutional Monarchy. The Constitution framers were thrown out overnight. [. . .] They [traditionalists] are the last to admit that they owe their tremendous power to the Namirembe Conference which democratised Buganda for the first time.

Eridadi M.K. Mulira[3]

---

[1] Kabaka Edward Mutesa II, *Desecration of My Kingdom* (London: Constable, 1967), p. 143.
[2] Interview, A.D. Lubowa, 23 November 2009, Maya, Mpigi District.
[3] Anonymous, 'A Background to the Political Scene in Buganda', *Uganda Church Review* (Winter 1958), 21–6 (p. 26). While published anonymously, the vocabulary and syntax of the article is Mulira's.

Throughout the 1940s the sovereignty of *Kabaka* Muteesa II was insecure. As I showed in Chapter 1, it was not entirely clear whether the young monarch would withstand populist critique and intrigue organised by princely rivals. Populist sentiment, though, changed drastically following the king's exile and return in the mid-1950s. It is not my intent to recount the events that precipitated Muteesa's deportation; this has been done elsewhere.[4] It is sufficient to note that Uganda's new governor, Andrew Cohen, removed Muteesa II from power between 1953 and 1955 for refusing to support the possibility of B/Uganda's federal unification with Kenya. Ganda elites worried that the future relationship between Kenya and Uganda would resemble the Central African Federation in southern Africa, which was established in August 1953. Muteesa's deportation was both a constitutional crisis and moment in Buganda's political history. It was a crisis because Buganda had indefinitely lost her king due to constitutional stipulations defined by the 1900 Agreement. It was a moment because it provided a platform upon which competing actors – such as Mulira (1905–95) – debated and advocated for diverging political agendas, a space in time when Buganda's monarchy was up for grabs. It was also a constitutional moment because Muteesa's deportation resulted in a new Agreement that set in motion the terms of B/Uganda's independence in 1962. The imminence of independence forced Buganda's parliament and dissenting activists to wrestle with the question of their monarchy's future position in a postcolonial Uganda. Until 1953, public debate in Buganda did not centre on the kingdom's constitutional relationship with the remaining Protectorate. For Mmengo politicians, the Agreements of 1894 and 1900 had provided adequate safeguards in the past. This was no longer the case after 1955.

The deportation of the king was the central event around which anti-colonial struggle in Buganda was largely organised. It fundamentally altered the emotional and political topography of the region. The *Lukiiko* convened an emergency session immediately after

---

[4] Paulo Kavuma, *Crisis in Buganda, 1953–55: The Story of the Exile and Return of the Kabaka, Mutesa II* (London: Rex Collings, 1979); D.A. Low and R.C. Pratt, eds., *Buganda and British Overrule, 1900–1955: Two Studies* (London: Oxford University Press, 1960), pp. 317–49; Caroline Howell, 'Church and State in Crisis: The Deposition of the Kabaka of Buganda, 1953–1955', in *Missions, Nationalism, and the End of Empire*, ed. by Brian Stanley and Alaine Low (Grand Rapids: William B. Eerdmans Publishing Co., 2003), pp. 194–211.

Figure 3.1 Outside of the *Lukiiko* hall, Mmengo, 1954
Source: D.A. Low, *Buganda in Modern History*

Muteesa was deported. Outside of the building, the meeting attracted approximately 10,000 spectators (Figure 3.1).[5] Within the chamber, the *Lukiiko* was overcrowded with people sitting on the floor and window seats.[6] During the assembly, the Kyaddondo representative Thomas Makumbi condemned Buganda's regents and shouted that they 'were useless',[7] before arguing that the *Lukiiko* should be disbanded.[8] Mulira referred to the initial days of the deportation as 'the darkest days Buganda had known in this century'.[9] He continued: 'We were like a ship at sea without a compass; nobody knew what should be done or what was going to happen.'[10]

Paulo Kavuma was Buganda's *katikkiro* during the period. With Nsibirwa's assassination in mind, he now feared being shot: 'Many

---

[5] *Gambuze*, 4 December 1953.
[6] CCAS MP E.M.K. Mulira, ['Autobiography'], Mss., n.d., p. 27 (hereafter 'Autobiography').
[7] Kavuma, *Crisis in Buganda*, p. 42.
[8] *Uganda Post*, 4 December 1953.
[9] 'Autobiography', p. 227.
[10] Ibid.

of my countrymen thought that I was an evil man and that I should be struck by lightning because, they said, I had sold the Kabaka to the Europeans [. . .] For 4 months I was unable to move freely about the country for fear of assassination.'[11] He further remembered: 'As I travelled about people pointed at me accusingly. Threatening letters reached me by post; one of them, addressed to my wife, contained a bullet. I received abusive telephone calls, and people passing by my house called out that I should be cursed.'[12]

Women exhibited distress throughout Buganda as they lamented the metaphorical loss of a husband.[13] E.M.K. Mulira's wife, Rebecca Mulira, was no exception. As early as January 1954, she initiated various campaigns throughout Buganda to guarantee the end of Muteesa's exile. With four women, she warned Bishop Leslie Brown that Muteesa's deportation 'might result in bloodshed, as God's just reprisal against the British Nation for destroying our God-given nation of Uganda'.[14] Drawing from Protestant theology and the history of Israel's monarchy, Rebecca Mulira argued that Muteesa had been forcibly 'divorced [. . .] from his people'.[15] In length she wrote:

[I]t is Your Lordship who crowns the King and invests him with the royal ring whereby he becomes united or married to his own people, according to the established Christian rites of our Church. Wherefore, 'THAT WHICH GOD HAS JOINED TOGETHER, LET NO MAN BREAK ASSUNDER'. By reason of the fact that King Mutesa II became united or married to his own people, the British Government has no right in all justice, to force his separation from us, without the previous unanimous consent of his people.

It pains us most deeply to see he, whom God did anoint in his royal position in a long and unbroken [dynasty] of Buganda Kings, should have been

---

[11] Kavuma, *Crisis in Buganda*, p. 1.
[12] Ibid., p. 2.
[13] For further discussion see Carol Summers, 'All the Kabaka's Wives: Baganda Women, the Kabaka Crisis (1953–6), and the Politics and Perils of Loyalty', Draft Paper, African Studies Association, New York, 2007. To review the activism of royal women during the deportation see ICS 29/1/10/14 Damali to Hancock, [c. 1954]; Musa K. Parma-Ntanda, *Deposition of H.H. The Kabaka of Buganda: The Representative in London of the Women of Uganda Challenges Her Majesty's Government's White Paper and the Secretary of State's Decision* (Sussex: Grange Press for The Women's League of Buganda, February 1954).
[14] UCU BA 1/113.7 Rebecca Mulira, et al., to Leslie Brown, 16 January 1954.
[15] Ibid.

'kidnapped', as it were, and hurried away from his own country! David, the holy Prophet, says, who can stretch his hand against him whom God has anointed, without being guilty of a sin.[16]

By the end of January, Rebecca, with twenty-four 'Christian women, who have our Nation at heart', petitioned Uganda's governor, reminding him that Muteesa's authority derived from the consent of the people and the Church; not the colonial government.[17] The following day, she mobilised three buses of women to protest before Governor Cohen.[18] Anguish was a pervasive and powerful force that propelled politics during Muteesa's absence.

In this chapter, I explore Buganda's ideational landscapes during the 1950s. The deportation of *Kabaka* Muteesa II opened new possibilities in late colonial Uganda. Prior to the early 1950s, activists in Buganda had directed much of their agitation against Buganda's young king and his colluding government. Following his deportation and return, though, Muteesa II became a symbol of patriotism and secessionist politicking. On the eve of independence, this culminated in efforts to assert political authority solely along the lines of kingship, *Kabaka Yekka* (the king alone). During this period, Mulira maintained that the authority of Buganda's king derived from democratic consensus, an argument that he developed by reclassifying syntax and power relations in Luganda grammar and a popular novel. As a member of the delegation charged to secure Muteesa's return, Mulira used the British and Luganda press to advance his constitutional platform. This shaped political language in Westminster and radicalised patriotic sentiment throughout Buganda. Following Muteesa's return in late 1955, the most prominent concern of high politics became Buganda's constitutional integration into Uganda. Mulira advocated for Buganda's federalist incorporation into Uganda. But in Buganda's conservative milieu, Mulira's project was largely unsuccessful, which pressured him to change political strategy. In consequence, Mulira publicly aligned with Buganda's two foremost partisan platforms: the Uganda National

---

[16] Ibid.
[17] UCU BA 1/113.7 Rebecca Mulira, et al., to Andrew Cohen, 27 January 1954.
[18] Rebecca Mulira, 'Rebecca Mulira', in *A Rising Tide: Ugandan Women's Struggle for a Public Voice 1940–2004*, ed. by Winnie Byanyima and Richard Mugisha (Kampala: Forum for Women in Democracy, 2005), pp. 38–46 (p. 41); UCU BA 1/113.7 O.G. Griffith to Rebecca Mulira, 13 February 1954.

Movement (UNM) and the political party *Kabaka Yekka*. A particular reading of global intellectual history and the Bible inspired this shift. Reading practices in colonial Uganda not only reinforced continuity with the past, for Mulira they were just as easily used to recalibrate local strategy and create unusual alliances.

The Syntax of Sovereignty

During the same period that *Teefe* was being written (Chapter 2), Mulira was also working on a Luganda grammar that was to be used in both schools in Buganda and in colonial training institutions. Mulira's engagement with Luganda grammar during this period illuminates the conceptual framework that undergirded his constitutional project during and after Muteesa's deportation. Through the production and revision of standardised grammar, Mulira, like other activists throughout eastern Africa,[19] sought to reformulate authority by evoking purposefully chosen illustrations that reinforced democratic metaphors.

From late 1947 to late 1950, Mulira worked with a small team of linguists at the School of Oriental and African Studies (SOAS). Mulira's fellowship was designed to enable him to teach and study Luganda 'in a scholarly way, with a view to becoming an acknowledged authority of its structure and authority'.[20] During his tenure, he worked on a Luganda orthographical project that resulted in two publications:[21] a Luganda–English dictionary published in 1952,[22] and a Luganda grammar published in 1954.[23] The purpose of Mulira's dictionary was to revise A.L. Kitching and Revd G.R. Blackledge's volume, which had been published in 1925 by the Anglican publisher the Society for Promoting Christian Knowledge. Its aim was to update the first edition's orthography according to the Standard Orthography

---

[19] Derek R. Peterson, *Creative Writing: Translation, Bookkeeping, and the Work of Imagination in Colonial Kenya* (Portsmouth, NH: Heinemann, 2004).

[20] CCAS MP Director of Education, Education Department, Kampala, to E.M.K. Mulira, 12 January 1948.

[21] For further insight see CCAS MP A.N. Tucker to E.M.K. Mulira, 23 May 1949; CCAS MP H. Moyse-Bartlett, Secretary, SOAS, to E.M.K. Mulira, 30 May 1949.

[22] E.M.K. Mulira and E.G.M. Ndawula, *A Luganda-English and English-Luganda Dictionary*, 2nd edn (London: Society for Promoting Christian Knowledge, 1952).

[23] E.O. Ashton, E.M.K. Mulira and others, *A Luganda Grammar* (London: Longmans, Green & Co., 1954).

recommended by the all-Baganda Conference in 1947.[24] The revised edition replaced the earlier dictionary and was 'accepted officially by the Government of Buganda and the Protectorate Government'.[25] As a standardised revision, though, there was minimal difference between the two editions. What is illuminating, however, is the parallel grammar that was published two years later; what Mulira and his colleague, E.G.M. Ndawula, described as 'an invaluable adjunct'.

Ethel O. Ashton, E.M.K. Mulira, E.G.M. Ndawula and A.N. Tucker authored *A Luganda Grammar*. The defined purpose of the book was 'to provide the beginner with a graded course in sentence construction, and to enable the more advanced student to appreciate some of the finer points of Luganda idiom'.[26] Mulira and Ndawula provided the 'great majority of the sentences illustrating the grammar, the exercises and the text of the Linguaphone Gramophone records'.[27] According to Ashton, the grammar reflected Mulira and Ndawula's 'intimate knowledge of the language and of the social life of their country',[28] insights that were considered 'essential to the book'. The gramophonic exercises recorded by Mulira and Ndawula were 'arranged in the form of drills, easy to learn by heart'.[29] The book was designed for Baganda students, educators and colonial officers.

In *A Grammar*, Mulira placed rural farmers, kings and appointed chiefs in the same grammatical category, which was not a prominent association in earlier linguistic books in Luganda. In ways that mirrored *Teefe*, Mulira emphasised the social and economic importance of labourers in Buganda, and presented to his readers a kingdom where no one is unemployed, *Tewalibaawo atalifuna mulimu*.[30] Cultivators and farmers were cast to contrast the cultural and political powerbrokers of Buganda's kingdom. Grammar exercises that referenced Kampala tended to describe Buganda's capital as a place of leisure,[31] European

---

[24] Mulira and Ndawula, *A Luganda-English and English-Luganda Dictionary*, p. v.
[25] Ibid.
[26] Ashton, Mulira and others, *A Luganda Grammar*, p. vii.
[27] Ibid.
[28] Ibid.
[29] Ibid., p. 471.
[30] Ibid., p. 238.
[31] Ibid., p. 228. '*Mwagenda kukola ki e Kampala? Twagenda ne tugula ebintu ne tulaba n'omupiira*', 'What did you (pl.) go to do in Kampala? We went and bought several articles and we saw a football match'.

dress and eroded work ethic.[32] People from the country, *abantu ab'omu kyalo*,[33] preserved Kiganda custom, not Buganda's official power-brokers. This theme was explicated through exercises on adjectives.

By using Buganda's rural landscape to illustrate the practice of custom, Mulira aimed to talk about power in a way that placed kings and commoners within the same theoretical and democratic framework. In colonial Luganda, nouns that typically involved personages of social importance did not have a prefix or initial vowel in the singular or an initial vowel in the plural.[34] And while such nouns often used the concord of the personal class (*-mu/-ba*), they were best understood as nouns *without* a class prefix.[35] Earlier grammars did not identify *Kabaka*, *Katikkiro* or similar entries with the personal noun class, such as *Katonda* (God) and proper names.[36] In *A Grammar*, though, the ambiguity of this syntax was accentuated by classifying the king, *kabaka*, in the social taxonomy of commoners, such as *muganda* (brother) and *muliraanwa* (neighbour). The entries *kabaka*, *muganda* and *muliraanwa* were grammatically elucidated alongside one another, which underscored equality between these social classes.

By placing these terms together, Mulira juxtaposed the glosses of power in colonial Buganda with a scathing reading of the kingdom's hierarchical structure. Mulira used *A Grammar* to remember a time when Buganda's kings wielded excessive power. He noted: '*Bajjajjaffe baatyanga Kabaka nga bwe batyanga ensolo, kubanga ejja kubaluma*', 'Our forefathers feared the King as they used to fear a wild animal lest it should bite them.'[37] Mulira offered a similar critique of Buganda's chiefs, who, at one time, had been esteemed commoners.[38] *A Grammar*, however, criticised chiefs who received unearned honour. In one case, the volume compared a chief whose 'position of authority should be taken from him' with *ssaza* chiefs who demanded food for simply making public appearances.[39]

[32] Ibid., pp. 230, 286 and 419.
[33] Ibid., p. 386.
[34] J.D. Chesswas, *The Essentials of Luganda*, 4th edn (Nairobi: Oxford University Press, 1967), p. 33.
[35] Ashton, Mulira and Others, *A Luganda Grammar*, pp. 217–18.
[36] Ibid., p. 89.
[37] Ibid., p. 318.
[38] Ibid., p. 332. '*Yakolerera okufuna obwami*', 'He strove hard to obtain a chieftainship'.
[39] Ibid., p. 339.

In short, Mulira imagined space for rural cultivators to be unhindered by kings who bite like untamed animals by emphasising the similar and *personal* character of Buganda's kings, chiefs and peasants. A *Grammar* reminded Ganda students and colonial officials of a time when chiefs were common labourers who toiled for their positions. To place kings, chiefs and commoners on equal footing, Mulira focused grammar to emphasise the universality of law in more than one instance, arguing that '[o]nce a law has been made, it should be obeyed by everybody',[40] including kings, chiefs and clan heads. In doing so, Mulira was formulating the possibility of democratic reform.

Within the context of Muteesa's deportation, Mulira translated his grammatical work into public discourse. By the early 1950s, he was a member of the *Lukiiko*. Without her king, Buganda's parliament was forced to debate if Buganda would constitutionally reform her monarchy, which was a principal concern for colonial bureaucrats. In an emergency session, Buganda's chiefs, clan heads and appointed members debated in earnest the future of their kingdom. In the past, it was argued, Buganda's king exercised 'direct rule over the natives of Uganda'.[41] Amid pandemonium, Mulira addressed Buganda's parliament. In his autobiography, Mulira recalled framing Muteesa's deportation as an affront to democratic practice in Buganda:

If we allowed foreigners to depose and make Kings for us then that institution would come to mean nothing to us, and if our forebearers had not allowed that institution to be humiliated by any foreigner, how could we live to be proud of our manhood, if during our time we let foreigners to tamper with that institution.[42]

Mulira's equalisation of power relations in Luganda grammar translated into a deliberate use of plural and possessive pronouns: 'If *we* allowed', 'make Kings for *us*', 'nothing to *us*', 'if *our* forebears', 'how could *we*', '*our* manhood', '*our* time', '*we* let', '*we* allowed', 'could *we* stand up' and 'respect any of *us*'. In refusing to cooperate with Cohen, Mulira argued, Muteesa was 'only expressing the wishes of his people; he was acting

---

[40] Ibid., p. 337. An earlier usage noted: 'Once a law has been passed it is proper that everyone should obey it' (ibid., p. 314).
[41] 'The Uganda Agreement of 1900', Article 6.
[42] 'Autobiography', p. 226.

in his capacity as the sole representative of his Kingdom'.[43] A few months after the *Lukiiko*'s emergency session, Buganda's parliament was reconvened to debate whether the kingdom would concede to colonial demands to negotiate a new constitutional arrangement. During the deliberation, Mulira collapsed onto his knees and argued that Buganda's king should 'be above politics' and democratised.[44] Through his plea, Mulira persuaded Buganda's government to pass a resolution to appoint a committee to explore constitutional reform in the kingdom.

International Lobbying

Omulamuzi Matayo Mugwanya, Apolo Kironde, Thomas Makumbi, Amos Sempa and E.M.K. Mulira were selected to serve on the *Lukiiko*'s international committee.[45] The delegation arrived in London in early December and implemented a comprehensive and purposefully amicable strategy to advocate for Muteesa's return.[46] The delegation received immediate attention in the British press,[47] which the *Lukiiko*'s appointees steered to shape British public opinion. Activists were not only pressed to calm emotional angst on the streets of Kampala, they were challenged to think about Buganda's monarchy in ways that would convince powerbrokers in London to orchestrate Muteesa's return.

The networks that Mulira forged in Britain in the 1940s proved useful for Buganda's committee. While at SOAS, Mulira had spent time with various Christian organisations and political societies. In July 1948, he attended a Keswickian convention where he observed

---

[43] Ibid.

[44] Kavuma, *Crisis in Buganda*, p. 71; ARP 7/6/125 Audrey Richards, Field Notes, May 1954.

[45] For further discussion on the controversy surrounding Mulira's appointment see Kevin Ward, 'The Church of Uganda and the Exile of Kabaka Muteesa II, 1953–55', *Journal of Religion in Africa*, 28 (1998), 411–49 (p. 423); Kavuma, *Crisis in Buganda*, pp. 14 and 43.

[46] '"The Mystery Deepens" Says Baganda', *Observer*, 31 January 1954, p. 7; James Griffiths, Parliamentary Debates (Hansard), House of Commons, 16 November 1954, Series 5 Vol. 533, cc 220.

[47] 'Delegation from Buganda', *The Times*, 9 December 1953; 'Buganda Chief Justice in London', *The Times*, 10 December 1953; 'Meeting Fixed for Buganda Talks', *Guardian*, 11 December 1953, p. 1; 'Uganda and Buganda', *Guardian*, 14 December 1953, p. 6; 'Great Lukiko of Buganda', *The Times*, 15 December 1953.

'real men and women of God'.[48] Politically, Mulira took an active role in the South East and Central African Student Union (SECASU), where he served as president.[49] SECASU afforded Mulira and other Africans in Great Britain an opportunity to network and become politically active.[50] Students such as Mulira, Kenya's Peter Koinange and Tanzania's H. Godfrey Kayamba[51] collaborated to draft 'memoranda after memoranda to Governments'.[52] The organisation took an active role in campaigning for the return of Botswana deportee Seretse Khama,[53] an experience upon which Mulira built to shape the tactics of the *Lukiiko's* delegation in England.[54] Through SECASU, Mulira was also introduced to the Fabian Colonial Bureau, who published his *Troubled Uganda* in 1950.[55] As early as March 1948, Mulira had attended Fabian seminars on topics such as 'The Socialist Approach to Politics'[56] and additional group discussions on colonial policy.[57] Participation with the Fabians introduced Mulira to the internal workings of Westminster,[58] and the activism of the anti-Apartheid

[48] CCAS MP 'Extract of Report of E.M.K. Mulira of His Travels in Great Britain', Mss., August 1948.

[49] CCAS MP E.M.K. Mulira, President, South East and Central African Student Union, to A. Chamier, for the Director of Colonial Scholars, 22 December 1949.

[50] 'Autobiography', section b, n.p.

[51] CCAS MP H. Godfrey Kayamba to E.M.K. Mulira, et al., 'Union Now', Memorandum, 23 October 1947. For further discussion see Martin Kayamba, 'The Story of Martin Kayamba Mdumi, M.B.E., of the Bondei Tribe', in *Ten Africans*, ed. by Margery Perham (London: Faber and Faber Limited, 1963), pp. 173–272; John Iliffe, 'The Spokesman: Martin Kayamba', in *Modern Tanzanians: A Volume of Biographies*, ed. by John Iliffe (Nairobi: East African Publishing House, 1973), pp. 66–94.

[52] 'Autobiography', section b, n.p. One memorandum, 'The Human Factor in East and Central African Development', stated: 'On behalf of the Executive Committee of SECASU, I am writing to bring to your notice our great concern as regards the development of the human element in the British Dependences which come under the term "East Africa and Central Africa"' (CCAS MP E.M.K. Mulira to Secretary of State for the Colonies, 24 January 1950).

[53] CCAS MP Ndawula, Secretary, SECASU, to E.M.K. Mulira, 16 March 1950.

[54] CCAS MP E.M.K. Mulira, 'A Christian in Public Life', 13 February 1966; 'Autobiography', p. 231.

[55] CCAS MP E.M.K. Mulira to Mr. Gayer, 20 December 1949.

[56] CCAS MP Rita Hinden, Fabian Colonial Bureau, to E.M.K. Mulira, 12 March 1948.

[57] CCAS MP Marjorie Nicholson, Fabian Colonial Bureau, to E.M.K. Mulira, 15 November 1949.

[58] CCAS MP Fabian Colonial Bureau to E.M.K. Mulira, n.d. In this letter, Mulira was provided with a parliamentary record: 'Hansard, 14 April 1948, Column 968'.

Anglican priest Michael Scott,[59] with whom the delegation worked closely during Muteesa's deportation.[60] The itinerary of the delegation shows that Mulira attended a meeting with leaders of the Society to explain their objectives and marshal support.

The delegation also solicited backing from the Church of England. In December 1953, the delegation and Uganda's former bishop, C.E. Stuart,[61] pressed for constitutional reform and Muteesa's return. Shortly after a meeting with the Archbishop of Canterbury, which Stuart attended,[62] the delegation met with the Secretary of State for the Colonies, Oliver Lyttelton. To Lyttelton, Mulira and the delegation argued that democratic consensus in Buganda warranted the return of Muteesa from exile: 'It is our sincere desire that our beloved Kabaka shall be restored to his people and that the present negotiations between the Colonial Secretary and ourselves will lead to acceptance of this most ardent wish of the Kabaka's subjects.'[63] Mulira and the delegates argued that Buganda's general population demanded the return of their king by using Protestant sensibility: 'The delegation and the people of Buganda still regard Mutesa II as their king. He was crowned in accordance with the rights of the Protestant Church.'[64] Bishop Stuart, 'the bishop who crowned *Kabaka* Mutesa II of Buganda', argued that

---

59 Mulira heard Scott speak as early as April 1950 at a conference organised by Christian Action on the theme of 'Christ and the Colour Problem' (CCAS MP 'Christ and the Colour Problem', Conference Program, 17 April 1950). Mulira's personal papers contain a pamphlet entitled 'Who Is Michael Scott?', published by the Social and Industrial Council of the Diocese of Johannesburg, printed around 1948.

60 'Autobiography', pp. 231–2. See also Colin Legum, *Must We Lose Africa?* (London: W.H. Allen, 1954), pp. 110–11.

61 Kevin Ward observes that Bishop Stuart strongly opposed Muteesa's deportation. In an article partially reproduced in the *Observer* on 27 December 1953 – and fully in *Ebifa mu Uganda* – Stuart asserted: 'Unless I am wrong there will be bloodshed in the whole of Africa and Mr Lyttelton will be responsible. If Mr Lyttleton were employed by the Russians he could not have served them better' (Ward, *The Exile of Kabaka Muteesa II*, p. 429).

62 Mulira recalled: 'Our first appointment was with the [Archbishop] of Canterbury, Dr. Fisher, because our first contact with the British people was with the Church' ('Autobiography', p. 233).

63 'Deposition of the Kabaka: Delegates' Version of Events', *The Times*, 22 December 1953.

64 'The Kabaka Not to Return: Final Decision by Cabinet', *The Times*, 23 December 1953. See also Kavuma, *Crisis in Buganda*, p. 44.

Muteesa 'was merely voicing the opinions of all his people and also of most of the rest of the Protectorate'.[65]

The delegation had also commenced a popular campaign throughout the United Kingdom to secure government reconsideration. In a press release, delegates stated that their campaign would vindicate the honour of the Kabaka, 'and seek his restoration as the lawful occupant of the Buganda throne'.[66] Meeting with trade unions, churches, university students and municipal councils,[67] Mulira and Makumbi addressed audiences in Edinburgh, St Andrews, Glasgow, Leeds, Manchester, Sheffield and Birmingham.[68] Amos Sempa travelled to Bristol and Bath before accompanying Mulira and Makumbi to Manchester and Sheffield. Buganda's delegates met with parliamentarians and numerous Protestant and Catholic leaders.

The constitutional ideals of Mulira, in particular, influenced debates in the House of Commons and the writings of Colin Legum. On 4 June 1954, the Labour parliamentarian John Dugdale underscored a press release that Mulira had made to criticise Buganda's colonial resident. It stated:

The work of the British Resident Commissioner in Buganda is to advise the Kabaka of Buganda and his ministers on behalf of Her Majesty's Government. The present Resident, Mr. Birch, however, instead of advising appears to be intent on undermining our native custom and the authority of the Great Lukiko. After the Lukiiko passed a resolution refusing to elect a new Kabaka, the Resident has tried to go direct to members of the Lukiko and persuade them to go back on their resolution. He has also backed elements in the country who are endeavouring to go against the wishes and decisions of the Lukiko in this matter. We protest very strongly against such a policy which aims at dividing our people into two rival factions.[69]

---

[65] C.E. Stuart, 'The Kabaka', *Observer*, 27 December 1953, p. 3.

[66] 'Buganda Delegation in London', *The Times*, 11 January 1954.

[67] 'Autobiography', p. 242.

[68] 'ICS 29/1/1/10c 'Report of the Buganda Kingdom Lukiiko Delegation to England on the Question of Arrest and Deportation of His Highness Kabaka Mutesa II of Buganda', 23 March 1954 (hereafter 'Report of the Buganda Kingdom Lukiiko Delegation to England').

[69] John Dugdale, Parliamentary Debates (Hansard), House of Commons, 4 June 1954, Series 5 Vol. 528, cc 1667.

After drawing attention to Mulira's comment, Dugdale highlighted the legitimacy of parliamentary power in Buganda: 'I should like to know whether it is the Minister's view that it is right for the Resident deliberately to try and persuade the people of Buganda to go back on a decision and to alter what their Lukiko has already decided to do.'

The *Observer* columnist Colin Legum took an active role in reporting on the activism of the delegation.[70] In their March report to the *Lukiiko*, the delegation reminded Buganda's parliament that the *Observer* 'was one of the most helpful papers during all the time of our mission'.[71] Indeed, as early as January 1954 Legum publicly questioned British policy and supported the undertaking of the delegates.[72] In the same month, an *Observer* correspondent, likely Legum, drew attention to Mulira's argument that Muteesa had been deported for consulting a democratically elected parliament:

Why did the Governor insist on keeping his protracted negotiations with the Kabaka secret, even forbidding him to consult his Parliament? Why, at a crucial stage in the talks, did he refuse in these matters? Only recently a new Lukiko, with a majority of elected Members, had come into being as a result of reforms initiated by the Governor. Did Sir Andrew Cohen have no confidence that our Parliament might be helpful in the crisis that had been reached?[73]

From February to June, Legum published no fewer than three additional articles on the deportation.[74] In one article, he portrayed Muteesa as the people's king.[75] In an additional piece, he drew exclusively from an interview with Mulira in London, citing: '[T]he [colonial] Government has no authority, direct or indirect, in making or unmaking Buganda's kings, the prerogative belongs to the Baganda, operating through the

---

[70] Examples of Legum's reporting include 'Clearer Picture of the Buganda Crisis', 21 February 1954, p. 7; 'At Grips with the African Crisis', 7 November 1954, p. 8; 'New Effort to End Crisis in Uganda', 5 June 1955, p. 2; 'Kabaka's Return: Talks to Continue', 19 June 1955, p. 4; 'Restoration of Kabaka Agreed On', 17 July 1955; 'The Kabaka is Triumph', 16 October 1955, p. 1.

[71] 'Report of the Buganda Kingdom Lukiiko Delegation to England'.

[72] Colin Legum, 'Uganda Rulers Back Kabaka', *Observer*, 24 January 1954, p. 7.

[73] E.M.K. Mulira, in 'The Mystery Deepens', p. 7.

[74] Legum, *Observer*: 'London Call to Governor of Uganda', 7 February 1954, p. 1; 'Clearer Picture of the Buganda Crisis', 21 February 1954, p. 7; '"Interference" in Buganda Palace: Protest against Resident's Letter to Regents, "Blows" over Actions of Pretender', 6 June 1954, p. 1.

[75] Legum, 'Clearer Picture of the Buganda Crisis', p. 7.

Lukiko.'[76] And when he published his book on late colonial Africa, *Must We Lose Africa?*, Legum incorporated Mulira's constitutional argument when he discussed Muteesa's deportation:[77] 'The Kabaka had been the victim of an unworkable constitutional set-up. He was condemned for voicing the opinion of his people, his parliament and his Ministers.'[78] Legum concluded his one hundred-page treatment of the deportation by citing an article Mulira published in *Uganda Empya* on 22 April 1954.[79] In the article, Mulira questioned what anyone had gained from the deportation and further stated that Buganda's citizenry would not 'be happy' as long as Muteesa lived in exile.

The international activism of the delegation and Mulira was successful.[80] On 28 February 1954, Lyttelton asserted that the 'long-term aim of Her Majesty's Government is to build the Protectorate into a self-governing State',[81] suggesting that Africans 'play a constantly increasing part in the political institutions of the country'.[82] Lyttelton utilised Mulira's language to outline the importance of constitutional reform in Buganda and the Protectorate, placing the future of Buganda's monarchy in the hands of democratically appointed representatives.[83] To examine constitutional reform in Buganda the Secretary of State appointed an 'independent expert', Professor Keith Hancock of the Institute of Commonwealth Studies.[84] The Namirembe Conference followed. By appropriating international networks and the British press, activists such as Mulira retooled Buganda's monarchy. Mulira's advocacy was

[76] E.M.K. Mulira in Legum, '"Interference" in Buganda Palace', p. 1.
[77] 'Autobiography', p. 238.
[78] Legum, *Must We Lose Africa?*, p. 101.
[79] Ibid., p. 125.
[80] Local activism accompanied international lobbying. While delegates engaged in campaigns throughout Britain, Apolo Kironde filed a case with the High Court in Kampala toward the end of January 1954. The case, which was won, was designed to challenge the legality of the deportation (*Ebifa mu Uganda*, 1 February 1951). For further discussion see 'Autobiography', pp. 244–5; Muteesa, *Desecration of My Kingdom*, pp. 130–6; Kavuma, *Crisis in Buganda*, pp. 84–99; Low and Pratt, *Buganda and British Overrule*, pp. 340–2.
[81] Oliver Lyttelton, Parliamentary Debates (Hansard), House of Commons, 23 February 1954, Series 5 Vol. 524, cc 212.
[82] Ibid.
[83] Ibid., cc 213.
[84] For additional material on Hancock's political activism in Uganda see 'Sir Keith Hancock Arrives To-day: A New Chapter for Buganda', *Uganda Mail*, 22 June 1954, p. 1; 'Sir K. Hancock on His Task', *The Times*, 24 June 1954; 'Constitution in Buganda: Reformed Agreed', *The Times*, 17 September 1954.

conceptually informed by his earlier literary work in Luganda, within which kings and commoners were described as equal participants in Buganda's political hierarchy. Mulira adapted these categories to help shape the terms under which Muteesa would assume power once again. Literary production not only facilitated creative politics in Uganda; it also shaped colonial policy in Britain's imperial capital.

Constitutional Debate in Buganda

The Namirembe negotiations began in the summer of 1954 and constituted fifty meetings between 24 June and 17 September (Figure 3.2).[85] During the sessions, activists pressed for competing political agendas,[86] some of which are explored more fully in the following two chapters. Mulira advocated for the democratisation of Buganda's monarchy, which Ganda representatives argued was a break from Buganda's political past.[87] In a report given on the fifth meeting of the Constitutional Committee, Mulira argued that in 'the old days full authority had been vested in the Kabaka, though the scope of his power had in practice varied in accordance with temporary personal factors'.[88] He asserted that 'now it was expected to derive from the people acting through their spokesmen'.[89] Mulira's recommendations repositioned Buganda's monarchy 'outside the sphere of politics [. . .]'.[90] Following the constitutional recommendations of Namirembe, Muteesa returned from exile on 18 October 1955, where in the presence of 900 official guests, Buganda's new constitution was ratified.[91] In theory, E.M.K. Mulira had successfully reconstituted Buganda's monarchy by ensuring that '[e]very Kabaka shall henceforward on becoming Kabaka enter a Solemn Engagement with the Great Lukiko and the people of Buganda [. . .]'.[92]

---

[85] ICS 29/1/12 & 29/1/17.
[86] ICS 29/1/12/2b 'Constitutional Committee & Steering Committee Minutes', Second Meeting, 25 June 1954, p. 1.
[87] Ibid., p. 2.
[88] ICS 29/1/12/5 'Constitutional Committee & Steering Committee Minutes', Fifth Meeting, 1 July 1954, p. 2.
[89] Ibid.
[90] UNAL 'Agreed Recommendations of the Namirembe Conference', Article 22, p. 5.
[91] *Uganda Argus*, 19 October 1955.
[92] UNAL 'Agreed Recommendations of the Namirembe Conference', Article 28, p. 7.

Figure 3.2 The Namirembe Conference, 1954

Row 1, left to right: Y. Kyaze; S.W. Kulubya; *Omulamuzi* M. Mugwanya; Professor K. Hancock; Governor A. Cohen; Bishop J. Kiwanuka; Resident of Buganda J.P. Birch.

Row 2, left to right: Father J.K. Masagazi; J.P. Musoke; A.K. Kironde; E.M.K. Mulira; E.Z. Kibuka; Y.K. Lule; J.G. Sengendo Zake; Thomas A.K. Makumbi; S.A. de Smith (secretary); Dr E.B. Kalibala; Father J. Kasule
Source: D.A. Low, *Buganda in Modern History*

Mulira's liberal project fuelled debate throughout the kingdom. One columnist in *Ebifa mu Uganda* praised Mulira for being 'a good Christian', but proceeded to state that he was misleading the *Lukiiko*: 'Mr. Mulira is well educated and a good Christian, but when he is in error the whole *Lukiiko* is in error. Who can tell whether Mr. Mulira has not some secret aim at the Kabakaship which is beyond the comprehension of the public?'[93] Three populists, who self-identified themselves as 'true patriots of this country', protested against Mulira's agenda, stating that 'it is undesirable that the Kabaka should

---

[93] *Ebifa mu Uganda*, 4 May 1954.

Figure 3.3 *Kabaka* Muteesa II's return from exile, October 1955: 'Your heroism is our glory'
Source: Fallers, *The King's Men*

be taken out of politics'.[94] Comments made by Buganda's *Ssaabaganzi*, Muteesa's eldest maternal uncle, were theologically weighty: 'The Kabaka of Buganda is the ruler of the country and its people, no muganda would like to transfer the political powers of the Kabaka to the Ministers, this would be unthinkable, just as it is unthinkable that God's power of creation would be transferred to His Angels' (Figure 3.3).[95] An elected member to the *Lukiiko* asserted that constitutional reforms would compromise the integrity of the kingdom's monarch, and asserted that Mulira's measures meant that 'the Kabaka would lose both power and dignity'.[96] In turn, when Mulira advocated for commoners to be appointed directly to Buganda's *Lukiiko* in 1958, the motion was barred by thirty votes.[97]

[94] ICS 29/1/13/21 Erukana Kiwanuka, et al., to Members of the Constitutional Committee, 22 June 1954.
[95] ICS 29/1/13/18 K.S. Katongole to Hancock Committee, 24 June 1954.
[96] ICS 29/1/13/26 S. Busulwa Kapere to Members of Constitutional Committee, 26 June 1954.
[97] *Uganda Argus*, 29 June 1956.

The constitutionalisation of Buganda's monarchy was part of a broader debate over the future legal state of Buganda in Uganda, a central issue that surrounded Muteesa's deportation.[98] Mulira advocated for Buganda's incorporation into Uganda: 'This is a grand opportunity to our generation to prepare a place for Buganda and the whole of Uganda, which will make it not a Country lagging behind but a progressive country in her natural greatness, not to be belittled by anyone.'[99] Mulira pressed for constitutional integration by proposing a six-part reform that framed Buganda's 1955 Constitution and 'the provisional terms on which Buganda could [. . .] be advised to join the central legislature'.[100] Throughout the mid-1950s, Mulira argued that incorporation was the best possible option for Buganda's political future. To make this argument, he borrowed from the federalist traditions of Europe.

To develop his platform, Mulira drew from the work of a group of scholars at Oxford whose research focused on federalism. Once Buganda's parliament agreed to participate in the Namirembe Conference Mulira began regular correspondence with Professor Hancock, a precedence that continued into 1956.[101] Early into their letter writing Mulira encouraged Hancock to study fourteen specific books, which may have been suggested to him by Margery Perham.[102] These works reinforced the scholarship of Oxford scholar Sir Kenneth Wheare, whose research examined the history and practice of international federalism.[103] Mulira also recommended Geoffrey Sawer's

---

[98] Ernest Z. Kibuuka, *Omulembe gwa Muteesa II* (Kampala: Crane Books, 2004), pp. 76–87.

[99] 'Report of the Buganda Kingdom Lukiiko Delegation to England'.

[100] ICS 29/1/17/3 'Namirembe Conference Minutes', Third Meeting, 4 August 1954, p. 1.

[101] ICS 29/1/10/38 E.M.K. Mulira to Hancock, 18 July 1954; ICS 29/1/29/21 E.M.K. Mulira to Hancock, 24 October 1954; ICS 29/1/29/32 E.M.K. Mulira to Hancock, 6 November 1954; ICS 29/1/29/41 Hancock to E.M.K. Mulira, 19 November 1954; ICS 29/1/29/67 E.M.K. Mulira to Hancock, 24 April 1955; ICS 29/1/29/68 Hancock to E.M.K. Mulira, 4 May 1955; ICS 29/1/29/81 E.M.K. Mulira to Hancock, 13 August 1955; ICS 29/1/29/96 E.M.K. Mulira to Hancock, 24 April 1956.

[102] ICS 29/1/3/80, n.d.

[103] Ibid. The list included: K.C. Wheare, *Federal Government* (London: Oxford University Press, 1953). Additional works included Lord Hailey, *Native Administration in the British African Territories (Part I)* (1950); Martin Wight, *Colonial Constitutions, 1947* (1950); Nicholas Mansergh, *The Government*

edited volume on federalism, which included an article by Wheare[104] and Christopher Hughes' translation of Switzerland's federal constitution,[105] a translation project that had been reviewed by Wheare.[106] Wheare's book on federalism was comprehensive and covered a number of subjects related to the topic: 'What Federal Government Is', 'When Federal Government is Appropriate' and 'How Federal Government should be Organised'. From the Constitution of the United States (1787) to the Austro-Hungarian *Ausgleich* (1867), modern constitutions had been built upon 'federal principle', argued Wheare, or 'the method of dividing powers so that the general and regional governments are each, within a sphere, co-ordinate and independent'.[107] For Wheare, federal governments were designed to mediate state control when 'the powers of government for a community are divided substantially according to the principle that there is a single independent authority for the whole area in respect of some matters and that there are independent regional authorities for other matters, each set of authorities being co-ordinate with and not sub-ordinate to the others within its own prescribed sphere'.[108] Wheare's federalist vision was useful. Mulira used it to advocate for Buganda's legal incorporation into Uganda, emphasising the importance of common national purpose, what Wheare considered 'essential' for the practice of federalism.

To advance his federalist project in the mid-1950s, Mulira organised the Progressive Party (PP). The Party's self-identified aim was to advocate for 'progressive African opinion',[109] which entailed 'progress "towards the building of a new self-governing Uganda" by providing

---

of *North Ireland* (1936); Sir Ivor Jennings, *Constitution of Ceylon* (1951); H.S. Nicholas, *The Australian Constitution* (1952); *Problems of Parliamentary Government in Colonies* (1952); Martin Wight, *The Development of the Legislative Council, 1606–1945* (1946); Martin Wight, *Constitution of India* (1946); D.N. Chester, *Central and Local Government* (1951); Ursula Hicks, *British Public Finances, 1880–1952* (1954); *Laws of Uganda* (1951).

104 ICS 29/1/3/80, n.d.; K.C. Wheare, 'When Federal Government Is Justifiable', in *Federalism: An Australian Jubilee Study*, ed. by Geoffrey Sawer (Melbourne: F.W. Cheshire, 1952), pp. 110–34.

105 ICS 29/1/3/80, n.d.

106 Christopher Hughes, *The Federal Constitution of Switzerland* (Oxford: Clarendon Press, 1954), Acknowledgements.

107 Wheare, *Federal Government*, p. 11.

108 Ibid., p. 35.

109 *Uganda Argus*, 31 January 1955.

leadership, encouraging education and supporting the economic development of the African'.[110] According to David Apter, by 1956 PP membership was approximately 1,400,[111] a relatively small number in comparison to I.K. Musazi's Uganda National Congress (UNC), whose membership included approximately 10,000 due-paying members and 50,000 sympathisers.[112] Apter further suggested that PP activists constituted twelve members in the *Lukiiko* with an additional twenty sympathisers in the same body.[113] The Party's administration consisted of two full-time leaders; twenty-one landlords and businessmen; two farmers; nine teachers; two women; and one newspaper proprietor, lawyer and doctor, respectively.[114] A survey of thirty-two remaining membership forms indicates that the Party's constituency was socio-economically diverse: cobbling, construction and painting, clerical/administrative, driving, estate management, farming, fishery, mechanical, printing, trade and sales, religious instruction, sewing and laundering, teaching and no description/illegible.[115]

Through party activism, Mulira sought to reconstitute a federal, or nationalised kingdom, a new Uganda, *Uganda Empya*, the title of a newspaper that he launched in late 1952.[116] Comparable to the pro-Bataka paper *Gambuze*, and the Catholic press *Munno*, colonial records indicate that 8,000 copies of *Uganda Empya* were in circulation by 1954.[117] Among privately owned papers, *Uganda Empya* was out-circulated only by *Uganda Eyogera*, owned by A.D. Lubowa and P.M.K. Lwanga, the son of James Miti, and the *Uganda Post*, owned by UNC activist 'Jolly' Joe Kiwanuka. *Uganda Empya*'s circulation increased to 8,500 by 1958, though distribution ratios with other presses remained fairly consistent.[118] The paper later merged with Aga Khan's *Taifa Uganda* to form *Taifa Empya*.[119]

---

[110] *Uganda Argus*, 7 February 1955.

[111] David E. Apter, *The Political Kingdom in Uganda: A Study of Bureaucratic Nationalism*, 2nd edn (Princeton: Princeton University Press, 1967), p. 338.

[112] Ibid., p. 332.

[113] Ibid., p. 338.

[114] Ibid.

[115] CCAS MP 'Progressive Party: *Olupapula Okuyingirirwa*', 1956.

[116] ARP 6/20/T2 E.M.K. Mulira, 'My Life since 1930', Mss., n.d., pp. 5–6.

[117] RHOP 529/2 'Uganda Department of Information', [c. 1954]).

[118] Apter, *The Political Kingdom in Uganda*, p. 274.

[119] CCAS MP E.M.K. Mulira, 'Curriculum Vitae', Mss., n.d.

Mulira's vision for *Uganda Empya*, a new Uganda, was most clearly developed in *Aligaweesa*, a short story that Mulira produced in May 1955 to offer a compelling case for the benefits of federalism.[120] The novel reinforced the federalist objectives of the Namirembe Recommendations. *Aligaweesa: Omuvubuka wa Uganda Empya* (*Aligaweesa: A Youth of the New Uganda*) was written intentionally short so that it could be easily memorised.[121] In keeping his story short, Mulira hoped to communicate 'only those things which provide the reader with a foundational message'.[122] To some extent, *Aligaweesa* is similar to *Teefe*; the protagonists in both books are of Kooki heritage. Aligaweesa was born in Kooki in 1890 and grew up in the court of *Omulangira* Ndawula. However, whereas *Teefe* chronicled the story of spiritual pilgrimage toward Buganda's periphery, *Aligaweesa* does just the opposite; it tells the story of a stranger's political promotion in Buganda's ethnic polity. Mulira highlighted that the terms 'nationalist' or 'citizen' were identical to the word used in Luganda for 'stranger'; each derived etymologically from *–ggwanga*.[123] To belong to the nation, *munnaggwanga*, it was not necessary to be a Muganda. Mobility within both the kingdom and the state, argued Mulira, was accommodated through comprehensive integration.

The novel followed a simple chronology: Chapter 1, *Obuto bwe* (Early Years); Chapter 2, Aligaweesa *Omuweereza* (the Servant; or 'one who serves'[124]); Chapter 3, Aligaweesa *mu Ssomero* (in School); Chapter 4, Aligaweesa *Akola Ewa* D.C. (works for the District Commissioner); and Chapter 5, Aligaweesa *Alya Obwami* (becomes a chief). In Chapter 1, Aligaweesa was presented as a hardworking labourer, who, through commendable behaviour, was selected to become the chief brewer before next being appointed palace treasurer. On account of his 'good conduct' (Chapter 2), Aligaweesa is chosen to manage Kooki's palace youths and entrusted to distribute work assignments and mediate internal disputes. During the course of his appointment, however, Aligaweesa is the target of 'jealousy

---

[120] E.M.K. Mulira, *Aligaweesa: Omuvubuka wa Uganda Empya* (Kampala: Uganda Bookshop Press, [1955]), *ebisookerwako* [Preface].

[121] Ibid.

[122] Ibid. '[. . .] *mpa ebyo byokka, asoma alyoke afune ebisengejje byokka*'.

[123] See also *A Grammar*, p. 372.

[124] John D. Murphy, *Luganda-English Dictionary* (Washington, DC: Catholic University of America Press, 1972), p. 391.

and envy'.[125] In time, a missionary visited Kooki's palace and noticed Aligaweesa's diligent work ethic. After negotiating with *Omulangira* Ndawula, the missionary secured an educational opportunity for Aligaweesa away from the palace. Now in his early twenties (Chapter 3), Aligaweesa undergoes formal education during a time when the children of Buganda's chiefs were already enrolled in university. Due to his natural intelligence, though, Aligaweesa's educational training is expedited and he is appointed head prefect of a school of eighty students. As a prefect, he initiates a series of reforms to instil discipline and manners among the students.

In Mulira's final two chapters, Aligaweesa's political advancement is outlined. In 1916, Aligaweesa takes a position in the district commissioner's office as a translator. During this time, he reads African American literature to improve his English. The rising Aligaweesa is particularly drawn to the work of Booker T. Washington, one who had forsaken everything to follow Jesus.[126] In Washington's footsteps, Aligaweesa 'decided to abandon' his colleagues in order to follow Jesus Christ, 'who would give him peace'.[127] After eight years of working with the district commissioner, Aligaweesa is appointed *ggombolola* chief, first in Ssingo and then in Kyaggwe, where he is recognised for his work ethic and commitment to education. In due course, Aligaweesa, who made '"truth" his guiding principle', is appointed *ssaza* chief, during which he established cooperatives and farmers' societies.[128] As the story concludes, Aligaweesa is preparing to contest the *katikkiro*ship.

In *Aligaweesa*, Mulira accentuated the importance of federalist integration. To make 'truth' a guiding political principle was to follow in the footsteps of Jesus and Booker T. Washington, which for Mulira was tantamount to forsaking separatist ideology. One month following the publication of *Aligaweesa*, without coincidence, the PP organised a rally entitled 'Uganda's Place in the World'.[129] The rally's proceedings

[125] Mulira, *Aligaweesa*, p. 14.
[126] Mulira, *Aligaweesa*, pp. 18–19. Mulira referenced Washington's autobiography, *Up from Slavery*, which emphasised the importance of Christianity in fostering social progress within African American communities in the post-bellum period (Booker T. Washington, *Up from Slavery: An Autobiography* (New York: Doubleday, Page & Co., 1902), p. 136).
[127] Mulira, *Aligaweesa*, p. 19.
[128] Ibid., pp. 23–4.
[129] *Uganda Eyogera*, 17 June 1955.

were published under the heading, 'God Chose Uganda to Develop the Whole of Africa', a theme attributed to Bishop John V. Taylor.[130] During the rally, Mulira argued that Taylor believed that the 'salvation of the entire world would come from Uganda'.[131] However, for 'world-leadership' to occur, it was necessary to develop a national government whose authority resided with its people, not its monarchs or appointed chiefs.[132] Development and Christian salvation throughout the continent were contingent upon Buganda's federalist integration in Uganda.

Mulira's position was overtly liberal; and he would spend much of the late 1950s battling court cases brought against him by the leadership of Mmengo and Ganda separatists.[133] Mulira's federalism instigated the formation of numerous protest parties throughout Buganda, such as the Labour Party, Uganda Landowners, All People's Party and the Uganda Nationalist Party.[134] The Uganda Nationalist Party organised a public burning of the Hancock Report, after which activists threw the ashes into Lake Victoria.[135] According to the Party, the report was burned for supporting the integration of Buganda into the national government.[136] Mulira was accused of 'betraying the country by urging acceptance of the Hancock Report'.[137] One columnist proposed that 'Mr. Mulira should go to his mother country Kooki, or should ask Sir Keith Hancock to make him Katikiro'.[138]

Following Mikaeri Kintu's election to the premiership,[139] Buganda's government followed various secessionist strategies and was reluctant to participate in the electoral trajectories set by the 1955 Agreement.[140] In 1958 Mmengo boycotted the General Election, which was designed to increase Ganda representation in Uganda's national legislature.

---

[130] *Uganda Empya*, 20 June 1955.
[131] Ibid.
[132] Ibid.
[133] In *Uganda Argus* alone, I have counted no less than twenty-five articles that chronicled Mulira's court hearings between 18 July 1956 and 26 February 1959. The Luganda press is equally saturated.
[134] *Gambuze*, 26 November 1954.
[135] *Uganda Eyogera*, 30 November 1954.
[136] Ibid.
[137] *Uganda Empya*, 27 June 1955.
[138] *Uganda Post*, 26 July 1955.
[139] 'Mr. Kintu Elected Katikiro', *The Times*, 25 August 1955; *Uganda Empya*, 29 August 1955; *Dobozi lya Buganda*, 29 August 1955.
[140] UNAL Constitutional Documents, 'Elections to Legislative Council', Sessional Paper 4, Paragraph 2, 1957/58.

And in 1960, Buganda's parliament declared formal secession from Uganda.[141] Conservatives argued that Buganda's 'special status' could only be maintained through its monarchy,[142] the 'source and strength of political, economic and social well-being'.[143] Buganda, argued Mmengo powerbrokers, would not 'sell her inheritance [heritage] in order to purchase the independence of Uganda',[144] nor 'sacrifice everything on the altar of Uganda's unity'.[145] Patriots asserted political authority along monarchical lines, distancing themselves from the demands of integration. In 1959, this translated into the formation of the UNM, whose meetings entailed activists facing Mmengo and singing Buganda's national anthem.[146] Through the organisational framework of the UNM, conservative Baganda protested political participation in Uganda's legislative council (Legco).[147] But the Movement was not only a patriotic campaign; within its membership, activists such as Mulira were driven by ulterior motives.

'I am like Moses': Competing Agendas in the Uganda National Movement

Until now, scholars have used the language of patriotic solidarity to describe the character of activism in the UNM. D.A. Low, for instance, argued that 'with the full support of the neo-traditionalists' following in Buganda the UNM quickly became the most powerful political party which either Buganda or Uganda had ever seen'.[148] I.R. Hancock concluded that '[b]ehind the alliance lay a determination to protect the

---

[141] The Kabaka's Government, *Okwefuga kwa Buganda* (Kampala: Uganda Printing & Publishing Co. Ltd, October 1960).

[142] Ibid., p. 28.

[143] Ibid. '*Kabaka gwe mwoyo era n'amaanyi agatambuza eby'obufuzi, eby'obugagga, awamu n'embeera ennungi.*'

[144] Ibid., p. 37. '*Buganda teyinza kutunda busika bwayo lwa kugula kwefuga kwa Uganda.*'

[145] Ibid. '*Era Buganda teyeteese kuwaayo nga saddaaka, buli kyonna, ku Kyoto ky'okwegatta kwa Uganda.*'

[146] 'U.N.M. is "A Buganda National Movement"', *Uganda Argus*, 18 March 1959.

[147] 'Boycott Aimed at "Privileges"', *Uganda Argus*, 12 March 1959; Interview, Samuel Mugwisa, Former UNM Branch Coordinator, 16 December 2009, Kampala.

[148] D.A. Low, *Buganda in Modern History* (Berkeley, CA: University of California Press, 1971, p. 193.

Ganda identity from foreign constitutions and economic enterprise'. For Hancock, the UNM organised 'in the stubborn resistance to the concept of "One Uganda", and in the increasing demand for the return of "our things" [. . .] and restoring the independence of Buganda's institutions'.[149] Mulira's activism in the Movement in 1959, though, complicates this monolithic interpretation. It also directly challenges the notion that there was a single vision of Buganda around which activists in the movement aspired.

By the late 1950s, Mulira considered his effort to advocate for constitutional federalism unsuccessful. In a political manifesto entitled, 'Why I am in the Uganda National Movement', Mulira explained that prior to the UNM his political project was ineffective: 'I have been a moderate all along, but with what result? – frustration and disappointment at every turn.'[150] Mulira compared himself to Kofi Busia, with whom he had studied at Achimota, who would 'die in opposition not because Dr. Nkrumah is opposed to him but because the majority of the nation do not accept him as one of them'.[151] Mulira concluded that in order to 'counteract traditionalism and at the same time mobilize the country against imperialism', it was necessary to launch a 'unity campaign that included the traditionalists'.[152] Mulira furthered: 'After joining we would see to it that we put their traditionalism to sleep, i.e., we would not allow it to arise above Nationalism.'[153] Participation in conservative politics was, Mulira argued, the art of co-optation, an effort to shepherd royalists and secessionists toward national and global politics, to 'unite the people of Uganda and to liberate the country from foreign rule'.[154]

Consistent with his earlier sensibilities, Mulira's subversive politics was shaped by global intellectual history and theological reflection. During a UNM rally in March 1959, conservatives organised what

---

[149] I.R. Hancock, 'Patriotism and Neo-Traditionalism in Buganda: The Kabaka Yekka ("The King Alone") Movement, 1961–1962', *The Journal of African History*, 11 (1970), 419–34 (p. 421).

[150] HMG E.M.K. Mulira, 'Why I am in the Uganda National Movement', April 1959.

[151] Ibid.

[152] CCAS MP E.M.K. Mulira to H.M. Grace, 'Explanation of My Political Creed in the Green Note Book', 4 October 1959.

[153] Ibid.

[154] 'Party Leaders Speak on Single Platform: Vast Crowd Urged to Join National Movement', *Uganda Argus*, 16 February 1959.

was hailed as 'the largest political meeting ever staged in Kampala'.[155] During the gathering, politicians, schoolmistresses, farmers and traders spoke for several hours amid 'applause and cheering'.[156] During the assembly, Mulira was allocated time by the event's organisers to articulate conservative talking points. Instead, he deviated from script to discuss the nationalism of Archbishop Makarios III, whose *Enosis* movement during the same period had advocated for the independence and incorporation of the community of Greek Cypriots into mainland Greece. For Mulira, Makarios championed integration, not separation. And from the platform, Mulira announced that Makarios 'set an example of determination in the fight for freedom',[157] and called for a two-minute period of silence to reflect on Makarios' life and activism. Following the moment of silence, Mulira concluded his speech by leading an antiphon between himself and the audience that focused on the name, 'Makarios'. Whereas other activists used their time to expound upon the legitimacy of Ganda separatism, Mulira shifted the audience's horizon, redirecting the tropes of patriotism toward anticolonial leaders who advocated for both independence and integration.

To bolster his peculiar patriotism, Mulira also drew from the Bible. In a manifesto that was drafted to explain his membership in the Movement to his European colleagues, Mulira interrogated the gospel of St Matthew, within which Jesus informed his followers that they were 'the salt of the earth [. . .]'.[158] From the passage, Mulira concluded that he, like Jesus' disciples, was called to work alongside the masses:

Salt is only useful if it mixes with food; salt apart from food is no use (except perhaps as medicine). Therefore, at this juncture we saw that without trying to change our principles why not take a plunge and mix with the masses and try to speak to them from within and speak to Government from a point of mass support which means strength instead of one of isolated moderation which it regards as weakness. Therefore, it was change of tactics and not of principles and it worked. The moment we did this we were accepted, and the masses can now listen to our counsels where before they frowned at and rejected us wholesale.[159]

---

[155] 'Inter-Party Group Announces Boycott Plan', *Uganda Argus*, 2 March 1959.
[156] Ibid.
[157] Ibid.
[158] Mulira, 'Why I am in the Uganda National Movement'.
[159] Ibid.

Mulira saw himself adapting the political methodology of Moses, whose biography demonstrated the importance of adaptability. Looking toward the Hebrew deliverer, whose early career and use of formal politics had resulted in disappointment and botched miracles, Mulira argued that his use of European political language had contributed to his own failure; it now behoved him to appropriate localised argumentation with greater diligence:

When Moses was called of God to deliver the children of Israel from Bondage he thought he would step out of the Palace of Pharaoh straight to the job and talk to people in the language of the palace.

That's why he failed. God sent him first to the wilderness, and, to my mind, he sent him there for one reason alone – to learn the language of the people and come back and speak to the Pharaoh in that language. In a way I am like Moses: I have been speaking to my people 'your language' (by which I mean that I have been selling to them what I have learnt from you), and they have not listened to me. I now speak to 'you' in their language and they listen to me. May be that is God's purpose. It wasn't all plain sailing with Moses nor was it unharmful to the Egyptians. I believe God is with me in this as He has been in other things – I have not turned against him.[160]

By identifying with Moses, Mulira recast his public politics. The uproar of the late 1950s required many of Buganda's liberalisers to become increasingly nuanced and elusive. Subtlety, though, must not be mistaken for similarity. The UNM was multifaceted.

Conclusion: Exile and *Kabaka Yekka*

On 23 May, the Protectorate government proscribed the UNM.[161] For his leadership in the Movement, Mulira was arrested and detained under the Deportation Ordinance.[162] On the morning of the arrest, Mulira gathered with supporters outside of his home to sing Christian hymns.[163] He spent the following year in political exile in Gulu. Mulira spent considerable time in political and spiritual reflection while in northern Uganda. Writing on her family's relocation, Rebecca Mulira

---

[160] Ibid.
[161] Low, *Buganda in Modern History*, p. 193.
[162] 'Leaders of Banned Uganda Movement Arrested', *The Times*, 1 June 1959.
[163] Ibid.

used the language of Christian devotion to explain the experience to
Bishop Leslie Brown: 'We have settled down here nicely. We are happy
with very clear minds, and have left everything in HIS HANDS. [. . .] A
prison where Jesus is discussed becomes a temple! We have more time
than we have ever had before to talk, to praise HIS LOVE, to us and
to be NEARER TO HIM!'.[164]

Rebecca's husband spent considerable time composing religious
works.[165] One extensive manuscript is worth addressing briefly: 'The
Way of Life: Dear Travellers this is the Way', later retitled, 'Jesus Christ:
"The Way of Life"'. Mulira's interest in the 'Way of Life' resulted in
no fewer than twelve exercise books filled with extensive sentence dia-
gramming of the gospels and hundreds of pages of typed manuscript.
In handwritten notation, Mulira introduced his piece by exploring the
work of God in biblical and world history. For Mulira, sinful humanity's social and moral restoration with God was contingent upon a
highly prescriptive political order, within which families were designed
to become tribes, and tribes unified nations:

Because he [Adam] ate the tree of knowledge which was forbidden him man
was punished with death and with [. . .] inevitable expulsion from the garden. But it remained God's constant wish to restore man by bringing life to
him Love, Righteousness (Righteousness is love to man), and Faith, but man
would not listen. So God chose Himself a family, then a tribe and finally a
nation through which to manifest his purposes to man.[166]

Mulira's theology suggested to him that God was actively using political history to restore humanity to an idyllic and divine space that
was characterised by love, righteousness and faith. Spiritual reflection
in exile reinforced the importance of seditious politics: God's desire
to transform distinctive 'tribes' or kingdoms into unified nations.
And following exile, Mulira built upon this line of reasoning to help
organise the patriotic politics of *Kabaka Yekka* (KY), the King Only

---

[164] UCU BA 1/136.5 Rebecca Mulira to Leslie Brown, 20 July 1959.
[165] The following memoirs were maintained in Mulira's private papers: 'The
Coming of Jesus Christ', Mss., 19 November 1959; 'About St. Paul', Mss., 22
November 1959; 'Personal Religion', Mss., 24 November 1959; 'About the
Churches', Mss., n.d.
[166] CCAS MP E.M.K. Mulira, 'The Way of Life: Dear Travellers This Is the Way',
Mss., [November 1959].

movement. Like the UNM, though, KY proved to be a vast political umbrella under which competing activists and religious communities asserted different political agendas. The extent to which Muslim activists used KY to reposition their community on the eve of independence is the subject of the following chapter.

4 | Abubakar K. Mayanja: Pluralism and Islamic Political Thought, c. 1844–c. 1962

[I]t is our express desire that you prevail upon him [A.K. Mayanja] appropriately as to how very much my Society is interested in his [career] at the College and for that reason the necessity of hi[m] becoming vigilant in his studies and habits ultimately proving useful to his co-brothers in Islam.

Hon. Secretary, East African Muslim Welfare Society[1]

Seriously – it is my sacred intention, nay, duty to be of use to my people. Although as yet I have only a dim glimpse of what it is I shall do, I have never had any doubt about my duty.

Abubakar K. Mayanja[2]

Well-connected to Buganda's conservative, small-scale farming communities, Ignatius Musazi, Abubakar Kakyama Mayanja (1929–2005) and the Uganda National Congress (UNC) spearheaded opposition against Mulira's constitutional reforms in the 1950s. But while Musazi's and Mulira's political projects conflicted, they were both shaped by Protestant social forces. Musazi's wife was the daughter of the heir of Apolo Kaggwa;[3] Mulira's wife was the daughter of Hamu Mukasa. Musazi was the son of a consequential Protestant chief in Bulemeezi; Mulira was a royal of Kooki heritage, whose family had routed Muslim exiles in their kingdom during the religious wars in the 1890s.[4] And shaped by the mentorship of Canon Harold M. Grace, both Musazi and Mulira were model disciples of the Native Anglican Church, at least during adolescence.

---

[1] KCBA Hon. Secretary, East African Muslim Welfare Society, to Timothy Cobb, 26 November 1948.

[2] KCBA A.K. Mayanja to Timothy Cobb, 18 March 1950.

[3] Interviews, Rita Naniskombi, 11 and 16 November 2009, Luteete, Wakiso District.

[4] James Kibuka Miti Kabazzi, *Buganda, 1875–1900: A Centenary Contribution*, trans. by G.K. Rock, 2 vols (London: United Society for Christian Literature, n.d.), I, p. 202.

Not royal, wealthy or Christian, Abubakar Mayanja was the organising secretary-treasurer of the UNC,[5] Uganda's foremost anti-colonial
party. Often enmeshed in public controversy and acutely practical in
his approach to politics, Mayanja, according to one activist, was the
'best political brain and potentially the hardest drive in Congress'.[6]
His forthright politics discomforted both Christian Baganda and
Britons. The Protestant activist Kawalya Kaggwa disclosed to Audrey
Richards that Mayanja, upon completing his course in history at
Cambridge, would 'come back and make trouble'.[7] And after hearing Mayanja speak at a World University Service conference in March
1954, Oxford's Margery Perham 'felt almost physically sick listening to him, because of the mingled ability, vanity and malice of his
speech'.[8] Perham surmised: '[Mayanja] gave a really horrifying speech,
in which he dropped carefully distilled poison, drop by drop. I should
say he is, or will be, an orator of great effect.'[9]

Educated at King's College, Budo, and King's College, Cambridge,
Mayanja was one of Uganda's most eloquent anti-colonial nationalists.
As D.A. Low observed, Mayanja was 'the ablest intellectually of the
politicians from Buganda [. . .]'.[10] By the early 1960s, though, he was
no longer an outspoken proponent of Uganda nationalism. Following
the death of Buganda's first Muslim minister of education, the titular
head of Buganda's Muslim community, *Omulangira* Badru Kakungulu,
approached Mayanja to fill a vacancy in Mmengo's government that
had been designated for the kingdom's Muslim community.[11] From
1960 onward, Mayanja was closely associated with the social activism

---

[5] NAP, Field Notes, p. 65, A.K. Mayanja to Neal Ascherson, June 1956.
See also 'Uganda National Congress Forming: "Should Prepare Plans for
Self-Government"', *East Africa and Rhodesia*, 20 March 1952.

[6] LFP 29/13/nf Neal Ascherson, 'The History of the Uganda National Congress',
n.d., p. 37.

[7] Interview, Audrey Richards with Kawalya Kaggwa, 8 February 1954, in ARP
7/6/69 Audrey Richards, Field Notes.

[8] ICS 29/1/3/26 Margery Perham to Keith Hancock, 15 March 1954.

[9] Ibid.

[10] D.A. Low, *Buganda in Modern History* (Berkeley, CA: University of California
Press, 1971), p. 248.

[11] SINP 'Autobiography of Hajj Mayanja', p. 54 (hereafter SINP). Political
columnist Ssemujju Ibrahim Nganda was appointed by Mayanja to assist in
writing the latter's biography (Interview, Ssemujju I. Nganda, 22 and 27 July
2010, Kampala). Ssemujju's notes contain seventy-two pages of interview
transcriptions.

of Buganda's Muslim community.[12] And he became the most prolific writer and negotiator in the patriotic party *Kabaka Yekka*. This has led scholars to argue that Mayanja was easily swayed by Uganda's constantly changing politics. More than political principle, Kenneth Ingham argued, Mayanja was driven by 'his irrepressible sense of fun [. . .]'.[13]

In this chapter, though, I argue that Mayanja's shifting political alliances are best understood in the context of Buganda's precolonial and colonial religious past, not an allegedly capricious disposition. Nor was Mayanja's political redirection mere expediency; what Max Weber, in a different context, associated with the emergence of power-hungry vocational politicians in industrialising societies.[14] For Mayanja, the emergence of anti-colonial nationalism in Buganda resonated with political arguments that had been generated much earlier by Muslim intellectuals, whom Mayanja argued were Buganda's proto-nationalists, the 'only community which really had stood for independence from the British and the French right from the very beginning'.[15] For two generations prior to the late 1950s Muslim historians argued that the colonial state, under the administration of Christian chiefs, was possessed with preserving its own power. For reasons explored throughout this chapter, Mayanja was well suited to expound upon this argument.

I begin this chapter by examining the early history of Islamic practice in Buganda, focusing on the activisms of *Kabaka* Muteesa I and *Omulangira* Nuhu Mbogo, the titular head of Buganda's Muslim community in the late 1800s and early 1900s. Muslim statebuilders used Islamic ritual and the Qur'an to realign political authority in a state afforded new possibilities through long-distance trade. Whereas most studies on colonial literacy and nationalism in Buganda have focused on the prominence of Christian production, I argue that Christian literacy became important in the colonial state precisely because Protestant and Catholic converts were challenged to recreate forms of textual authority that were already being developed in Muslim communities. In the second section, I turn to the mid-twentieth century, when a new generation

---

[12] Interviews: Al-Hajj Isa Lukwago, 11 February 2010, Kampala; Al-Hajj Mustafa Mutiaba, 3 March 2010, Kampala.

[13] Kenneth Ingham, *Obote: A Political Biography* (London: Routledge, 1994), p. 51.

[14] Max Weber, 'Politics as a Vocation', in *From Max Weber: Essays in Sociology*, ed. by H.H. Gerth and C. Wright Mills, trans. by H.H. Gerth and C. Wright Mills (New York: Oxford University Press, 1946), pp. 77–128 (p. 116).

[15] Interview, Neal Ascherson, 17 August 2010, London.

of Muslim historians used Arabic and Luganda literacy to begin to rewrite the state's official histories. After five decades of colonial rule, Sheikh Ali Kulumba returned to the kingship of Muteesa I. Contrary to arguments being made by Christian historians, Kulumba asserted that the emergence of political calm and religious pluralism in the 1800s had followed a king's conversion to Islam. I address the political thought of Abubakar Mayanja in the final section. Mayanja's liberal education in the 1940s and 1950s was largely the result of educational strategies that were being utilised throughout eastern Africa to train future Muslim legislators. In the early 1960s, Mayanja used his secular education to work alongside *Omulangira* Badru Kakungulu and Sheikh Kulumba to reassert the prominence of Buganda's Muslim community in kingdom politics. For two to three generations, Muslim activists had been ostracised from the heart of Ganda politics. By 1963, Mayanja and Sheikh Kulumba were not only representatives of Buganda's Muslim community – they represented the formal voice of the kingdom's patriotic government.

Shifting Textual Practices: From Qur'ans to Bibles

Half a century before the Protestant historian Apolo Kaggwa published *Bassekabaka be Buganda*, Buganda received her first Muslim guests, Zanzibari missionary-traders.[16] Emin Pasha (Eduard Carl Oscar Theodor Schnitzer) recorded that the Zanzibari Ahmed bin Ibrahim reached the court of Kabaka Ssuuna in 1260 AH/CE 1844.[17] Early sources suggested that Medi Ibulaimu, the Luganda form of Ahmed bin Ibrahim,[18] reproved Ssuuna for what appeared to be the indiscriminate killing of Ganda subjects.[19] When Pasha reached Buganda's court

---

[16] For further discussion on the expansion of Zanzibar's trading interests throughout eastern Africa see John M. Gray, 'Ahmed Bin Ibrahim – The First Arab to Reach Buganda', *Uganda Journal*, 10 (1947), 80–97; James de Vere Allen, *Swahili Origins: Swahili Culture and the Shungwaya Phenomenon* (London: James Currey, 1993), pp. 55–98.

[17] Emin Pasha, 'The Diaries of Emin Pasha – Extracts I', ed. by John M. Gray, *Uganda Journal*, 25 (1961), 1–15 (pp. 9–10 & 14–15).

[18] T.W. Gee, 'A Century of Mohammedan Influence in Buganda, 1852–1951', *Uganda Journal*, 22 (1958), 139–50 (p. 139).

[19] Apolo Kaggwa, *Ekitabo Kye Bika Bya Baganda* (Kampala: Uganda Bookshop and Uganda Society, 1949), pp. 115–16; Badru Kakungulu and A.B.K. Kasozi, *Abaasimba Obuyisiraamu mu Uganda* (Kampala: Equator Books, 1977), pp. 2–3. For further discussion on Ibrahim see Gray, 'Ahmed Bin Ibrahim', pp. 80–97.

in the mid-1870s, he found Ssuuna's son, Muteesa I, sitting on Persian carpets, wearing Arab clothes, and donning a gold-trimmed turban that had been imported from the eastern African coast.[20] According to Pasha, Muteesa had learned some Arabic, though his ministers spoke the language fluently.[21] By the end of his life, Kaggwa noted, Muteesa could read and speak Arabic and Swahili.[22] Muteesa I was instructed in Islam under the tutelage of Muley bin Salim and soon instituted Ramadan and implemented the *Hijri*, the Muslim calendar.[23] Following the construction of Muteesa's palace mosque (*muzigiti*) in Nakawa, chiefs followed suit, erecting structures freely and under conscription. Muteesa's brother, Nuhu Kyabasinga Mbogo, was appointed to ensure that mosques were built in accordance with Islamic tradition.

During a period of considerable social change in Buganda's military history, Muteesa I incorporated Islam to extend the reach of the state.[24] The ability to legislate prayer and fasting among subjects, who were increasingly able to participate in transregional markets between Buganda and the Swahili coast, was tantamount to commanding political allegiance. Keeping with Islamic custom, Muteesa commanded Baganda to pray five times per day (*okuyimiriza esswala etano buli lunaku*).[25] To ensure obedience to royal edict and Islamic teaching, Muslim chiefs renamed their wives according to prayer times. One early convert recalled: 'One wife could be called Subuyi – morning. She would go to her master in the morning to remind him that it was time

---

[20] Pasha, 'Diaries – Extracts I', p. 6.

[21] Ibid., p. 7.

[22] Apolo Kaggwa, *Bassekabaka be Buganda*, trans. by Semakula Kiwanuka (Nairobi, Dar Es Salaam, Kampala: East African Publishing House, 1971), p. 182.

[23] Ibid., pp. 158–61.

[24] For further insight into the impact of long-distance trade on nineteenth-century eastern Africa see John A. Rowe, 'Revolution in Buganda, 1856–1900. Part One: The Reign of Kabaka Mukabya Mutesa, 1856–1884' (unpublished PhD, The University of Wisconsin, 1966); John Iliffe, *A Modern History of Tanganyika* (Cambridge: Cambridge University Press, 1979), pp. 40–87; Jeremy Prestholdt, *Domesticating the World: African Consumerism and the Genealogies of Globalization* (Berkeley, CA: University of California Press, 2008); Catherine Coquery-Vidrovitch, *Africa and the Africans in the Nineteenth Century: A Turbulent History* (Armonk, NY: M.E. Sharpe, 2009), pp. 70–134.

[25] Ali Kulumba, *Empagi Z'obusiramu mu Luganda* (Kampala: Sapoba Book Press, 1953), p. 1.

for the morning prayer. Another wife was called Zukuli – i.e. 12:30 noon.'[26] Hamu Mukasa, who was an early convert to Islam, recalled Muslim chiefs in the royal court suggesting to Muteesa that the practice of prayer and qur'anic study should replace leisurely hunting, a policy that Muteesa implemented. Muteesa's subjects were required to maintain the fast of Ramadan (*okusiiba omwezi gwa Ramazane*),[27] for which Muteesa created a chieftainship 'to teach Buganda to fast'.[28]

The reorganisation of time and ritual constituted one way to recreate alternative political mobilities. The conclusion of Ramadan became a season when Muteesa moved his capital and shuffled chieftaincies.[29] Critical engagement with the Qur'an resulted in new ways of constituting authority. By wielding the Qur'an to directionalise political change, Muslim statebuilders invented a textual approach to legitimising rule that was eventually adopted by Christian chiefs in the early 1900s. Indeed, the development of Protestant literacy was central to the processes of instituting colonial power, precisely because literacy was integral to how Muslims had begun to reorganise society prior to the 1890s. By the early 1900s, statebuilders in Buganda had largely stopped looking toward the Qur'an; Christian chiefs and Protestant kings began using their bibles. But the potency of biblical exegesis in Buganda during the 1900s dated to the mid-1800s, a time when critical engagement with Islamic literacy reshaped the way power was practised and negotiated between monarchs, chiefs and labourers.

The introduction of Arabic literacy facilitated the production of new ways of talking about older conceptions of death and divine favour in high politics. By the nineteenth century, communities throughout Buganda largely believed that death was the result of divine will or witchcraft. 'Death from natural causes rarely presented itself [. . .] as a feasible explanation for the end of life', observed the missionary

---

[26] Interview, Arye Oded with Shaikh al-Islām Ahmad Nsambo, 16 December 1967, Natete, in Arye Oded, *Islam in Uganda: Islamization through a Centralized State in Pre-Colonial Africa* (New York: Israel Universities Press, 1974), pp. 337–41 (p. 337).

[27] Kulumba, *Empagi Z'obusiramu mu Luganda*, p. 1.

[28] LFP 54/7/172 Ali Kulumba, *Ebyafayo By'obusiramu mu Uganda*, trans. by John Rowe (Kampala: Sapoba Bookshop Press, 1953). See also MUA M.M. Katungulu, *Islam in Buganda*, Mss., trans. by J. Busulwa (n.d.), pp. 4–5.

[29] Kaggwa, *Bassekabaka be Buganda*, pp. 158–61.

anthropologist John Roscoe.[30] In 1882, in a letter forwarded to the British officer Sir John Kirk, Muteesa used Arabic to reflect on the death of Buganda's queen mother (*nnamasole*). Buganda's Muslim king opened his letter by using the *basmala*,[31] 'In the name of God, the Lord of Mercy, the Giver of Mercy'.[32] When he turned to discuss the death of the *nnamasole*, he cited al-Baqara, a supplication often referenced during periods of duress or loss: 'We belong to God and to Him we shall return.'[33] The *nnamasole*'s passing was caused by *maqadīr*, it was believed, or divine decree.[34] And to conclude the letter, Muteesa incorporated a Muslim benediction, asking God to bestow protection, mercy and favour upon Kirk.[35] The language of divine blessing was one way of talking about earlier practices of hospitality and extravagance extended to guests during visits at the royal court.[36]

For Muteesa, the adaptation of writing was connected with the materiality of bounded texts; Buganda's king utilised the physicality of the Qur'an to assert monarchical authority against clan heads and burial chiefs. Prior to the arrival of Muslim traders in central Uganda, the death of Buganda's kings elicited a complex set of burial rituals performed mostly by clan heads.[37] Burial chiefs, who possessed considerable political power, required compensation from their king(s) for the future performance of embalmment.[38] In his writings on Ganda custom, Apolo Kaggwa recounted when Muteesa called the practice into question: 'When Mukabya became king he inquired of his chiefs

---

[30] John Roscoe, *The Baganda: An Account of Their Native Customs and Beliefs*, 2nd edn (London: Frank Cass and Co. Ltd, 1965), p. 98.

[31] My discussion draws largely from Sheikh Isaac Ssettuba's analysis of Muteesa I's Arabic (Varied correspondence, May 2011).

[32] Muteesa to Sir John Kirk, 19 May 1882, in Arye Oded, *Islam in Uganda*, p. 321. The *basmala* introduces each chapter of the Qur'an, with the exception of sūrah Al-Tawba.

[33] Muteesa to Sir John Kirk, 19 May 1882. See M.A.S. Abdel Haleem, trans., *The Qur'an* (Oxford: Oxford University Press, 2004), p. 2.

[34] Muteesa to Sir John Kirk, 19 May 1882.

[35] Ibid.

[36] Henry M. Stanley, *Through the Dark Continent (Through the Dark Continent (The Sources of the Nile Around the Great Lakes of Equatorial Africa and Down the Livingstone River to the Atlantic Ocean)*, 2 vols (New York: Sampson Low, Marston, Searle, & Rivington, 1878), I, p. 190.

[37] Benjamin C. Ray, *Myth, Ritual, and Kingship in Buganda* (Oxford: Oxford University Press, 1991), pp. 108–14.

[38] Apolo Kaggwa, *Ekitabo Kye Mpisa Za Baganda*, ed. by May M. Edel, trans. by Ernest B. Kalibala (New York: Columbia University Press, 1934), pp. 13–14.

as to the reason why these chiefs demanded to be paid in advance for these services [. . .] Then the king became very angry and ordered all the participants in the funeral ceremonies arrested and held for execution.'[39] Similarly, according to Muslim oral sources, Muteesa ordered his *katikkiro*, Mukasa, to prevent the king's body from being passed into the stewardship of Buganda's clan heads. His body was not to be disembowelled or deified according to earlier traditions. Burial custodians and clan heads were to be given qur'ans,[40] however, not the bodies of kings.[41] By removing the bodies of kings from the hands of Buganda's hereditary morticians, Muteesa renegotiated the extent to which political competitors could regulate the economies of kings between investiture and internment.

Conversion to Islam in southern Buganda also empowered local communities – Islam was not only an instrument used by centralising kings. Dissenters adapted Islamic teachings to legitimise the coronation and removal of kings. By debating the prohibition of circumcision and food impurities, Ganda Muslims sought to regulate the successions of power in the state. In the mid-nineteenth century, Ganda custom prohibited the shedding of royal blood, proscription to which Muteesa also subscribed.[42] According to the Muslim nineteenth-century historian Sheikh al-Islām Ahmad Nsambo, Muteesa refused to undergo circumcision because he feared that he would die for violating this particular custom.[43] Another early convert suggested that Buganda's king was to have a subject vicariously circumcised on his behalf. However, during the ceremony, the subject's penis was cleaved: 'You see, the princes those days were cheeky and at times behaved childishly. Mutesa then exclaimed that those operations were really tantamount to murder.'[44] Muteesa's unwillingness to practice circumcision resulted in considerable debate throughout southern Buganda, which was compounded by the king's refusal to dismiss the court's

---

[39] Ibid., p. 14.
[40] Interview, Arye Oded with Shaikh al-Islām Ahmad Nsambo, 11 November 1967, Natete, in Arye Oded, *Islam in Uganda*, pp. 332–7.
[41] LFP 54/7/173 Kulumba, *Ebyafayo By'obusiramu mu Uganda*.
[42] Interview, Arye Oded with Shaikh al-Islām Ahmad Nsambo, 11 November 1967, Natete, in Oded, *Islam in Uganda*, pp. 332–7 (pp. 333–4).
[43] Ibid.
[44] Interview, Arye Oded with Yusufu Kiwanuka, 12 November 1967, Lwanjaza, Ssingo County, in Oded, *Islam in Uganda*, pp. 327–32 (p. 327).

non-circumcised butcher. From 1874 to 1875, Muteesa had no fewer than sixteen Ganda Muslims killed for refusing to eat meat prepared by his butcher, food considered *haraam*, forbidden by Islamic law.[45] Following the first dethronement of Muteesa's abstruse son, Mwanga, Buganda's throne was 'eaten' by Muteesa's eldest son, Kiweewa. Kiweewa's commitment to creating an Islamic state was unclear; like his father, he refused to be circumcised. During the second month of his reign, politically powerful Muslims usurped Kiweewa's throne.[46] Kiweewa's younger brother, Kalema, an austere Muslim, was subsequently invested, circumcised and given the name Nuhu.[47] By renaming Buganda's king, Muslim historians reminded Baganda of a time in the Qur'an when God saved his followers through Noah's ark, *Nabbi Nuhu*.[48] Ali Kulumba suggested that by using the qur'anic name Nuhu, Muslims demonstrated that Buganda's king had guided the state into God's ark, a covenant to protect the kingdom from the 'sin of not being circumcised'.[49] Concerned that Christian chiefs would remove the state's Islamic king from the throne, Muslims used weapons acquired through long-distance trade to displace Christians from the capital. Following a short period of exile in Ankole, Christian revolutionaries returned to Buganda's capital (Lungujja) in October 1889 to claim political control.[50] While Muslims made concerted effort to maintain power, they were ultimately unsuccessful due to inferior weaponry. Colonial-backed Christians re-invested Mwanga, and *Kabaka* Kalema, who was driven into exile, died of smallpox near Kijungute, where the majority of Buganda's Muslims fled after Christians stormed the capital (Figure 4.1).

---

[45] Oded, *Islam in Uganda*, pp. 317–18. For further discussion see Ahmed Katumba and Fred B. Welbourn, 'Muslim Martyrs of Buganda', *Uganda Journal*, 28 (1964), 151–63.

[46] John M. Gray, 'The Year of the Three Kings of Buganda', *Uganda Journal*, 14 (1949), 15–52 (p. 27).

[47] Katungulu, *Islam in Buganda*, p. 10. For further discussion see Ali Kulumba and Mustafa Mutyaba, *Nuhu Kalema N'Obusiraamu mu Buganda* (Kampala: Crane Publishers Ltd, 1994).

[48] LFP 54/7/167 Kulumba, *Ebyafayo By'obusiramu mu Uganda*.

[49] Ibid.

[50] The two best overviews are Michael Twaddle, 'The Muslim Revolution in Buganda', *African Affairs*, 71 (1972), 54–72 (pp. 66–72); C.C. Wrigley, 'The Christian Revolution in Buganda', *Comparative Studies in Society and History*, 2 (1959), 33–48.

Figure 4.1 'The Battle Against the Mohammedans', 1891
Source: Lugard, *The Rise of Our East African Empire*, II, p. 132.

After Kalema's death, *Omulangira* Nuhu Kyabasinga Mbogo (c. 1835–10 March 1921) was appointed titular head of Buganda's Muslim community.[51] Whereas the past provided political space for Muslims to administer power in the state, Christian chiefs and colonial officials used discriminating land policies to push Muslim activists into unknown political territory – the social periphery. According to the Ganda historian Jemusi Miti, Mbogo led Ganda Muslims back into Buganda's capital following negotiations with Captain Fredrick Lugard.[52] Fearful that Nubian and Ganda Muslims would install *Omulangira* Mbogo

---

[51] Interview, Amin Mutyaba, A.K. Kasozi, Noel King, and William M. Watt with Osmani Wamala, May and September 1967, Buyanga, Butambala County, in Noel Quinton King, A.B.K. Kasozi and Arye Oded, *Islam and the Confluence of Religions in Uganda, 1840–1966* (Tallahassee, FL: American Academy of Religion, 1973), pp. 11–12 (p. 12).

[52] James Miti Kabazzi, Buganda, 1875–1900, pp. 22–3. For additional accounts see Apolo Kaggwa, *The Reign of Mwanga II (A Later Addition to Ekitabo Kya Basekabaka Be Buganda)*, trans. by Simon Musoke (Kampala: Typescript, University of Cambridge Library, 1953), pp. 164–82; B. Musoke Zimbe, *Buganda and the King*, trans. by F. Kamoga (Mengo, 1978), pp. 164–416. For Lugard's version see Frederick D. Lugard, *The Rise of Our East African Empire: Early Efforts in Nyasaland and Uganda*, 2 vols (London: Frank Cass & Co. Ltd, 1968), II, pp. 473–503. The best secondary overview is John A. Rowe, *Lugard at Kampala* (Kampala: Makerere University, History Paper, No. 3, 1969).

as the next king of Buganda,[53] British officers exiled the prince to Zanzibar from 1893 to June 1895.[54] While Buganda's Muslim prince was in exile, the kingdom became an official Christian state. Militarily disadvantaged, following his return, Mbogo was not in a position to reassert his community's claim to Buganda's throne. In 1897, Nubian soldiers in central Uganda offered Mbogo military support to incite revolt and to reclaim the capital.[55] They pronounced Mbogo's kingship: 'You, Mbogo, are the King, look after your work in Kampala.'[56] Aware of his precarious position in a Protectorate policed by Christian captains, Mbogo refused to storm the royal palace:

I received your letter and understood the contents. You have done a wrong thing because you are gone out of obedience [sic], and I am not with you in this affair. The best thing for you is to leave this disturbance and agitation. You will repent when you find the result of your action.

If you do not listen to my advice I am not on your side. When the fight commences I will be on the Government side and fight against you. I am not powerful to fight the English [. . .] I have not the power to fight them. You also have not the power to fight the British Government. If I had not been to the coast perhaps I might have taken your part. I have seen with my own eyes their power, how they in about half an hour bombarded even Zanzibar.[57]

Following the signing of the 1900 Agreement, which stated that the line of descent from which monarchs could be selected in Buganda was

---

[53] Co-authored with Mbogo's daughter, *Nnaalinnya* Hafiswa Nakabiri, Mustafa Mutyaba's book is the foremost account of the life and activism of Mbogo (*Omulangira Nuhu Kyabasinga Mbogo* (Kampala: Crane Books, 2009), pp. 51–5). See also Amin Mutyaba's currently unpublished manuscript, 'The Development of Islam in Uganda', Mss., n.d.

[54] RCMS 150/5/1/1 G. Wilson to Marquess [sic] of Salisbury, 5 October 1897. Mbogo's return is commemorated annually by Buganda's Muslim community, which I attended in 2010.

[55] RCMS 150/5/1/1 G. Wilson to Marquess [sic] of Salisbury, 9 November 1897. For fuller treatment see J.V. Wild, *The Uganda Mutiny, 1897* (Kampala: Uganda Bookshop, 1954). To place the Nubian revolt within the transnational context of Sudan's Mahdist state see P.M. Holt, *The Mahdist State in the Sudan: 1881–1898: A Study of Its Origins, Development and Overthrow*, 2nd edn (Oxford: Oxford University Press, 1979).

[56] RCMS 150/5/1/1 Mabruk Effendi, Bilal Effendi Amin and Suliman Effendi to N. Mbogo, n.d.

[57] RCMS 150/5/1/1 N. Mbogo to Officers of Soudanese Mutineers, 19 October 1897.

restricted 'to the descendants of King Mutesa', Mbogo's enthronement was no longer a viable option.[58] During the distribution of private land, Muslims were allotted only 1.4 per cent of total land distributions. They were given the county of Butambala.[59] Politically marginalised and militarily enclosed by adjacent Protestant and Catholic counties, Ganda Muslims would have to think and advocate creatively from the margins for the foreseeable future.

When Mukaabya Became Muteesa: Fictions of Calm in Ganda Historiography

By the 1940s, Muslim historians had begun to rethink the controversies of the last two decades of the nineteenth century. The postwar period had begun to unravel the logic of colonial rule, and the ability to associate political calm with one's community in Buganda was part of a broader effort to maintain legitimacy amid emerging postwar dissent. Indeed, the capacity to exhibit political calm had long been central to how ritual and power was practised and debated in eastern Africa. As David Schoenbrun has shown, during a period of environmental catastrophe in sixteenth-century Bunyoro, the aspirant Rukidi reenacted public calm with drums, stools, copper bangles and beads to give weight to words about the past and to help people confront a ruined world in which life had to move forward.[60] In 1940s Buganda, history writers worked to produce such fictions. Activists showed the ways in which their respective communities had been solely instrumental, allegedly, in stabilising society during the uncertain sovereignty of *Kabaka* Muteesa I.

In 1946, the anxieties of the past prompted Hamu Mukasa to publish a brief history entitled, 'The Rule of the Kings of Buganda', whose English translation was reproduced in *The Uganda Journal*. In his history, Mukasa argued that prior to the arrival of Christian missionaries the state had experienced perpetual warfare. Mukasa identified no fewer than fifteen kingdoms with which Buganda frequently warred.[61]

[58] 'The Uganda Agreement of 1900' (Article 6).
[59] UNA SMP 44/255 'Report on the Kingdom of Buganda, 1907–08'.
[60] David Schoenbrun, 'A Mask of Calm: Emotion and Founding the Kingdom of Bunyoro in the Sixteenth Century', *Comparative Studies in Society and History*, 55 (2013), 634–64 (pp. 644 & 660).
[61] Hamu Mukasa, 'The Rule of the Kings of Buganda', *Uganda Journal*, 10 (1946), 136–43 (p. 138).

Buganda's kings were *Ma'nyonku-zisa-busolo*, those with large teeth who eat all other animals. Ganda monarchs demonstrated 'power to destroy the life of anyone [they] wished'.[62] For Mukasa, Muteesa I, whose earlier name was Mukaabya, one who causes suffering or tears, exemplified a long tradition of autocratic power in the region. Mukasa suggested that Mukaabya did not become Muteesa until much later in life, when Christian missionaries 'had a far-reaching influence on him'.[63] Through the influence of Christian chiefs, Mukasa continued, Mukaabya recognised the importance of changing his name and moving away from violent approaches to statebuilding. Recounting Muteesa's transformation, Mukasa noted: 'Mukabya suddenly remarked, "And my name Mukabya strikes terror among my people. I will henceforward be called Mutesa, the peace maker." From that day onwards, he was known as Mutesa and his conduct changed to suit the name.'[64] Through the process of Christian conversion, political calm returned to Buganda. Muteesa renounced 'the evils of war', abolished slavery, and taught his chiefs to bathe. Muteesa, who ordered the kingdom's chiefs to stop slandering one another, prohibited drunkenness and 'abolished the heathen religion and introduced Christianity'. During a decade when government officials were being 'misled by irresponsible people, who do not care a whit as to the things that do matter in the development of nations', Mukasa called upon Baganda and colonial officials to scrutinise the past. 'Many of the old customs were repressive of individual freedom', Mukasa concluded, 'and to try to revert to them, after the advent of Christianity and the Union Jack, is to lose sight of the meaning of the principles of Christianity and the British Empire.'[65] The identification of Mukaabya's makeover – the invention of Muteesa – with Christian conversion was central to Protestant ways of talking about the past. Imagining Protestant calm in the nineteenth century was one particular way of legitimising the monopolisation of power during the interwar and postwar periods. If Christianity had been central to healing societies impacted by state violence in the 1800s, Mukasa inferred, it would facilitate a return to calm in the twentieth century.

---

[62] Ibid., p. 136.
[63] Ibid., p. 141.
[64] Ibid.
[65] Ibid., p. 142.

Figure 4.2 Detail of 'King Mtesa and his chiefs', 1875
Source: Stanley Archives/5184, King Baudouin Foundation collection, on deposit in the Royal Museum for Central Africa, Tervuren.
I wish to thank Andrea Stultiens for drawing this image to my attention.[66]

Muslim historians recalled Mukaabya's political conversion and the 1890s differently. They remembered a time when Muslim powerbrokers, unlike Christian activists in the 1900s, were willing to overlook religious differences for the welfare of the state (Figure 4.2). On 27 August 1943, a cadre of Ganda Muslims, speaking 'for and on behalf of the Buganda Muslims under Prince Badru Kakungulu's leadership', forwarded a three-page missive to Uganda's governor to critique 'the

---

[66] This nineteenth-century image is currently being explored by History in Progress Uganda, in their project, *Ekifananyi Kya Muteesa*, which can be reviewed here: www.hipuganda.org/blog/ekifananyi-kya-muteesa-the-show-is-on.

Buganda Government on account of its unhelpful attitude towards our religious practice and its indifference to our requests for consideration'.[67] With no fewer than eighteen detailed historical references, Ganda Muslims chronicled an unconventional past, a time when Muslims helped to orchestrate national development in partnership with other religious parties. 'It is not out of place,' suggested Kibuli historians, 'to mention that the Muslim, and Roman Catholic and Protestant have always stood side by side in discharging their respective duties to the King, the Kabaka and country.'[68] In the 1890s, they argued, Ganda Christians were unwilling to share power and practice political negotiation in a long season of competing religious agendas. Failure to explore the possibilities of power sharing resulted in political violence toward the end of the 1800s. Religious civil war had not been the result of Muslim and Arab influence, as colonial historians argued; it was the outcome of Christian chiefs placing rigid demands upon Muslim kings and chiefs. Muslims reminded colonial officials that with the support of communities in northern Uganda and Sudan they could have reclaimed power after Kalema was removed from the throne:

After revolting, the Nubians on October 8th, 1897, sent a message to Prince Nuhu Mbogo inviting him and the whole of the Mohammedan community in this country to their side, holding out to him the promise that, after a successful issue of the war, they would install him on the throne of Buganda.[69]

Under the 'leadership and inspiration' of *Omulangira* Nuhu Mbogo, however, a 'unanimous motion was declared against the Nubians' suggestions and offers'.[70] Muslim writers recalled that at precisely '3 a.m. on the 18th October, 1897, a message was despatched to the Protectorate Government disclosing the Nubians' plot and revolt'.[71]

Using the precision of colonial time, Muslim activists argued that they had set aside legitimate political claims to stabilise the kingdom. Muslims now challenged Christian rulers to do the same, to learn to share power.

---

[67] MUA Unmarked Buganda Government File/2 Buganda Muslims to Governor of Uganda, 27 August 1943.
[68] Ibid.
[69] Ibid.
[70] Ibid.
[71] Ibid.

Rewriting the nineteenth century – the fictions of calm – was central to claiming political power in the twentieth. This not only resulted in extensive Christian historiography, it inspired the publication of alternative histories written by Muslims. As both John Rowe and Michael Twaddle have shown, disputed claims in the 1880s and 1890s gave rise to a concerted effort by Muslim intellectuals to imagine dissenting pasts, to call into question the Protestant histories of Apolo Kaggwa, Hamu Mukasa and Bartolomayo Zimbe.[72] In 1937, Bakale Mukasa bin Mayanja published the first edition of *Akatabo k'Ebyafayo Ebyantalo za Kabaka Mwanga, Kiwewa ne Kalema* (An Introduction to the History of the Wars of Kings Mwanga, Kiweewa and Kalema).[73] Whereas Kaggwa's *Bassekabaka be Buganda* completely ignored Buganda's Muslim king, Kalema, Mukasa bin Mayanja reminded Baganda of the kingdom's Muslim ruler, who was militarily removed from power by Catholic and Protestant collaborators. In the 1940s, Sheikh Abdallah Ssekimwanyi published a second edition of *Ebyafayo Ebitonotono Kudini ye Kisiramu Mu Buganda* (A Short History of the Introduction of Islam in Buganda). And in 1953, Sheikh Ali Kulumba published his important *Ebyafayo By'Obusiramu mu Uganda* (A History of Islam in Uganda), concerned that the history of Islam in B/Uganda would increasingly 'sink out of sight' should appropriate measures not be taken.[74] Whereas Hamu Mukasa associated Mukaabya's calming with the arrival of Christian missionaries, Kulumba argued that Muslim teaching had resulted in political calm. The adoption of the Muslim calendar created innovative ways of regulating the political authority of kings, whose mobilities were realigned according to new conceptions and implementations of time. Kulumba noted that while fasting during Ramadan, Mukaabya experienced a moral conversion, during which he 'saw that it is not a good thing for a reader to remain with savage customs and be a Kabaka who does not

---

[72] John A. Rowe, 'Myth, Memoir, and Moral Admonition: Luganda Historical Writing, 1893–1969', *Uganda Journal*, 33 (1969), 17–40, 217–19 (pp. 25–7); Michael Twaddle, 'On Ganda Historiography', *History in Africa*, 1 (1974), 85–100 (p. 88).

[73] Amin Mutyaba suggests that the 1937 copy is a second edition. He dates the first edition to 1932 (Mutyaba, 'The Development of Islam in Uganda', p. 30).

[74] LFP 54/7/171 Kulumba, *Ebyafayo By'obusiramu mu Uganda*. To explore Kulumba's biography further see '*Okujjukira* Sheik Islaam-Ali Saad Kulumba', Mss., 2004.

know God'.[75] Following Kulumba, one Muslim recalled that Islamic traders 'taught Mutesa religion so that the country might improve, so that there would not be any more murder, any more selling of each other and generally so that there might be stability'.[76]

Debates about political calm raised additional questions regarding the relationship between authenticity and power. To undermine Muslim legitimacy, Christian historians argued that Muslims had adopted a foreign religion, through which Arabs and Egyptians introduced cultural practices that were alien to Buganda, such as particular sexual habits. In his autobiographical history, *The Life of Ham Mukasa*, Mukasa suggested that he had been pressured in the royal court to participate in 'profane' customs:

I think I must have been about twelve years old when I entered the king's household. I found the king's court full of the vilest customs, introduced by the Arabs and the Turks (the people who came from Egypt). I was much afraid, for my parents had told me not to agree to such things; for they told me that if I did such things I should die at once. But in spite of this I was compelled to join with the rest.[77]

By tracing the genealogies of vile customs in Buganda to the arrival of Muslim traders, Mukasa legitimised Christian power and the necessity of marginalising Muslim communities.

Christian activists largely accepted Mukasa's interpretation of the past. In turn, for Muslim historians in the colonial period, it was crucial to argue that the advent of Islam in Buganda reinforced legitimate precolonial cultures. To suggest that Buganda's Muslims were sons and daughters of the soil, Kulumba placed the history and development of Muslim ritual in concert with Bataka dissent in the late 1940s. Kulumba showed that Muslim powerbrokers had a proven track record of responding to populist sentiment and authentic culture, sensibilities that allowed Muslims to exercise religious and political

---

[75] LFP 54/7/172–73 Kulumba, *Ebyafayo By'obusiramu mu Uganda*.

[76] Interview, Arye Oded with Yusufu Kiwanuka, 12 November 1967, Lwanjaza, Ssingo County, in Oded, *Islam in Uganda*, pp. 327–32 (p. 327).

[77] Ham Mukasa, 'The Life of Ham Mukasa', in *The Wonderful Story of Uganda*, trans. by Ven Archdeacon Walker (London: Church Missionary Society, 1904), pp. 173–208 (p. 176).

discretion for the welfare of Buganda's kingdom. Kulumba explained that by becoming calm through Muslim fasting, Muteesa I developed a newfound appreciation for Buganda's clan heads and their customs. Early Muslim converts had suggested that while Muteesa was initially willing to undergo circumcision, he was persuaded otherwise because he feared that he would die for violating custom. In the early 1950s, Kulumba pushed this argument further, suggesting that Muteesa refused to be circumcised in order to allay political tension between Buganda's throne and the kingdom's clan heads: 'He [Muteesa] himself wished to be circumcised but people frightened him much saying "if you are circumcised, the Bataka are going to remove you from the throne["]; for the Kabaka must not shed blood in Buganda.'[78] In ways that contradicted Mukasa, Kulumba showed that Muslim powerbrokers in the past practised discretion. Not only were Muslims sensitive to the regulation of Ganda custom, Kulumba argued, they were willing to self-regulate Muslim teachings for the purposes of creating social calm – peace, *–teesa*, not suffering, *–kaabya*.

Islamic Patriotism and the Changing Politics of Abubakar K. Mayanja

Sheikh Kulumba's history writing was part of a wider initiative to support the production of a new generation of Muslim leadership in kingdom politics. Through missionary education and textual practices, Ganda Christians had dominated the regulation and production of official knowledge. Education policies favoured Christian powerbrokers; and the development of primary and secondary education was tied to the development of Christian mission.[79] Without their own institutions, Muslim parents were pressured to send their children to Protestant and Catholic schools, something they often refused to do

---

[78] LFP 54/7/173 Kulumba, *Ebyafayo By'obusiramu mu Uganda*.
[79] 'Annual Report of the Education Department for the Year Ended 31st December, 1930' (Entebbe: Government Printer, 1931), p. 3. For further discussion see A. Hughes, 'The Early Days of Education in the Protectorate: White Fathers' Mission', *Uganda Teachers' Journal*, 1 (1939), 18–23; Felice Carter, 'The Education of African Muslims in Uganda', *Uganda Journal*, 29 (1965), 193–9 (p. 194); J. Sykes, 'A Further Note on the Education of African Muslims', *Uganda Journal*, 30 (1966), 227–8.

'for fear that their children would be converted to Christianity'.[80] In 1935, there were only eighteen registered Muslim schools throughout the Protectorate.[81] Toward the end of the following decade, there existed a total of forty-six primary, secondary and post-secondary Muslim schools aided by colonial or local government funds. There were still significantly more Christian schools – colonial or local government monies aided 614 Protestant schools and 769 Catholic schools during the same period.[82]

Muslim leaders theorised education as a tool to produce a younger generation of activists. Educational strategies among the kingdom's Muslim communities were developed under the leadership of Nuhu Mbogo's heir, *Omulangira* Badru Kakungulu Wasajja (1907–91), and the Young Men's Muslim Association (YMMA). Through international partnerships with the Uganda Muslim Education Association (UMEA) and the East African Muslim Welfare Society (EAMWS), Muslims in Buganda developed international partnerships to sponsor their students.

Registered by *Omulangira* Kakungulu no later than 1940,[83] the YMMA was established 'to bring up young Muslims in the culture of Islam while, at the same time, promoting an appreciation of modern secular western knowledge and organization'.[84] Activists in the movement aimed to construct mosques and schools in pairs. From these multipurpose sites it was hoped that young activists would engage in the arena of Ganda politics. Article 2 of the 1959 Certificate of Registration stated that the founding objective of the YMMA was 'to acquire and/or erect a building or buildings to be used by members as a Mosque, School, and/or for social charitable or instructional

---

[80] Musa Musoke, 'Muslim Education in the Uganda Protectorate', *Uganda Teachers' Journal*, 1 (1939), 242–3 (p. 242).

[81] 'Annual Report of the Education Department for the Year Ended 31st December, 1935' (Entebbe: Government Printer, 1936), p. 30.

[82] 'Annual Report of the Education Department for the Year Ended 31st December, 1949' (Entebbe: Government Printer, 1951), p. 87.

[83] JLEP Sulaiman Kiggundu to Commissioner of Land Registration, 17 October 1996. YMMA historians suggest that the organisation was established as early as 1932 (Young Men's Muslim Association, *Prince Badru Kakungulu* (Kampala: Wood Printers & Stationers Ltd, 1990), pp. 9–10).

[84] A.B.K. Kasozi, *The Life of Prince Badru Kakungulu Wasajja: And the Development of a Forward Looking Muslim Community in Uganda, 1907–1991* (Kampala: Progressive Publishing House, 1996), p. 69.

purposes'.[85] Organisers encouraged Ganda Muslims to contest Ganda politics, 'to subscribe to any charity or other good cause for the relief and assistance of mankind in general, and adherents of Islam in particular'.[86] Muslims were instructed to 'help, whether in money or otherwise, [. . .] members and visitors in time of need, sickness or death'.[87] Organisers admonished the faithful to 'observe and procure the due observance of all feasts and fasts celebrated by Muslims'.[88]

Muslim activists used the Association to orchestrate political critique early into its formation. On 7 August 1941, organisers forwarded a two-page letter to Buganda's three Christian regents. Ramadan K.K. Gava (YMMA secretary) and J.H. Semakula (YMMA chairman) expressed 'grievances which are of sore anxiety' for Buganda's Muslim community.[89] The two denounced religious inequality in Buganda's chieftaincies, especially at the upper levels of Ganda governance: '[W]e have no voice when the three Ministers take their seats to discuss affairs which affect the nation.'[90] The two further argued that Muslim schools were underfunded and 'youths who have had education are not recommended for employment in the senior offices of this Government'. It was noted that Buganda's Muslims were pressured to forfeit land, while the state simultaneously pushed the faithful to subject their community of imams to 'drastic reduction'. If Buganda was going to be a 'great, peaceful and loyal kingdom, which lends an attentive ear to whosoever has a reasonable complaint', it was expected that Christian politicians would not 'fail to listen' to their grievances.

Muslim educational politics in Buganda in the 1940s coincided with initiatives to create Islamic solidarity throughout eastern Africa. In Uganda, cosmopolitan associations were developed through the UMEA and the EAMWS. In 1944, Badru Kakungulu convened Buganda's Muslim leaders to establish UMEA,[91] through which he

---

[85] JLEP '[YMMA] Certificate of Registration as a Corporate Body under the Trustees (Incorporation) Ordinance, 1959', 2.b.
[86] Ibid., 2.a.
[87] Ibid., 2.d.
[88] Ibid., 2.e.
[89] MUA Unmarked Buganda Government File/2 Ramadan K.K. Gava and J.H. Semakula to Honorable Three Ministers, Mengo Lukiiko, 7 August 1941.
[90] Ibid.
[91] *60 Years of Uganda Muslim Education Association (UMEA)* (Kampala: New Limited, n.d.), pp. 11–12; A.B.K. Kasozi, *The Spread of Islam in Uganda* (Nairobi: Oxford University Press, 1986), pp. 95–6.

developed a partnership between B/Uganda's Muslim community and Aga Khan and the EAMWS, an organisation that aimed to cultivate Islamic camaraderie and Isma'ili spirituality throughout eastern Africa.[92] In association with the YMMA, UMEA advocated for the importance of Muslim education to the Ministry of Education, supervising Muslim schools, appointing head teachers, developing syllabi and marking examinations.[93] In so doing, UMEA campaigned for the kingdom's Muslim community 'in the developmental process of their country WITHOUT APOLOGY OR UNNECESSARY PATRONAGE'.[94] By providing Muslim children with an 'overall appreciation of the world',[95] UMEA and EAMWS sought to 'equip children with the tools to defend their religion from an intellectual stand point' and to ensure 'Islamic Culture is respected and expanded'.[96] Through the development of educational opportunities in eastern Africa and Buganda, it was hoped that Muslims would be aptly suited to shape local and regional politics following the Second World War.

Abu Mayanja was born into a Muslim family in 1929, in Zziba (Ngoggwe), Kyaggwe.[97] His career was increasingly intertwined with these strategies from the late 1940s onward. While Mayanja adapted classical liberalism and secular education to help organise Uganda's first national party, the UNC, his dissent could be traced to earlier Muslim grievances against the state, first mediated to him during adolescence. Mayanja learned to read and write Latin-script Luganda from his

---

[92] For the history of Aga Khan see Farhad Daftary, *Mediaeval Isma'ili History and Thought* (Cambridge: Cambridge University Press, 2001); Farhad Daftary, *The Isma'ilis: Their History and Doctrines*, 2nd edn (Cambridge: Cambridge University Press, 2007). For additional analysis on the history of Aga Khan in eastern Africa see H.S. Morris, 'The Divine Kingship of the Aga Khan: A Study of Theocracy in East Africa', *Southwestern Journal of Anthropology*, 14 (1958), 454–72; A.K. Adatia and N.Q. King, 'Some East African Firmans of H.H. Aga Khan III', *Journal of Religion in Africa*, 2 (1969), 179–91. To explore the educational policies of Aga Khan in Uganda see CCAS 676.1/370 H.H. The Aga Khan's Shia Imami Ismailia Education Department for Uganda, 'A Review of Islamilia Education in the Uganda Protectorate', (n.d.).

[93] Kasozi, *The Spread of Islam in Uganda*, p. 107.

[94] *60 Years of Uganda Muslim Education Association*, p. 12.

[95] Ibid.

[96] Ibid.

[97] My discussion on Mayanja's early life draws from Ssemujju Ibrahim Nganda's interviews with Mayanja.

Muvuma mother,[98] Maimuna Kayaga, with whom he was particularly close.[99] Mayanja's father, Abdallah Waswa Kambuga Kakyama, was an early convert to Islam. His father was also an *omukijungute*: he had fought for Buganda's Muslim party during the religious wars, during which he was shot in the leg. Mayanja's father, like other early Muslim converts, learned to read and write Arabic and to use Arabic script to write Luganda. Abdallah Kakyama began teaching the Qur'an and Muslim oral history to Mayanja at the age of five. During school holidays, Mayanja and at least one additional brother were frequently sent to a *mwalimu* (religious instructor) to learn how to cite the Qur'an.[100] From his father, Mayanja and his siblings learned the pattern of daily Muslim prayer. Mayanja's sister, Asiya Kakyama, recalled: '[W]hen I was growing up, everybody, each of us in turn, used to imitate dad, so each one of us, in turn, knew how to pray like [him].'[101] When Abdallah Kakyama was away during prayer, Abubakar Mayanja and a small number of his extended family were responsible to call the family and their servants to worship.[102] Like Buganda's first generation of Muslims under the rule of *Kabaka* Muteesa I, the Muslim calendar and daily regulations of time became a way that Mayanja and his family delegated responsibilities among themselves and within the community.

As small-scale coffee and cotton farmers, Mayanja's family was economically poor. To increase agricultural productivity, in a county where by 1950 45 per cent of the population was comprised of migrant workers, Mayanja's parents employed Rwandan and Bagisu labourers.[103] With little money and without easy access to Muslim schools, Mayanja attended Baskerville Primary, where he learned to hold his Muslim

---

[98] The family of Mayanja's mother converted to Catholicism in the late 1800s, when Kayaga began to learn to read and write Luganda in Latin script.

[99] Addressing Abubakar Mayanja's close relationship with his mother, Mayanja's sister recalled: 'Oh, there is something I cannot put into words. We always said if two hearts were beating as one, Abu and my mother's hearts were beating as one. They were very, *very* close; they were intensely close' (Interview, Asiya Kakyama, 9 December 2009, Kampala).

[100] Interview, Asiya Makyama, 9 December 2009, Kampala.

[101] Ibid.

[102] Ibid.

[103] For additional discussion see Audrey I. Richards, ed., *Economic Development and Tribal Change: A Study of Immigrant Labour in Buganda*, 2nd edn (Nairobi: Oxford University Press, 1973).

faith in tension with missionary education.[104] Mayanja secured placement at King's College, Budo, in 1945, where he studied until matric-
ulating at Makerere College in March 1950.[105] At Budo, the YMMA
and EAMWS identified Mayanja as a future leader in Buganda's
Muslim community. As early as October 1948, Budo headmaster,
Timothy Cobb,[106] discussed Mayanja's future with the leadership of
EAMWS.[107] Muslim activists were interested in Mayanja's 'moral
standard',[108] with aspiration that 'his studies and habits ultimately
[prove] useful to his co-brothers in Islam'.[109] In their effort to pastor
Mayanja, EAMWS subsidised considerable portions of his education
at Budo.[110] Through frequent discussion,[111] Cobb and the EAMWS
worked to secure additional educational opportunities for Mayanja,
whom Cobb considered Budo's 'cleverest boy'.[112]

Initially, the Muslim Welfare Society worked to secure post-secondary education for Mayanja in a Muslim university. On 24 March 1949,
Mayanja, a self-identified 'Moslem [of] nearly 18 years of age', pur-
sued the possibility of education in Pakistan, whose universities were
preoccupied with the question of Islamic statebuilding.[113] However,
the Society decided that Mayanja should concentrate on admission to
Makerere College, after which he would later apply to study abroad
through the Muslim Society of Mombasa.[114] At Makerere, it was

---

[104] SINP, p. 10.
[105] Ibid., pp. 11 & 19.
[106] Cobb replaced Dennis George Herbert, who had served as headmaster from
    1939 to 1947 (Gordon P. McGregor, *King's College Budo: A Centenary
    History, 1906–2006* (Kampala: Fountain Publishers, 2006), pp. 99–123).
[107] KCBA Timothy Cobb to Hon. Secretary, EAMWS, 1 October 1948.
[108] KCBA Hon. Secretary, EAMWS, to Timothy Cobb, 5 November 1948.
[109] KCBA Hon. Secretary, EAMWS, to Timothy Cobb, 26 November 1948.
[110] For Mayanja's education, EAMWS provided Shs. 464.55/– for 1948 and 1949
    (ibid.), a sizeable scholarship (KCBA Hon. Secretary, EAMWS, to Timothy
    Cobb, 16 November 1950).
[111] Available records indicate that letters between the two parties were exchanged
    on no fewer than eleven occasions between 1948 and 1950.
[112] KCBA Timothy Cobb to Hon. Secretary, EAMWS, 1 October 1948.
[113] KCBA A.K. Mayanja to Prime Minister, Pakistan, 24 March 1949. Mayanja
    expressed jubilation to Pakistan's prime minister, noting that 'one of our
    leading Moslem countries has become an independent state'. For reasons
    that are not evident, however, correspondence between Timothy Cobb and
    EAMWS suggests that Mayanja's letter was not posted (KCBA Timothy Cobb
    to Hon. Secretary, EAMWS, 1 April 1949).
[114] KCBA EAMWS to A.K. Mayanja, n.d.

hoped, Mayanja would become 'the best educated and most intelligent African Muslim of his age'.[115] Leaders in the EAMWS admonished Mayanja to work toward becoming a leading advocate for Muslims in Buganda and eastern Africa: 'I beg you earnestly to do this well so that your fellow men may not call you lazy in taking opportunity for Moslems.'[116] Mayanja's political career was entangled with regional Muslim political strategy by the early 1950s. Reflecting on his obligation to serve Buganda's marginalised Muslim community, Mayanja confided to Cobb: 'Seriously – it is my sacred intention, nay, duty to be of use to my people. Although as yet I have only a dim glimpse of what it is I shall do, I have never had any doubt about my duty.'[117]

Mayanja's denunciation of colonial discrimination against Muslims in Uganda coincided with many of the economic and political arguments that were being directed against colonial rule in the 1950s. During his studies at Makerere, Mayanja became a noteworthy activist in Ignatius Musazi's anti-colonial project, first with the Farmers' Union,[118] and then with the UNC as organising secretary in 1952.[119] Mayanja worked with Musazi to draft the party's constitution.[120] If Christian leadership in the kingdom of Buganda had aimed to prevent young Muslims from directly shaping Mmengo politics, as YMMA activists concluded in the early 1940s, party nationalism was for Mayanja Islam's Trojan horse, a way to accumulate critical mass on behalf of the kingdom's Muslim community.

---

[115] KCBA Timothy Cobb to Hon. Secretary, EAMWS, 20 October 1949.
[116] KCBA EAMWS to A.K. Mayanja, n.d.
[117] KCBA A.K. Mayanja to Timothy Cobb, 18 March 1950.
[118] KCBA A.K. Mayanja to Timothy Cobb, 14 February 1952.
[119] 'Uganda National Congress Forming'. According to Musazi, the idea of establishing Congress emerged in 1949 (Interview, Neal Ascherson with I.K. Musazi, 9 June 1956, Uganda Club, Kampala, in NAP). According to Mayanja, the idea developed out of a conversation between Musazi and British socialists Fenner Brockway and George Padmore (Abu Mayanja to Neal Ascherson, June 1956, in NAP Field Notes, pp. 62–3). For further insight see Ascherson, 'The History of the Uganda National Congress', pp. 1–11; Sallie S. Kayunga, *Uganda National Congress and the Struggle for Democracy: 1952–1962* (Kampala: Centre for Basic Research, Working Paper, No. 14, 1995), pp. 21–30.
[120] Interview, Neal Ascherson with I.K. Musazi, 9 June 1956, Uganda Club, Kampala, in NAP.

Shortly after the formation of Congress, Mayanja was expelled from Makerere College for organising a food strike.[121] To curb Mayanja's anti-colonial nationalism, Andrew Cohen and Peter Kitcatt, Oliver Lyttelton's assistant private secretary, secured placement for Mayanja at King's College, Cambridge.[122] At Cambridge, Mayanja read history from 1953 to 1955 and law from 1955 to 1957, after which he was called to the bar at Lincoln's Inn in 1959.[123] Despite what colonial officials had hoped would occur, Mayanja's time at Cambridge bolstered his anti-colonial fervour. Following Muteesa's deposition Mayanja spent his evenings at King's, which was a centre of Marxist ideology in Great Britain during the Cold War,[124] in the company of politically-minded Erisa Kironde and Neal Ascheron,[125] 'drawing up constitutions for the future of Uganda that [were] then sent in to Hancock'.[126] For Mayanja, Muteesa's deposition reflected the infeasibility of imperial policy throughout Britain's empire.[127] As early as January 1954, Mayanja used Aneurin Bevan's *Tribune* to critique what he viewed as the social consequences of colonialism in eastern Africa.[128] Colonialism, argued Mayanja, created African doctors who were not allowed to 'use certain drugs without permission'.[129] Through the intended design of

---

[121] SINP, pp. 34–5.

[122] Tam Dalyell [Thomas D. Loch], 'Sir Peter Kitcatt', *Independent*, 2 April 2007.

[123] 'Abubakar (Abu) Kakyama Bakijukire Mayanja', in KKCA 'Annual Report: King's College', Cambridge (2009), p. 180.

[124] Hobsbawm explored King's Marxist community in his autobiography (Eric J. Hobsbawm, *Interesting Times: A Twentieth-Century Life* (New York: Pantheon Books, 2002).

[125] Erisa C.N. Kironde (1926–86) attended King's College, Cambridge, from 1950 to 1954, where he read English and eventually archaeology and anthropology ('Erisa Christopher Ndawula Kironde', in KKCA 'Annual Report: King's College, Cambridge' (1987), pp. 56–8). Kironde was interested in the interplay between media and politics. While attending Cambridge, Kironde befriended the family of Sir George Reginald Barnes, a prominent broadcaster and educationalist. Shortly after his return to Uganda, Kironde wrote to 'Lady Barnes', criticising the response of Labour to the *Kabaka* crisis: 'some of us were so annoyed at the soppy Socialist reaction on the Kabaka's "deposition" and particularly for their attacks on his private life which was outside their scope of politics [*sic*]' (KKCA GRB 2/1/7 E.C.N. Kironde to Lady Barnes, Kent, 15 May 1955).

[126] Interview, Neal Ascherson, 17 August 2010, London.

[127] A.K. Mayanja, 'We Call This Plan a Fraud!', *Tribune*, 24 December 1954, p. 2.

[128] From 1953 to 1956, Mayanja published in *Tribune* on no fewer than ten occasions.

[129] Mayanja, 'The African Who Fell Off His Bicycle', 22 January 1954, p. 5.

the government, Uganda's system of education entrenched discrimination and religious division: non-Catholics were declined entrance into parochial schools, and Protestant institutions permitted admittance on the condition that students commit themselves to 'scripture lessons'.[130] Colonialism entailed ruthless exploitation and resulted inevitably in pitting Africans and non-Africans against one another, what Mayanja defined as 'the tragedy of Uganda'.[131]

Unlike Eridadi Mulira, Mayanja did not conclude that Muteesa's deportation was the result of a constitutional crisis. He criticised E.M.K. Mulira's and Colin Legum's suggestion that Muteesa and Cohen 'were both the victims of an outmoded, unworkable constitution'.[132] For Mayanja, this was an 'inadequate' explanation. He suggested that throughout the first half of the twentieth century, B/Uganda had undergone 'far-reaching' constitutional and economic reforms – measures that Uganda's governor was now 'disregarding'.[133] Uganda's governor refused to work with Buganda's king and parliament; in so doing, he demonstrated contempt toward Buganda's political institutions. Mayanja argued that Uganda's governor publicly scolded 'the ancient Ganda Parliament as though it were a kindergarten', while further castigating Britain's government for exploring the possibility of coronating a new king and for petitioning the removal of Buganda's queen and officials from the royal palace. In short, Uganda's political impasse was not constitutional in character, but the consequence of being governed by 'a proconsul intoxicated by the possession of unlimited power'.[134]

In Buganda, Muslims used Muteesa's deportation to renegotiate power in ways that were more attuned to the early 1880s than the early 1950s. By supporting the immediate return of Muteesa II, Kibuli Muslims advocated for Muslim representation in the state. Predominantly Kampala-based Muslims identified with the social aims of the Uganda Peoples' Party (UPP), which organised at Mmengo on 1 February 1953.[135] Like the YMMA, the primary objective of the

---

[130] Mayanja, 'Well, at Least They Built Us a Reformatory', 5 February 1954, p. 2.
[131] Mayanja, 'The Struggle for Democracy in Uganda', *United Asia [Bombay]*, 7 (1955), 97–101 (p. 97).
[132] Mayanja, 'Sir Andrew Cohen Challenged', 12 November 1954, p. 9.
[133] Ibid.
[134] Ibid.
[135] BNA CO 822/854/5 'The Uganda Peoples' Party', Colonial Report, 22 July 1955, p. 1.

party was to 'improve all African educational facilities in Uganda'.[136] Patriotic Muslims used the party to advocate for the immediate return of Buganda's monarch.[137] Badru Kakungulu worked with activists in the UPP and a small cadre of royalists to scrutinise the Namirembe recommendations.[138] Kakungulu also called upon Ganda Muslims to support the candidacy of Michael Kintu for the office of *katikkiro*. If Muslim activists supported Kintu, it was concluded, the kingdom's Muslim community would be offered a principal position in the Kintu government. After considerable parliamentary debate following the election, the community was given the Ministry of Education, which was first appointed to Kassim Male.[139]

Following Muteesa's return, Muslim devotees demonstrated their allegiance to Buganda's throne by presenting elaborate gifts to Muteesa II. Under the leadership of Badru Kakungulu, Uganda's African and Asian Muslims obtained 9336/- worth of uncirculated silver coins.[140] During an extravagant ceremony performed within the first week of his return from deportation, Muteesa sat in an equal-arm beam balance, poised by 146 pounds of coinage, the equivalency of Muteesa's physical weight. The gift was accompanied with a silver replica of Buganda's Kibuli Mosque. By giving elaborate gifts and demonstrating able negotiation, Ganda Muslims showed that they were indispensable mediators in Buganda's political landscape. Through Muslim counterbalance, Buganda's monarchy was stable and politically calm.

Throughout the mid- to late 1950s Mayanja, like E.M.K. Mulira, was enmeshed in various political controversies.[141] At Cambridge,

---

136 Ibid.
137 Ibid., p. 2. See also ICS 29/1/13/95 N.R. Kayondo, Secretary, UPP, to Constitutional Committee, 23 July and 13 & 17 August 1954; *Uganda Eyogera*, 17 November 1954; *Uganda Mail*, 17 June 1955.
138 Paulo Kavuma, *Crisis in Buganda, 1953–55: The Story of the Exile and Return of the Kabaka, Mutesa II* (London: Rex Collings, 1979), p. 95.
139 Fred B. Welbourn, *Religion and Politics in Uganda: 1952–1962* (Nairobi: East African Publishing House, 1965), p. 17. For further discussion see Kasozi, *The Life of Prince Badru Kakungulu Wasajja*, pp. 125–8; Anonymous, *A Short History of the Democratic Party*, ed. by Richard Muscat (Rome: Foundation for African Development, 1984), pp. 25–32.
140 *Uganda Argus*, 5 November 1955; 'Uganda Muslims present 9336/– to the Kabaka, 146lbs', *Uganda Argus*, 15 November 1955.
141 For further insight see Mayanja, 'Sir Andrew Challenged', p. 9; Mayanja, 'The Struggle for Democracy', pp. 97–101. See also A.K. Mayanja, 'Tribal Politics in Kenya', *Guardian*, 9 January 1956, p. 6; A.K. Mayanja, 'Bases',

Mayanja studied British economic and constitutional history, American history and the history of modern European political thought.[142] Through the process of learning to read history, Mayanja acquired a particular analytic skill set that enabled him to scrutinise historical argumentation in the public sphere. In March 1958, he explored both the long history of power in central Uganda and international political history to question the refusal of Buganda's government to participate in national elections, which had resulted from secessionist campaigning orchestrated by Mmengo activists following *Kabaka* Muteesa II's return from exile. In an article in the Kampala press, 'Elections and Traditions', Mayanja criticised Buganda's conservative government for opposing the appointment of an elected representatives from Buganda into the national legislature:

The threat by the Kabaka's Government to sabotage direct elections for Legislative Council in Buganda is so full of ugly possibilities for the future that it is high time somebody did some very straight talking to the reactionary elements in Buganda who seems to imagine that somehow Buganda can contract out of the 20th century, and revert to a system of administration when the efficiency of guns used to be tested on human beings.[143]

For Mayanja, the policies of Buganda's government were antiquated, driven by the legacies of a time when Buganda's kings ruled the state with violence and a small class of military chiefs. Mayanja continued his diatribe by contending that Buganda, despite the claims of conservatives at Mmengo, was an integral constituency in Uganda:

If they want Buganda to go back to the 18th century, with the Kabaka ruling through hand-picked men and clan heads, let them say so – they owe it to the country to speak the truth. I also think that the notion that the Kabaka's Government – which is but part of the Government of Uganda – can defy

---

Uganda Argus, 5 July 1956; A.K. Mayanja, 'Background to Events in Uganda: Sir Andrew Gets Tough', *Tribune*, 13 July 1956, p. 10; A.K. Mayanja, Mwai Kibaki, et al., 'Rhodesian Electoral Bill: Changing the Constitution', *Guardian*, 18 February 1958, p. 8; A.K. Mayanja, 'Kenya's Constitution', *The Times*, 20 March 1958; 'Reserved Seats', *Uganda Argus*, 23 May 1958; A.K. Mayanja, 'Evictions in Kariba: Natives not Consulted', *Guardian*, 15 September 1958, p. 6.

[142] SINP, p. 43.

[143] A.K. Mayanja, 'Elections and Traditions', *Uganda Argus*, 6 March 1958.

Figure 4.3 Kampala, January 1959. L to R: I.K. Musazi (with flag);
Dr B.N. Kununka; Abu Mayanja (rear centre, shouting with glasses)
Source: DRUM Magazine

the latter is a matter so grave that it must be clarified and the correct position authoritatively stated.[144]

Independence extended the possibility of a state governing its own affairs without foreign interference, not the secession of the state's pre-colonial kingdoms (Figure 4.3).

By failing to appoint representatives through general election and by moving toward secession, Mayanja suggested that Buganda's rulers were instituting political despotism. He scrutinised Buganda's policymakers by comparing his activism with the insurrection of Julius Caesar in the mid-first century BCE:

Speaking for myself, I have crossed the Rubicon. I have set my face firmly against any autocracy whether it be foreign and imperialist or native and feudal. I stake my future and dedicate my life to the realisation of democratic principles in my country no matter from which side the obstacles may emanate. This is a declaration of political faith, and I call on other intellectuals to do likewise.[145]

[144] Ibid.
[145] Ibid.

Mayanja argued that the practice of power in Buganda was being developed along lines similar to the autocratic governments of Francisco Franco's Spain and the Saudi monarchy. Mayanja contended that *Katikkiro* Kintu 'should realise that political parties have come to stay. There is no chance of a Saudi Arabia in Buganda'.[146]

Mayanja's analysis evoked considerable debate in the local press. H. Bukomeko was a member of Buganda's Electoral College. He questioned Mayanja's interpretation of Buganda's past, and suggested that Mayanja exemplified an 'unquestionable foolishness and ignorance of the history of the country, Buganda [. . .]'.[147] Bukomeko berated Mayanja, whose political argument was compared to a colonial administrator's:

Look, how dare Mr. Mayanja call the Great Lukiko a stumbling block? Nonsense! How can he call the Great Lukiko unrepresentative? Shame! Poor boy, he should learn from me that in no way should he call the Buganda Great Lukiko an unrepresentative body [. . .] [H]e appears to be a colonial administrator.[148]

Bukomeko concluded by cautioning Mayanja to forego 'nonsensical political views, which are half-baked, incomplete and untrue'.

Mayanja cited economic and labour policies in early twentieth-century Buganda to respond to Bukomeko. He argued that while Buganda's *Lukiiko* had 'brought about many things beneficial to Buganda, and indeed to the whole of Uganda', her parliament exhibited political mismanagement.[149] Throughout the late 1950s, *Lukiiko* propaganda suggested that the kingdom's government was successfully safeguarding the political interests of ordinary citizens in the arena of national politics. The government of Buganda, polemists argued, aimed to protect Baganda in the postcolony from what one activist called 'diluted democracy'.[150] Mayanja challenged this assertion, writing that 'if the Lukiko is so confident that what it says reflects what the majority in Buganda thinks, why not allow the people the chance to say so by means of their own elected representatives?' By averting elections within Buganda, Mayanja noted, Ganda statebuilders were returning to

[146] A.K. Mayanja, 'Buganda Voting', *Uganda Argus*, 29 March 1958.
[147] H. Bukomeko, 'Lukiko Defended', *Uganda Argus*, 4 April 1958, p. 2.
[148] Ibid.
[149] A.K. Mayanja, 'Buganda Lukiko', *Uganda Argus*, 16 April 1958, p. 4.
[150] A.F. Mpanga, 'Lukiko Supported', *Uganda Argus*, 18 April 1958.

a time when autocracy characterised the practice of power in the state, a political order that 'the majority of Baganda do not agree with [. . .]'.[151]

According to Mayanja, political calm had eluded rural communities in the past; the kingdom was governed by 'feudal tyranny based on the debasement of the human personality and the vagaries of the so-called native customary law'.[152] Mayanja advised Bukomeko to question his selective use of sources, to 'reread' Buganda's political history.[153] Mayanja's argument, like Sheikh Ali Kulumba's, questioned the fictions of calm in twentieth-century Buganda, whose Christian parliament claimed to represent the entire kingdom. In fact, Mayanja underscored, Buganda's *Lukiiko* had supported partisan interests following a period of religious conflict: 'Really, Mr Bukomeko! I do know some history of our country, and it is because of this knowledge that even the Lukiko is capable of making mistakes that I am so anxious that they should be pointed out before it is too late.'[154] The logic of criticising patriotism in Buganda, for Mayanja, was tied to a much longer history of trying to create political space for the kingdom's Muslim community or, in the least, showing the extent to which Buganda's parliament had privileged the kingdom's Christian subjects.

In the early 1960s, Mayanja's concealed agenda became overt. Badru Kakungulu needed to replace his Minister of Education, who had died. Mayanja was appointed. During this same period, on the eve of independence, Mayanja, with Skeikh Kulumba, became leading spokesmen for the state's most conservative political party, *Kabaka Yekka* (KY). By joining the government of Mmengo and KY, Mayanja committed to fulfil what he had identified earlier as a 'sacred intention' to serve Buganda's Muslim community. His decision to support patriotic politics in Buganda was consistent with his liberal sensibilities, the hope of creating political space for Buganda's largest marginalised community. There was more than one way to cross the Rubicon.

Kabaka Yekka, the 'King Alone' party, was founded in the early 1960s to push Mmengo's conservative agenda forward in the context of national electoral politics in Uganda. Its intellectual progenitors constituted a small, close-knit group of Muteesa's friends who spent

[151] Mayanja, 'Buganda Lukiko'.
[152] Mayanja, 'Elections and Traditions'.
[153] Mayanja, 'Buganda Lukiko'.
[154] Ibid.

time in sport and leisure.[155] The founders of the party were mostly 'palace men',[156] prominent Protestants who helped constitute the state's landed aristocracy. On the eve of independence, Muteesa's palace men had increasing influence over Buganda's internal affairs. Preeminent Protestants – including *Katikkiro* Kintu, S.K. Masembe-Kabali and Amos Sempa – used their influence to fuel secessionist sympathy throughout Buganda. In so doing, conservative Protestants aimed to prevent Catholics and Muslims from gaining political traction during a period of electoral uncertainty. Interviews conducted by Professor Kasozi with *Omulangira* Badru Kakungulu show that Buganda's Muslim leaders were increasingly marginalised in the late 1950s: 'Prince Badru began to perceive the increasing influence the "palace men" were having on Sir Edward as evidenced by his inability to influence his king on key issues and his being kept uninformed of crucial matters of the state that he would have been privy to in the former days.'[157]

However, while conservative Protestants largely orchestrated the genesis of KY, party records show that KY constituted a complicated arena of interests, where activists such as E.M.K. Mulira advocated for a constitutional agenda that undermined secessionist policy. Muslims, by contrast, used KY to advocate for their community's causes, such as education and representation in government administration. Kakungulu advocated for the political merger between KY and Milton Obote's Uganda People's Congress (UPC) – the official party programme of KY among B/Uganda's Muslim communities. He advised Muslims in Ankole, Bugisu and Busoga to vote for the UPC during the upcoming national elections, and Muslims in Buganda to vote KY.[158] Partisan constitutional strategists hoped that UPC and KY would be able to effectively share power in postcolonial Uganda, with UPC controlling the state outside of Buganda and KY governing Buganda.

---

[155] I.R. Hancock, 'The Kakamega Club of Buganda', *The Journal of Modern African Studies*, 12 (1974), 131–5. Hancock notes that Muteesa's associates were mostly the sons and grandsons of landholding Protestant chiefs (p. 133). See also I.R. Hancock, 'Patriotism and Neo-Traditionalism in Buganda: The Kabaka Yekka ("The King Alone") Movement, 1961–1962', *The Journal of African History*, 11 (1970), 419–34.

[156] Whereas I.R. Hancock uses the term '*Kakamega* Club', A.B.K. Kasozi uses the phrase 'palace men' (Kasozi, *The Life of Prince Badru Kakungulu Wasajja*, pp. 130–1 & 133–5).

[157] Ibid., p. 140.

[158] Ibid., pp. 143–4.

Figure 4.4 Abubakar Mayanja with *Kabaka* Muteesa II, c. 1963
Kabaka Muteesa II (centre); Abubakar Mayanja (right)
Source: 'Abubakar Kakyama Mayanja' (Kampala: Crane Books, 2005)

Through well-calculated politics, 40 per cent of KY's central executive and seven out of fifteen of the members of the elected policy-making body were Muslim by 1963, though Muslims constituted only 15 per cent of Buganda's total population.[159] Kakungulu's strategy proved effective – Muslims in Buganda were beginning to occupy leading roles in high politics (Figure 4.4).

Kakungulu's effort to renegotiate political space in the early 1960s was further orchestrated by Abubakar Mayanja and Sheikh Ali Kulumba, who, as I have shown, was one of Buganda's premier Muslim historians by the early 1950s. Early into the partnership between KY and UPC, Mayanja facilitated negotiations between Muteesa II and Milton Obote.[160] And by 1961 he was one of the key

[159] Ibid., p. 144.
[160] SINP, pp. 55–9. See also Edward Muteesa II, *Desecration of My Kingdom* (London: Constable, 1967), pp. 159–60; Milton Obote, 'Notes on

public intellectuals of KY, drafting the majority of the party's numerous pamphlets.[161] He participated in private meetings between KY
and UPC in 1963,[162] where, with Sheikh Kulumba, he sought to represent both the kingdom of Buganda and the interests of her Muslim
subjects. Mayanja simultaneously served as a translator for Sheikh
Kulumba, who only spoke Luganda and Arabic.[163] Available minutes
provide insight into the eventual dissolution of the KY/UPC coalition,
which had been created to prevent Benedicto Kiwanuka's Democratic
Party from securing power (Chapter 5). Minutes show that Mayanja
dominated discussions, and advocated for Buganda's political interests in Uganda. Often in the height of debate, Kulumba proffered his
assessment alongside Mayanja's, critiquing nationalist politicians who
tended to go 'round and round and round',[164] or those who leaned
toward 'wishful-thinking'.[165]

In the past, Muslims advocated for kings who responded to Muslim
counsel. In the late 1800s, Muslim powerbrokers replaced one king
who did not demonstrate equity, Kiweewa, with another, Kalema,
one who sought to protect the state from self-aggrandising Christian
chiefs. In the mid-twentieth century Sheikh Kulumba showed that
Buganda's king, Mukaabya, while practising the teachings of Islam,
became Muteesa, one who administered peace. Through wise guidance Muteesa II's grandfather had implemented the Muslim calendar
to regulate power, while governing in concert with Buganda's clan
heads, whom Muteesa pleased by forgoing the rite of circumcision.

Concealment of Genocide in Uganda', 55 (1990) <www.upcparty.net/obote/
   genocide.htm>.

[161] Authored pamphlets included ICS PP.UG.KY/4 *'Kabaka Yekka Amulisa
   Obulimba bwa D.P.'* [*'Kabaka Yekka Exposes the Lies of DP'*] (Kampala:
   Kabaka Yekka Publication, n.d.); ICS PP.UG.KY/12 Abu Mayanja, *You
   and Your Vote: A Guide to the Lukiiko Election* (Kampala: Kabaka Yekka
   Publication, 18 May 1962).

[162] Minutes indicate that Mayanja played an important role mediating disputes
   between UPC and KY following independence. Minutes include MUA KY/2
   'Record [. . .] between Leaders of UPC and KY', 12 July 1963; MUA KY/1
   'Record [. . .] between Leaders of UPC and KY', 19 July 1963; MUA KY/2
   'Record [. . .] between Leaders of UPC and KY', 8 August 1963; MUA KY/1
   'Record [. . .] between Leaders of UPC and KY', 4 September 1963.

[163] MUA KY/2 'Record [. . .] between Leaders of UPC and KY', 12 July 1963,
   pp. 13–14.

[164] MUA KY/2 Sheikh Ali Kulumba, 'Record [. . .] between Leaders of UPC and
   KY', 19 July 1963, p. 18.

[165] Ibid., p. 17.

Whereas Christian powerbrokers had been unwilling to delegate power, Muslims argued that they exhibited a long history of foregoing political claims for the purpose of ensuring political calm, which they dated to Nuhu Mbogo's resignation in the 1890s. Like Muslim historians before him, Mayanja now advocated for the political purposes of Buganda's kingship in the postcolony, even if that required reworking his earlier nationalism:

> Now, we in Kabaka Yekka hold that only a government based on the institution of Kabakaship can be stable in Buganda. The monarchy in Buganda is the focal point and the corner-stone of stability and order. The Baganda cannot really imagine or fathom a government, for Buganda anyway, that is not headed by the Kabaka.[166]

In the same document, Mayanja continued, 'as its name implies, [*Kabaka Yekka*] believes that the first duty of government is to maintain and uphold the institution of monarchy as the foundation of order, security, unity and patriotism in Buganda'.[167]

Similar to Muslim statebuilders one century earlier, Mayanja reminded Baganda of what was at stake in the early 1960s, a political kingdom that had been safeguarded for hundreds of years.[168] In due course, to condemn the alleged intrusion of Obote's national party into Buganda's internal affairs – the formal pretence under which KY moved to dissolve the coalition in the mid-1960s – Mayanja drew from the history of Islamic political thought in Buganda. This enabled him to chide the state's Christian powerbrokers, which, once again, were obsessed with acquiring and maintaining absolute power. For Mayanja, the continuities of power in the state between Buganda's late nineteenth-century Christian chiefs and the predominantly Protestant party of Milton Obote were eerily similar.

Conclusion: The Disruption of Catholic Politics

By the time of independence, Muslim activists had effectively liberalised the state for the kingdom's Muslim community.[169] Rising conservative

---

[166] Mayanja, 'You and Your Vote'.
[167] Ibid.
[168] Mayanja, '*Kabaka Yekka Amulisa Obulimba bwa D.P.*': '[. . .] *bajjajja ffe byebaatukuumira nebabitulekera okumala emyaka ebikumi n'ebikumi*'.
[169] Kulumba and Mayanja were leading spokesmen for the government of Buganda throughout the 1960s. After May 1966, they worked under the

Figure 4.5 Buganda's Muslim leaders, c. late 1960s
L to R: Sheikh Ali Kulumba; Sheikh Asuman Kitti; Abubakar Mayanja;
Omulangira Badru Kakungulu; Hajji Senyojo
Source: 'Abubakar Kakyama Mayanja' (Kampala: Crane Books, 2005)

sentiment throughout Buganda in the late 1950s provided a platform
on which Muslims asserted their community's interests. For Ganda
Muslims, such as Mayanja and Kulumba, it was vital to reclaim
political territory that had been surrendered in the 1890s. This helps
explain why Mayanja, when given the opportunity, distanced himself
from national politics. His seeming shift in solidarity did not signify a
recantation of democratic values; it merely demonstrated the extent to
which religious loyalties complicated the practice of coalition building
during the 1950s (Figure 4.5).

auspice of Kakungulu's Uganda Muslim Community (UMC) to challenge
the formation of the National Association for the Advancement of Muslims,
a pro-Obote political organisation. For further discussion see RDA D/128.5
A.K. Mayanja to Archbishop of Uganda, Rwanda and Burundi, and the
Archbishop of Kampala, 29 November 1967; RDA D/128.5 A.K. Mayanja,
Ali Kulumba, and Yusufu Sirimani Matovu, 'Press Statement', Uganda Muslim
Community, 1967.

Buganda's Muslims, however, were not the only politically marginalised actors in Buganda. By creating political space for Muslims, activists such as Mayanja developed alliances that intentionally prevented a Catholic commoner, Benedicto Kiwanuka, from becoming Uganda's prime minister. Catholic devotees constituted the majority of Buganda's population in the twentieth century. But colonial bureaucrats and Protestant chiefs following the 1890s had displaced them. On the eve of independence, Ganda Catholics became the focal point of ridicule and opposition among patriots and secessionists. A demographic majority, yet politically ostracised, Catholic activists throughout the twentieth century developed innovative ways of contesting and re-imagining power. Catholic political imagination and practice in Buganda found its strongest expression in the slogan of the Democratic Party, 'Truth and Justice', *Amazima ne Obwekanya*, to which I now turn.

5 | *Benedicto K.M. Kiwanuka: Justice and Catholic Dissent, c. 1879–c. 1962*

Therefore anything or anybody that tries to alienate the Baganda's loyalty to his Highness the Kabaka is like the Nnabe (Termite-eater) which invades an ant-hill and drives out or kills not only the Queen but also the termites; the ant-hill becomes empty and desolate. The Baganda curse such an event in relation to the Kabaka, anybody who tries to play the Nnabe as far as this Kingdom is concerned will be condemned both by God and by history [. . .] If the party supported by the Roman Catholic Church comes into power that will be the end of this Kingdom. We have been warned.

Kabaka Yekka pamphlet[1]

I turned to the Holy Bible for guidance. What had we done? Why should everyone be working against us? At Chapter 11 of St. Paul's Epistle to the Romans I came across Verse 33: 'Oh the depth of the riches of the wisdom and the knowledge of God! How incomprehensible are his judgements, and how unsearchable his ways!' How unsearchable indeed! We were defeated, but was it genuine? Then I remembered another saying: '[. . .] for the children of this world are wiser in their generation than the children of light.' Indeed they are! But there was another saying against these children: 'You serpents, generation of vipers, how will you flee from the judgement of hell?' and again, 'Woe to you, [. . .] because you are like to whited sepulchres, which outwardly appear to men beautiful but within are full of dead men's bones and of all filthiness.' (Matt. 23). How meaningful were the words in this Holy Book!

Benedicto K.M. Kiwanuka[2]

This chapter examines the history of the conception of political justice in colonial Buganda. It begins by showing how colonial change fostered the emergence of competing interpretations of social justice in the kingdom's Protestant and Catholic communities. It next

---

[1] ICS PP.UG.KY 'Kabaka Yekka: A Thought on His Grace the Archbishop of Rubaga and Metropolitan Letter', [c. Late 1961].
[2] RDA 904.4 B.M. Kiwanuka, '1962 Uganda Elections', Mss., n.d., p. 26.

explores the political settlement of Buddu, where Ganda Catholics fled
after the religious wars of the early 1890s. From Buddu, Catholics
worked to unsettle Buganda's Protestant hierarchy. Whereas elite
Protestants used the language of *sala 'musango* to talk about justice
in the state, Catholics tended to talk about *obwenkanya*, whose noun
stem derived from *–kkaanya*, a word that emphasised political inclusivity and the practice of two disparate communities coming together
to be equally heard. I next turn to the political career of Benedicto
Kiwanuka (1922–72). The force of Catholic history in Uganda influenced Kiwanuka's early sensibilities, which were reshaped in time by
European political thought. As Buganda's monarchy was politically
shaken during the *Kabaka* crisis in the mid-1950s, Kiwanuka studied law and European intellectual history at the University of London.
After two years of practising law in Kampala, Kiwanuka became the
president of the Democratic Party (DP), Uganda's preeminent Catholic
party. Kiwanuka was appointed Uganda's first prime minister on 1
March 1962. The DP used the slogan of *amazima n'obwenkanya* (truth
and justice) to complicate authoritative conceptions of political participation. Kiwanuka used both Catholic theology and classical liberalism
to develop this idea further. Using the autobiography of the erstwhile
Protestant John Henry Cardinal Newman, *Apologia Pro Vita Sua*,
Kiwanuka created a moral vocabulary that challenged Protestants and
nationalists, such as Abubakar Mayanja, to stop obstructing Catholic
political participation. Kiwanuka also drew from John Locke and
Jean-Jacques Rousseau to envision a state without politically obstructive sovereigns, a liberal kingdom whose 'people can live in harmony
without fear, want or discrimination based on tribe, religion or race'.

In the previous chapter, I showed that Buganda's marginalised
Muslim communities used history to pluralise a past from which
they could talk about power in ways that were consistent with the
mid-1800s, a moment when the state was governed by Muslim kings.
Ganda Muslims, led by a Ganda prince, sought to recapture political
space in Buganda that had been lost during the 1890s. Ali Kulumba
and Abubakar Mayanja marketed themselves as patriots and polemists,
gatekeepers of Buganda's monarchy in the postcolonial state. In consequence, Ganda Muslims shaped the internal affairs of Buganda's kingdom in the early 1960s in ways that were not possible during colonial
rule. By contrast, Benedicto Kiwanuka was not a royal; nor was
Buganda's Catholic community a demographic minority. This altered

the dynamics significantly. Protestant powerbrokers in Buganda and Uganda were willing to partner with B/Uganda's Muslim minority population to contest Catholic claims to state power. Whereas Muslim activists, such as Abubakar Mayanja, considered themselves defenders of Buganda's monarchy during decolonisation, Kiwanuka pushed Buganda's monarchy away from royal patronage, ethnicity and Protestant devotion. He contended that Buganda's kingdom should be subject to the political processes of national liberalisation and undergo complete integration into a unified state. His liberalising project was too radical for many Baganda; he maintained power for less than one year.

Justice in Kaggwa's Historiography

Two years following the signing of the 1900 Agreement, *Katikkiro* Apolo Kaggwa published *Engero za Baganda*, *Folktales of the Baganda*. In the collection, he produced eighteen stories that were selected 'for all our young people in Uganda to read and learn'.[3] Kaggwa's fables were politically instructive; each story was designed to produce 'some helpful lesson [. . .]' that called readers to 'think out carefully what it all means, and what it should teach'.[4] In his collection, Kaggwa recounted the story of Lunzi, one who journeyed 'from village lad to judge'.[5] One day, the story begins, the woodcutter Lunzi was chopping trees in a forest. After a hard day's work, he set out toward home with a piece of timber. But along the way, Lunzi passed the home of a friend, who insisted that he should stop and rest. Lunzi then placed the log against the stem of a nearby banana tree and joined his friend for a drink inside of the home. After the two entered, a hunter walked past the compound with his dogs, which frightened a sheep that was tied near the timber. When the sheep ran from the dogs, its rope snapped. The animal then slammed into the log, which collapsed onto and killed a young child.

Members of the community quickly apprehended Lunzi, whom they accused of murder. The child's death instigated a complicated

---

[3] Apolo Kaggwa, *The Tales of Sir Apolo: Uganda Folklore and Proverbs*, trans. by F. Rowling (London: The Religious Tract Society, 1934), p. 7.

[4] Ibid., p. 8.

[5] Ibid., pp. 54–8.

debate – Lunzi blamed the owner of the sheep; and the owner of the sheep accused the hunter, whose dogs triggered the immediate chain of events that resulted in the child's death. The three men were brought before a local court, whose chief was unable to reach a verdict. It was then decided that the trial should be moved to the *kabaka*'s high court in the capital. As the party travelled to Mmengo, a young man, Kalali, asked the delegation about their journey. Each of the three defendants narrated a different story:

The log cutter said: 'If the sheep had not butted my log, it would never have killed the child.' Then the sheep's owner said: 'If there had been no dogs to make my sheep break its rope and butt the log, the child would not have died.' But the hunter pleaded: 'If your sheep had not been scared without reason and broken its rope – since the dogs did not touch your sheep – then the child would not have died.'

After listening, Kalali concluded that each of the objects and animals in question were responsible for the child's death: 'If I had to judge the case, I should take the log, and the sheep, and the dogs, and burn them all: *they* are the wizards who have killed the child.' Without giving Kalali much consideration, though, the party continued their journey toward the court of the king, who, after listening to the case, was unable to 'come to any fair decision'.

After the king and his principal chiefs were unable to offer 'just judgment', the king learned about Kalali, whose 'good judgement' impressed the court. For his ability to cut cases with considerable discernment, Kalali was given the county of Busujju to govern, from whence he judged 'all matters concerning the princes and princesses of the land'. In Kaggwa's court, a commoner exhibited the wisdom of a king who was unable to mediate complicated cases. To resolve the hearing, Buganda's king handed the court over to Kalali. By demonstrating superior judgement, Kalali quickly ascended the state's hierarchy: the kingdom's royals were placed under his authority.

Kaggwa's story was both autobiographical and hagiographical. By recounting nineteenth-century folktales, he sought to illustrate his own ability and willingness to 'cut cases' on behalf of Buganda's monarchs, like Kalali. In the past, conceptions of political peace were tied to the institution and health of Buganda's monarchy. One dictionary defined peace in the early 1900s as *–mirembe*, the 'duration of

[a] king's reign'.[6] As guardians of peace and protectors of social welfare, respectable kings were believed to be superb adjudicators, willing to execute subjects who instigated violence and instability in the
state. 'The king is not the one who kills', suggested one proverb, 'but
the unjust accuser.'[7] By wielding oral traditions 'from the old people
who knew them best',[8] Kaggwa demonstrated that '[i]t does not matter whether good counsel comes from small or great – to those who
profit by it'.[9]

Kaggwa's argument reinforced broader claims that were being
developed by Buganda's Protestant chiefs to legitimise their control
of the state. Indeed, Kaggwa concluded *Bassekabaka be Buganda* by
recounting the history of the Ganda prime minister Mukasa, not the
history of a king.[10] Like Kalali, Mukasa's 'political career had humble
beginnings'. By the end of Muteesa I's kingship, however, Mukasa was
'the real ruler of the country, and Muteesa himself knew it'. And while
Kaggwa argued that Mukasa demonstrated ruthlessness, he was also
described as a real statesman who, with political skill and calm dignity, ensured political order through firmness.[11] The Protestant chief
Jemusi Miti suggested that Buganda's precolonial hierarchy entailed
a complex series of courts that were designed to facilitate an optimal
'administration of justice to all classes [. . .]'[12] Bartolomayo Zimbe,
in his comprehensive history, *Buganda ne Kabaka*, noted that Kintu,
Kintu kya Mukama, 'Kintu of God', had been divinely endowed to
administer justice. He argued that Baganda mostly believed that 'God
gave only Kabaka the power of killing another person and also to
give judgement to the people'.[13] Hamu Mukasa suggested that the
kings of Buganda were proverbially addressed, *Segulu ligamba enjuba*

---

[6] A.L. Kitching and G.R. Blackledge, *A Luganda-English and English-Luganda
Dictionary* (London: Society for Promoting Christian Knowledge, 1925), p. 64.

[7] Ferdinand Walser, *Luganda Proverbs* (Berlin: Reimer, 1982), no. 2041.

[8] Kaggwa, *The Tales of Sir Apolo*, p. 7.

[9] Ibid., p. 58.

[10] Apolo Kaggwa, *Bassekabaka be Buganda*, trans. by Semakula Kiwanuka (Nairobi,
Dar Es Salaam, Kampala: East African Publishing House, 1971), pp. 183–4.

[11] Ibid., p. 184.

[12] James Kibuka Miti Kabazzi, *Buganda, 1875–1900: A Centenary Contribution*,
trans. by G.K. Rock, 2 vols (London: United Society for Christian Literature,
n.d.), I, p. 22.

[13] B. Musoke Zimbe, *Buganda and the King*, trans. by F. Kamoga (Mengo,
Uganda, 1978), p. 8.

tegana munyazi', 'Heaven's word is not final, sunlight cannot prevent thieves'.[14] This implied that while the sun may give its light without prejudice, the *kabaka* could not. Pernicious subjects would be judged inevitably. By standardising the accounts of how arbitration operated in precolonial Buganda, Kaggwa and likeminded historians suggested that the responsibility of regulating justice rested with the kingdom's Protestant rulers, who, like Kalali, now controlled the state's courts.

Kaggwa and Mukasa used the language of authority to explain how jurisprudence supposedly worked in the past. Protestants recalled a period when kings held absolute power to administer justice. In the early 1880s, the linguist C.T. Wilson 'began collecting vocabularies of words from the natives with whom [he] came in contact',[15] and suggested that the infinitive form of the verb 'to judge', or its cognate 'judgement', centred on *msala* or *msangu*.[16] The Anglican missionary George L. Pilkington clarified Wilson's earlier entry in the late 1800s, and noted that *sala 'musango* meant to give a verdict during a case, derived from *sala*, defined, 'cut (as with saw or knife)'.[17] From the early to mid-twentieth century, Protestant dictionaries and grammars consistently categorised 'justice' and its derivatives as *sala (o)musango*.[18] This particular concept of 'justice' accentuated the legal qualities of juridical decisiveness, an authoritarian process of cutting and dividing off.[19] Justice was to be *decided* and *given* by a party in authority,[20] not negotiated. Following this tradition, E.M.K. Mulira and

---

[14] Ham Mukasa, 'The Rule of the Kings of Buganda', *Uganda Journal*, 10 (1946), 136–43 (pp. 136–7).

[15] C.T. Wilson, *An Outline Grammar of the Luganda Language* (London: Society for Promoting Christian Knowledge, 1882), p. vii.

[16] Ibid., p. 68.

[17] George L. Pilkington, *Luganda-English and English-Luganda Vocabulary* (London: Society for Promoting Christian Knowledge, 1899), p. 97.

[18] Henry W. Duta, *Elements of Luganda Grammar Together with Exercises and Vocabulary* (London: Society for Promoting Christian Knowledge, 1902), pp. 224 & 235; G.R. Blackledge, *Luganda-English and English-Luganda Vocabulary* (London: Society for Promoting Christian Knowledge, 1904), pp. 154 & 202; Charles W. Hattersley and Henry W. Duta, *Luganda Phrases and Idioms: For New Arrivals and Travellers in Uganda* (London: Society for Promoting Christian Knowledge, 1904), p. 49; W.A. Crabtree, *A Manual of Lu-Ganda* (Cambridge: Cambridge University Press, 1921), pp. 172 & 220; Kitching and Blackledge, *A Luganda-English and English-Luganda Dictionary*, p. 91.

[19] Kitching and Blackledge, *A Luganda-English and English-Luganda Dictionary*, p. 91.

[20] Crabtree, *A Manual of Lu-Ganda*, p. 172.

E.G.M. Ndawula in 1952, while revising Kitching and Blackledge's dictionary (1925), defined 'justice' as *èby'ênsonga, èby-obutuukìrìvu*;[21] the former derived its meaning from an earlier usage of the transitive verb *–kusonga*, meaning to 'prod, poke, pierce',[22] or *òkugoba ensonga*, to 'stick to the point'.[23] By adopting the metaphors of saws and poking irons, Protestants reinforced the boundaries of colonial jurisprudence: those with saws and prodding sticks (Protestants), and those without (Muslims and Catholics).

Catholic intellectuals, by contrast, argued that by the early 1900s the state's Protestant rulers were not practising justice in ways that were consistent with the past, a time when negotiation and discussion characterised social justice. For Catholics, the inequities of Protestant justice were energised by a disproportionate allocation of land and the practice of withholding government employment based upon religious devotion. While Catholics constituted the majority of Buganda's early twentieth-century population, they were apportioned only 37.4 per cent of general land in Buganda, whereas 61.7 per cent was allotted to Protestant counties.[24] Catholic chiefs, moreover, received approximately 35.5 per cent of *mailo* distribution between 1900 and 1905, whereas approximately 60.6 per cent was distributed to Protestant chiefs. Administrative appointments and salaries were also considerably less for Catholic chiefs.[25] One report suggested that whereas Catholics constituted 14 per cent more of Buganda's general population

---

[21] E.M.K. Mulira and E.G.M. Ndawula, *A Luganda-English and English-Luganda Dictionary*, 2nd edn (London: Society for Promoting Christian Knowledge, 1952), p. 174.

[22] Blackledge, *Luganda-English and English-Luganda Vocabulary*, p. 88; Kitching and Blackledge, *A Luganda-English and English-Luganda Dictionary*, p. 97.

[23] Mulira and Ndawula, *A Luganda-English and English-Luganda Dictionary*, p. 89.

[24] Henry W. West, *The Mailo System in Buganda: A Preliminary Case Study in African Land Tenure* (Entebbe: Government Printer, 1965), p. 173.

[25] In his history of religions in Uganda, Revd Fr J.L. Ddiba suggested that Protestants had argued that they were pressured by colonial officers to distribute land while Catholics were away from the capital: *Olwo obuganda bwonna aba Protestanti nga babwekomya. N'okugamba nga bagamba nti 'abakatoliki bwe balidda tujja kubagamba nti twalaba temuliiwo obwami bwammwe netubugabana kati tewaliiwo bwami butalina nnyinibwo: Tunakola tutya'* (Rev Fr J.L. Ddiba, *Eddini mu Uganda*, 2 vols (Masaka, Uganda: St. Liberatum Printing Press, 1967), II, pp. 174–5).

by 1934, they occupied 22 per cent fewer chieftaincies, resulting in 35 per cent less in salary earnings.[26]

As a consequence of social discrimination, Catholics argued that Protestant justice was tantamount to political disorder. It was concluded that Kaggwa was a purveyor of confusion in Buganda's courts and legislative bodies. Catholics created songs that critiqued Kaggwa's inability to adjudicate: 'My friends, people confuse me, // They have that man // They call him 'kaggwa' (thorn) // What type of (thorn) kaggwa? // The one used to remove jiggers!'[27] In the lyrics, Catholic innovators played on the *li-ma* noun class in Luganda, which was often used to describe items that were hard, bare or flat.[28] Kaggwa, like a thorn (*erigwa*), typified a short and pointed object that lacked grace and sophistication.

Among Catholics, Kaggwa was colloquially referred to as Gulemye, a phrase that he purportedly used in court to describe a difficult case that could not be easily settled.[29] One proverb read: *Gulemye: eyalemera e Mmengo*, 'A trial unable to be settled: so says the one who can't settle it at Mmengo.'[30] Conversely, Catholics lauded the Catholic chief minister of justice Stanislaus Mugwanya for the ability to practice conversational and inclusive politics.[31] Mugwanya was compared to a proverbial rope that could be used to tie the one who could not administer equity in Buganda's capital, Kaggwa (Gulemye): 'We have a man here // I don't announce his name // I call him a strong 'mugwa' (rope) // The woven mugwa (rope) // Which will tie Gulemye.'[32] Not only did the song associate Kaggwa to a thorn; it likened Mugwanya to a long and elaborate rope, as opposed to a small rope or a simple string, *akagwa*, a word that resembled the intonation of 'Kaggwa'.

[26] RDA 31.6 'Synopsis of Comparative List of Catholic and Protestant Chiefs in Buganda', 1934.

[27] Joseph S. Kasirye, *Obulamu bwa Stanislaus Mugwanya* (Dublin: Typescript found in Seeley Library, University of Cambridge, 1963), p. 45.

[28] W.A. Crabtree, *Elements of Luganda Grammar: Together with Exercises and Vocabulary* (Kampala: Uganda Bookshop), 1923, p. 84.

[29] Walser, *Luganda Proverbs*, no. 1927.

[30] Henry W. Duta, *Engero za Baganda* (London: Society for Promoting Christian Knowledge, 1902), 1152.

[31] 'Stanislas Mugwanya G.C.S.S.', *Munno*, 23/2 1912, pp. 164–5; '*Ebaluwa ya S. Mugwanya (Ng'eyita eri His Highness Kabaka we Buganda)*', *Munno*, April 1921, pp. 85–6; Kasirye, *Obulamu bwa Stanislaus Mugwanya*, p. 46.

[32] Kasirye, *Obulamu bwa Stanislaus Mugwanya*, p. 45.

Catholic intellectuals employed the language of thorns and string to show that social challenges should be addressed through extensive talks and inclusivity. Like a long woven rope, debates were remembered as being lengthy and involving multiple parties (or strands). It suggested that developed forms of justice are characterised by prolonged arbitration and drawn-out conversations. As one Luganda proverb recalled, *Embozi teba nkadde*, 'A conversation does not grow old'. Gulemye's vision of justice was problematic precisely because it undercut power sharing and inclusive forms of justice. Social conversation had halted; political stability was improbable. If the story of Lunzi was autobiographical, in that it recounted a king who handed his court over to an able adjudicator, Catholic songs could just as convincingly argue that Kalali (Kaggwa or Gulemye) was as incompetent as an earlier generation of kings.

Contesting Kaggwa: Early Catholic Society and the Invention of –*kkaanya*

Military conflict in Buganda's capital during the 1890s resulted in extensive migration, during which Catholics resettled in the western region of Buddu, a territory that was removed from the king's palace by two counties. John Mary Waliggo's research indicated that approximately 15,000 to 20,000 Catholics emigrated in 1892, leaving only one-third of Buganda's Catholic population outside of Buddu.[33] Catholic chiefs by 1894 had begun to articulate concerns about exclusion to the Anglican bishop Alfred R. Tucker, to whom it was argued that Catholics were distanced from the practice of power in the kingdom through forced migration and underrepresentation. Catholics, recalled Tucker, 'contended that they had been unjustly treated and that more territorial chieftainships had been promised to them than had actually been assigned to them; that their isolation in Budu prevented them from taking any part in the government of their country [. . .]'.[34] Narratives about marginalisation circulated widely

---

[33] John M. Waliggo, 'The Catholic Church in the Buddu Province of Buganda, 1879–1925' (unpublished PhD, Cambridge: University of Cambridge, 1976), pp. 81–4.
[34] Alfred R. Tucker, *Eighteen Years in Uganda and East Africa*, 2 vols (London: Edward Arnold, 1908), I, p. 243.

between Ganda and French Catholics by the early twentieth century. Stories that accentuated discrimination and violence were commonly discussed in missionary letters, sermons and Catholic historiography. As one account poignantly noted, '[i]t is therefore appropriate to remark that Catholic missionaries and their neophytes were being intensely tracked by hostile agents of [the Imperial British East Africa Company] and their proponents [. . .]'.[35]

Society in Buddu was restructured around Catholic practice. As the historian Father Waliggo argued, Buddu 'became for [Catholics] "a place to feel at home", a "wilderness" to which God called them for spiritual renewal before expanding to other areas [. . .] a worthy substitute for the wider political and religious kingdom they had hoped and prayed for but lost'.[36] Catholic chiefs enforced catechism, employed catechists as civil chaplains and marched devotees to church on Sunday.[37] Catholic and Buganda's royal material culture were blended together to produce administration and architecture in Buddu. By July 1892, Buddu's *ppookino* (*ssaza* chief), Alikisi Ssebowa, established four administrative departments near the Villa Maria mission, Buddu's foremost Catholic centre. Each department was named after an administrative unit in Buganda's monarchy: *ekitongole ekirowooza* (office of planning); *ekitongole ekitabaazi* (warriors' department); *ekitongole ekigo* (construction department); and *ekitongole ekijjomanyi*, a department that fined converts who failed to devote ample time toward the work of the church.[38]

The architecture of Villa Maria was constructed to reflect Buganda's capital. The central cathedral was built according to royal protocol and subsequently titled *Twekobe*, the official residence of the king.[39] The Catholic God was also given monarchical titles: *Kabaka* (king),

---

[35] Ernest Layer, *Les Pères Blancs et la Civilisation dans l'Ouganda* (Rouen: Imprimerie Cagniard, 1909), p. 25. For further discussion see J.J. Hirth to A.S.L.J. Livinhac, 15 June 1892, in *L'ouganda et les Agissements de la Compagnie Anglaise "East-Africa"* (Paris: Missions D'Afrique, 1892), pp. 114–25 (p. 115); Aylward Shorter, *Cross and Flag in Africa: The "White Fathers" During the Colonial Scramble (1892–1914)* (Maryknoll, MD: Orbis Books, 2006), pp. 4–14.

[36] Waliggo, 'The Catholic Church in the Buddu Province of Buganda', p. 5.

[37] John Iliffe, *Honour in African History* (Cambridge: Cambridge University Press, 2005), p. 178.

[38] Waliggo, 'The Catholic Church in the Buddu Province of Buganda', pp. 105–6.

[39] Ibid., pp. 106–7.

Ssalongo (father of twins), *Ssebintu* (an extravagantly wealthy person), *Ssemanda* (all-powerful) and *Kamalabyonna* (one with final say).[40] The White Fathers' compound was constructed near *Twekobe* and was encircled with decorated fencing that mirrored *lubaale* shrines.[41] The residence of Buddu's queen mother (*nnamasole*), the Virgin Mary, also reflected precolonial topography. Like the *nnamasole*, the Virgin was provided with a separate residence on an adjacent hill, the *Chapelle de Notre Dame*, where converts prayed for children. Mary was given the variant titles of Buganda's *nnamasole*, including *nnaluggi* (head-door) and *nnabijjano* (one who is full of surprises) (Figure 5.1).

The intensity of Catholic fervour and the replication of royal culture unsettled colonial officials, who suggested that it was 'the very universal belief that Buddu-ese obstruct the introduction of any outside element into their province'.[42] Colonial reports indicated that the question of religious loyalties had to be particularly taken into account when distributing chieftaincies in Buddu and neighbouring Kooki, whose chiefs and activists were decisively Protestant (Figure 5.2).[43] Catholic and Protestant tensions in Buddu and Kooki were a prominent concern throughout the early colonial period. And reports show that the burning of Catholic churches continued to be a problem in Kooki into the 1910s.[44] The long history of this tension may help partially explain, in time, why the Kooki and Buddu politicians E.M.K. Mulira and Benedicto Kiwanuka were not fully able to bring themselves to consolidate their respective political parties, which had been initially discussed between the two.

Tensions in western Buganda were also evident between Catholic factions in northern Buddu and Protestants in southern Ggomba, two counties that were divided along the Katonga River. On the river's northern bank, Protestants sang toward Buddu, evoking images that concerned manners and etiquette to shame their neighbours: 'I don't want to sit where a papist sits. I don't want to sit where a papist eats. I don't want to dip my fingers in the same place with a papist.'[45]

---

[40] Ibid., p. 126.
[41] Ibid., p. 107.
[42] UNA SMP A43/43/25 Deputy Commissioner to Sub-Commissioner, Kampala, 2 December 1907.
[43] UNA SMP A43/43/24 'District Report, Buddu', October 1907.
[44] UNA SMP A46/668 'Acting Commissioner of Masaka's Report on Koki Tour', 17 December 1912.
[45] Waliggo, 'The Catholic Church in the Buddu Province of Buganda', p. 84.

Figure 5.1 Chapelle de Notre Dame, Villa Maria, Buddu, late 1800s
Source: MA Photothèque Missionnaires d'Afrique Rome

Protestants mocked Catholics by arguing that one could not be both a
Catholic and a Muganda. '*Ssi muganda mukatoliki*', asserted one saying, He's not a Muganda; he's a Catholic.[46] In response to Protestant
ridicule, Catholics chanted the threat of war across Katonga toward
Ggomba: 'The person who crosses [. . .], Will open the gun muzzles.'[47]

Throughout the early colonial period, Catholic intellectuals were
challenged to adapt their theology and history to think about the (re)
invention of equitable hierarchies in Ganda society. As Carol Summers
has usefully argued, the creation of hierarchies that could actually be
ascended was never far removed from the activism of Catholic dissenters during the interwar period.[48] Like Muslim historians, Catholic
writers worked to imagine an idyllic past, a period when all Baganda
could expect to have an opportunity to participate fully in the life of
high politics. Whereas Protestant historians such as Kaggwa chroni-

[46] Fred B. Welbourn, *Religion and Politics in Uganda: 1952–1962* (Nairobi: East
African Publishing House, 1965), p. 6.
[47] Kasirye, *Obulamu bwa Stanislaus Mugwanya*, p. 39.
[48] Carol Summers, 'Catholic Action and Ugandan Radicalism: Political Activism
in Buganda, 1930–1950', *Journal of Religion in Africa*, 39 (2009), 60–90.

Figure 5.2 'Bridge across the river Kisoma the boundary of Koki and Budu
The river is overgrown with papyrus, and the water is probably 4 or 5 ft
deep', c. early 1900s
Source: EEPA 1998–002–0049. Uganda Photographs, 1897–1903,
Eliot Elisofon Photographic Archives, National Museum of African Art,
Smithsonian Institution

cled the emergence and legitimacy of non-royalist authority, seen in
the likes of Kalali, Catholic missionaries and Baganda talked about
returning to the capital to participate in the life of the high court.
Shaped by conversations with Ganda Catholics in the 1910s, Henri
LeVeux's *Vocabulaire Luganda-Français* elucidated the meaning of a
court trial (*omusango*) by talking about the possibility of adjudica-
tion before the *kabaka*. For LeVeux, this process entailed returning to
Mmengo to partake in the process of negotiation: *Yadza omusango ku
Kabaka*, 'S/He has returned to court before the *kabaka*.'[49] Buganda's
capital was described as a place where Baganda distinctly returned
('faire ramener') in order to win trials: *Yabidza ku Kibuga*, 'S/he has

[49] R.P. LeVeux, *Premier Essai de Vocabulaire Luganda-Français d'Après l'Ordre
Étymologique* (Alger: Maison-Carrée, 1917), p. 669.

won [obtained justice] in the capital.'[50] By juxtaposing the processes of returning to Buganda's capital alongside the institution of justice, Catholics recalled a moment in the past when due process was not obstructed.

In time, Catholics employed *–bwenkanya* to talk about justice, a word that starkly contrasted the restrictive language of *sala 'musango*. Prior to the Second World War, there does not appear to be any extensive use of *–bwenkanya* (*–kkaanya*) to describe legal or political justice.[51] Its earliest appearances emphasised the importance of social inclusivity. In an article entitled *Omukristu Omutegevu Ky'alowoza ku by'Olutalo*, 'What a True Christian Thinks about War',[52] for instance, one writer maintained that 'truth and justice' (*amazima n'obwenkanya*) called Christians to attend to the travail of a weaker person or disenfranchised citizens. Consistent with the definition of *–kkaanya* (to discuss or to agree), then, the writer used *–bwenkanya* to underscore the correlation between social stability and attainable justice. Created by conjoining the conditional prefix *bwe*[53] with the infinitive form of the verb *–kukkanya*, the gloss simply meant to be in a 'state in which' *–kkaanya* was observable. Earlier definitions interpreted *–kkaanya* as to 'discuss matters'[54] or 'recognise by careful scrutiny';[55] it implied togetherness or the practice of paying attention to somebody.[56] In a society governed by *–bwenkanya*, competing parties are guaranteed unencumbered due process and equal representation in the affairs of statebuilding, both of which were not extended to Buganda's Catholic faction by the Protestant architects of Buganda's colonial order.

---

[50] Ibid., p. 107.

[51] This is based upon an analysis of *Munno* prior to the 1950s and a review of six Catholic grammars and dictionaries published between the mid-1890s and 1932. For this word study, I also interrogated twelve Protestant dictionaries and grammars published between the late 1890s and 1951. For further discussion on these sources see Jonathon L. Earle, 'Political Theologies in Late Colonial Buganda' (unpublished PhD, Cambridge: University of Cambridge, 2012), p. 206.

[52] 'Omukristu omutegevu ky'alowoza ku by'olutalo', *Munno*, April 1940.

[53] J.D. Chesswas, *The Essentials of Luganda*, 4th edn (Nairobi: Oxford University Press, 1963), p. 109.

[54] *Elements of Luganda Grammar Together with Exercises and Vocabulary*, p. 188; Blackledge, *Luganda-English and English-Luganda Vocabulary*, p. 30.

[55] *Elements of Luganda Grammar Together with Exercises and Vocabulary*, p. 188.

[56] LeVeux, *Premier Essai de Vocabulaire Luganda-Français d'Après l'Ordre Étymologique*, p. 398.

Amazima n'obwenkanya and the Birth of the Democratic Party

By the mid-1950s, the language of participatory justice had begun to shape the way that Catholic intellectuals talked about monarchical power and popular representation. Throughout *Kabaka* Muteesa II's exile, Catholics worked to insert themselves into a political process from which they had been noticeably removed for five decades. During the Namirembe Conference (Chapter 3), Eridadi M.K. Mulira advocated for the constitutional rights of Buganda's rural peasantry. His vision for a commoners' kingdom, though, further entrenched Protestant control of the state.[57] Three Catholic priests worked to undermine Mulira's project during the Negotiations: Father J.K. Masagazi, Father J. Kasule and Bishop Joseph Kiwanuka. With Buganda's Catholic *omulamuzi*, Matayo Mugwanya, these delegates constituted the most outspoken critics of B/Uganda's Protestant government. The implementation of colonial rule, they argued, had created a kingdom where due process was no longer guaranteed. The majority of citizens in Buganda were unable to participate in the arena of kingdom politics. 'Historically', noted Mugwanya, 'the Baganda had the right of direct access [. . .] but in Luganda the office of the Resident is called "Kagangu", which means an ante-chamber.'[58] Building upon Mugwanya's point, Father Masagazi asserted that there was no difference between a provincial commissioner and Buganda's resident;[59] both obstructed due process. Baganda chiefs and colonial residents were inexperienced, observed Bishop Kiwanuka, 'often immature young men who adopted a super-cilious attitude, and were incapable of co-operating with the Baganda'.[60]

Catholic activists used the Conference to renegotiate representative ratios in Buganda's government that would accurately mirror the state's religious demographics. In the sixteenth meeting, Mugwanya and Father Masagazi challenged Article 31 of the recommendations

---

[57] ICS 29/1/17/17 Namirembe Conference Minutes, Seventeenth Meeting, 7 September 1954, p. 4; *Uganda Protectorate: Buganda* (London: Her Majesty's Stationary Office, 1954), p. 13.

[58] ICS 29/1/17/5 Namirembe Conference Minutes, Fifth Meeting, 6 August 1954, p. 5.

[59] ICS 29/1/17/16 Namirembe Conference Minutes, Sixteenth Meeting, 6 September 1954, p. 8.

[60] Ibid., p. 10.

and Article 5 of the 1900 Agreement. Article 5 had stipulated an 'equally applicable' clause to the administration of statutory law within Buganda. It emphasised the moral responsibility of 'Her Majesty's Government' to faithfully administer justice without discrimination.[61] In Article 31 of the new recommendations, the constitutional burden of national governance was placed on the kingdom's Protestant parliament: 'The *Buganda Government* shall administer the services for which it is responsible in accordance with the general policy of the Protectorate Government and in conformity with the laws governing those services.'[62] Mugwanya and Father Masagazi saw this as a Protestant attempt to reify power. Mugwanya argued that 'long before the British came to the country, the Baganda had developed a system of settling their disputes that resembled the British'.[63] The practice of justice 'worked excellently', furthered Mugwanya, 'and the Baganda dreamt of nothing better'.[64] He contended that under British rule, however, courts were often disrupted by Protestant chiefs, who by 'virtue of their social status attended the court [and] took part in judgement'.[65] By pointing toward an idyllic past, Buganda's foremost Catholic chief worked to weaken Protestant control of the state's local and high courts. But the argument ultimately failed to guarantee religious quotas.

In a further attempt to dislodge Protestant power in the 1950s, Mugwanya contested the state's foremost seat in the *Lukiiko*, the *katikkiro*ship, which had been a *de facto* Protestant post from the 1890s onward. According to one Catholic historian, Mugwanya was predicted to win the election. *Kabaka* Muteesa II, however, ordered members of the *Lukiiko* to vote for the Protestant conservative Mikaeri Kintu, which secured his bid.[66] A.D. Lubowa was Buganda's *omulamuzi* in the late 1950s and a member of the *Lukiiko* during the *katikkiro* election in the mid-1950s. When I interviewed him, he

---

[61] 'The Uganda Agreement of 1900' (Article 5).

[62] *Uganda Protectorate: Buganda*, p. 12. (Italics added.)

[63] ICS 29/1/12/18 Constitutional Committee Minutes, Eighteenth Meeting, 23 July 1954, p. 2.

[64] Ibid.

[65] Ibid.

[66] Anonymous, *A Short History of the Democratic Party*, ed. by Richard Muscat (Rome: Foundation for African Development, 1984), p. 26.

recalled the use of unethical voting practices to secure Mugwanya's defeat:

[J]ust before the *kabaka* came back, there was a need to form a government and there was a need to elect a *katikkiro*. Then, I'm sorry to say, religion became very much at play. And the reason why Matayo Mugwanya lost was not because he was inferior [. . .], no; he was much, much better than Kintu [. . .] But what spoilt him was religion.[67]

After Kintu secured the election, non-Catholic writers in the Luganda press gave thanks to God for Mugwanya's defeat. Mugwanya's supporters were identified as the *kabaka*'s enemies,[68] a precedence that continued up until independence.

Following the election, Mugwanya secured a vacant seat in the *Lukiiko* for the county of Mawokota, an election that he won in a landslide.[69] In 1957, though, Muteesa II and Kintu revoked Mugwanya's appointment. They argued that Mugwanya could not maintain the appointment due to his membership in the East African Traffic Advisory Board, which, it was suggested, would compromise the economic interests of the kingdom.[70] In less than two years following Muteesa's return from exile, Buganda's political hierarchy effectively crushed Buganda's foremost Catholic politician. Evident discrimination against Mugwanya accelerated the intensification of Catholic nationalism in the 1950s, which was given its most robust expression in the rise of DP politics.

The DP was organised by eight Ganda Catholics on 6 October 1954. Joseph Kasolo, an engineer who had worked in northern Uganda, was the party's first president.[71] Before he passed away, I spent time interviewing L. Mathias Tyaba, who was the last surviving founder of DP. Across several afternoons, we discussed the circumstances surrounding the emergence of the Party in the mid-1950s. Tyaba recalled that the Party was organised to challenge Protestantism and communism

---

[67] Interview, A.D. Lubowa, 23 November 2009, Maya, Mpigi District.
[68] *Uganda Post*, 26 August 1955; *Dobozi lya Buganda*, 29 August 1955.
[69] Anonymous, *A Short History of the Democratic Party*, p. 27.
[70] *Sekanyolya*, 16 November 1956; Welbourn, *Religion and Politics in Uganda*, p. 18.
[71] Simon Mwebe and Anthony Sserubiri, *Ebyafaayo bya D.P., 1954–1984* (Kampala: Foundation for African Development, [c.] 1984), pp. 12–14.

during the Cold War.[72] For founding members, the threat of communism reflected older tensions between Buganda's Catholic and Protestant factions. According to Tyaba, by 1954 he had concluded that leading Protestant thinkers, such as Ignatius K. Musazi and Thomas Makumbi (E.M.K. Mulira's brother-in-law), were communists. During a period when Protestants were obstructing Catholic mobility in the _Lukiiko_, Tyaba and his colleagues believed that Protestants would use communist teaching and policies to further legitimise the discrimination of Catholic communities.

To confront Protestant communism and religious discrimination, DP activists used the language of _amazima n'obwenkanya_. The term _amazima_, which focused on 'truth', was used to talk about creating political realities that correctly reflected Buganda's religious demographics. It called for fair political representation and Catholic employment opportunities, land distributions and appointments in the _Lukiiko_. _Obwenkanya_, as I have shown, embodied a particular reading of justice that contrasted _sala 'musango_ by the mid-1940s: the former emphasised participation and conversation; the latter authority and decisiveness. By implementing 'truth' and 'justice', Catholics sought to legitimise the integrity and divine character of their project, calling Protestants to turn away from prejudicial politics. After losing his bid for the post of _katikkiro_, Mugwanya cited _amazima n'obwenkanya_ to respond to claims that he was an enemy of Buganda's throne. Mugwanya advised his opponents to turn toward God, 'to walk in the path of Truth'.[73] He observed that 'God notes everyone's action and Satan cannot erase it'.[74] Whereas DP activists aimed to create a society along the lines of _amazima n'obwenkanya_, Protestants had created 'a game for deceit and cunning'.[75]

---

[72] Ganda Catholics critiqued communism in print as early as 1940. It was argued that communism would adversely impact 35 million Catholics living in central Europe (_'Ensonga Ennungi Ey'abangereza N'abafransa mu Lutalo Luno'_, _Munno_, 1 March 1940, p. 30). In 1947, concerns were further heightened when Semakula Mulumba petitioned the United Nations through the Soviet delegate Andrei Gromyko (James Mulira, 'Nationalism and Communist Phobia in Colonial Uganda, 1945–1960', _Mawazo_, 5 (1983), 3–16 (pp. 3–4).

[73] _Uganda Eyogera_, 11 October 1955.

[74] Ibid.

[75] _'Ebbaluwa ya Mgr. J. Kiwanuka'_, _Munno_, 10 April 1957, pp. 3 & 5. For further discussion see 'New Political Party Formed in Uganda: To Prepare Blue-Print for Self-Government', _Uganda Argus_, 21 August 1956, p. 1; 'Democratic

Simon Mwebe was a leading DP activist in the late 1950s. During our discussions, he shared with me that he was first attracted to the Party while studying at Aggrey Memorial, where he observed social discrimination against Catholics and Muslims.[76] For Mwebe, DP provided organised space to dispute religious discrimination. Reflecting on the Party's early ethos, he recalled: 'Because for us, we don't believe in segregation at all, because that is the declared philosophy of the Democratic Party. That's why the Democratic Party came into being, for opposing discrimination [. . .] because of [the faith] he believes in [. . .] This is fundamental for the Democratic Party!'[77] When Mwebe talked about *amazima n'obwenkanya*, he discussed the gospels. Jesus Christ laboured to create a society governed by a universal franchise, within which communities were not excluded due to religious affiliation. Whereas Protestants in colonial Buganda only 'spoke' with other Protestants, Jesus, he stated, interacted with everyone; he was willing to delegate power. Mwebe recalled:

The problem was during those days, in the fifties, there was very much discrimination in government circles, when giving jobs and all that between the Protestants and the Catholics. So, when these people wanted to fight, *Catholics* wanted *to fight* that imbalance, they used the slogan of "Truth and Justice" [. . .] *Religious difference* was the most important drive, yes [. . .] It's a *very big* problem.[78]

Amazima n'obwenkanya was not abstract political theology for Mwebe and the early founders of the Party; it called communities to undo and recreate the kingdom's colonial order. By instituting *amazima n'obwenkanya*, activists believed that they were redressing a fundamental social wrong, a kingdom skewed by religious politics.

Benedicto Kiwanuka became the president of the Democratic Party in August 1958. Under his leadership, the Party transitioned from being a predominantly Catholic organisation in Buganda to a religiously

---

Party', *Munno*, 22 August 1956, p. 5; '*Ebigambo bya Mugwanya By'agamba*', *Munno*, 4 June 1957.

[76] Interview, Simon Mwebe, 17 March 2010, Kampala.
[77] Ibid., 11 February 2010, Kampala.
[78] Emphases are Mwebe's.

inclusive national movement.[79] But while his party moved onto the stage of national politics to oppose Milton Obote's Uganda People's Congress (UPC), which had superseded Musazi's Uganda National Congress by the late 1950s, Kiwanuka's politics were clearly informed by Buganda's Catholic historiography. His library included bound volumes of the Catholic newspaper *Munno* from the 1920s, and he collected editions throughout the 1950s that he frequently annotated. In the early 1960s, Kiwanuka ordered a copy of Joseph S. Kasirye's *Obulamu bwa Stanislaus Mugwanya, The Life of Stanslaus Mugwanya*,[80] whose Catholic focus complicated Protestant biographies. And in 1962, Kiwanuka circulated a sixty-one-page political manifesto on colonial Uganda, which he began by scrutinising the history of religions in Buganda.[81] For Kiwanuka, the motivations driving Protestant and Muslim efforts in the UPC and *Kabaka Yekka* (KY) to derail Catholic politics were traceable to the kingdom's religious wars during the late nineteenth-century. Kiwanuka asked: 'Haven't Kabaka Yekka Leaders declared openly that their aim is to destroy the Democratic Party not only in Buganda but throughout Uganda? And why "to destroy?"'[82] He continued: 'There is no other reason, in my way of thinking, than the one I have given which is based on our history rather than on anything else. You have got to know our history in order to understand Mengo behaviour.'

Party intellectuals had translated 'truth and justice' into moral capital to equalise lopsided representative ratios in Buganda's parliament. Kiwanuka's project pushed these claims even further. For Kiwanuka, *amazima n'obwenkanya* promised the possibility of creating a liberalised kingdom, where political representation in Buganda and Uganda was not predetermined by religious boundaries or disruptive Protestant kings. During a period of escalating secessionist politicking

---

[79] Michael Twaddle, 'Was the Democratic Party of Uganda a Purely Confessional Party?', in *Christianity in Independent Africa*, ed. by Edward Fasholé-Luke (Bloomington, IN: Indiana University Press, 1978), pp. 255–66. On 2 December 2009 and 17 February 2012, I conducted two interviews with Professor William Senteza Kajubi, who was the most prominent Protestant in the Democratic Party. For discussion on the role of Protestants within the larger move toward nationalisation see Earle, *Political Theologies in Late Colonial Buganda*, pp. 227–8.

[80] BKMKP Minister without Portfolio: Miscellaneous 'Educational Secretary General for Catholic Missions', order form, n.d.

[81] RDA 904.4 Kiwanuka, '1962 Uganda Election', p. 2.

[82] Ibid., p. 21.

in Mmengo, Kiwanuka advocated for the constitutional integration of Buganda into a unified state with the country's eastern and northern provinces. In the late 1950s, Mulira and Abubakar Mayanja worked in concert with Buganda's foremost patriotic organisations, the Uganda National Movement (UNM) and *Kabaka Yekka* (KY). To undermine Mulira and Mayanja, Kiwanuka harnessed Catholic theology and European constitutional theory. But to understand Kiwanuka's political vision, we need to return to his early biography.

Benedicto K.M. Kiwanuka and Buganda's Catholic Historiography, c. 1955–c. 1962

Benedicto Kagimu Mugumba Kiwanuka was born in Musale (Bukomansimbi), Buddu, on 8 May 1922.[83] Consistent with what we know about early twentieth-century society in Buddu, Catholic teachings and traditions influenced Kiwanuka's emerging sensibilities. Kiwanuka's father was an alcoholic, which adversely impacted the stability of the home.[84] From an early age, the Catholic Church provided stability for Kiwanuka and by the age of twelve he had completed catechism.[85] Kiwanuka enrolled in the Catholic school at Villa Maria, the principal mission in early Catholic Buganda (Figure 5.3).[86] The school's superior, Father Benedicto Nsubuga, mentored Kiwanuka. Building upon Nsubuga's instruction, Kiwanuka developed an austere approach to religious practice. Kiwanuka attributed his success in school to prayer and advised his brother to integrate his studies with devotion to the Virgin and practice of the rosary.[87] Throughout his political career, Kiwanuka routinely attended mass and his closest

---

[83] BKMKP Government House Copies of Minutes, Etc. 'My Early Life', Mss., n.d., p. 1. My biographical discussion draws from this manuscript in addition to various pages found throughout Kiwanuka's private papers. Formal and informal interviews with family members provided me with a general 'sense' of Kiwanuka's personality. Beyond this, I am grateful to Ambassador Maurice P.K. Kiwanuka for providing me with access to the unabridged copy of Albert Bade, *Benedicto Kiwanuka: The Man and His Politics* (Kampala: Foundation Publishers, 1996).

[84] Bade, *Benedicto Kiwanuka*, p. 2; BKMKP Government House Copies of Minutes, Etc. 'My Early Life', p. 1.

[85] Bade, *Benedicto Kiwanuka*, p. 3.

[86] BKMKP Confidential Information Department (MP/29) 'Biographical Details', n.d.

[87] Bade, *Benedicto Kiwanuka*, pp. 3–4.

Figure 5.3 Villa Maria, Buddu, early 1900s
Source: MA Photothèque Missionnaires d'Afrique Rome

confidants were Catholic priests, including Archbishop Joseph Kiwanuka (Figure 5.4).[88]

Following his studies at Villa Maria, Kiwanuka transferred to St Peter's Secondary School, Nsambya, in 1940.[89] From 1942 to 1946, he enlisted in the King's African Rifles and served as a clerk in Palestine and Egypt.[90] While abroad, Kiwanuka devoted his spare time to studying French, Swahili and economics.[91] Comparable to the experiences of other postwar nationalists throughout Africa,[92] international service provided cosmopolitan space for Kiwanuka to reflect upon the particularities of empire at home. Early into his commission, Kiwanuka, who was eventually honourably decommissioned as sergeant major,[93]

---

[88] Interviews: Ambassador Maurice P.K. Kiwanuka, 29 May 2010, Kampala; Josephine Kiwanuka, 7 July 2011, London.

[89] Bade, *Benedicto Kiwanuka*, p. 4.

[90] BKMKP Confidential Information Department (MP/29) 'Biographical Details'; Bade, *Benedicto Kiwanuka*, pp. 5–6.

[91] BKMKP Confidential Information Department (MP/29) 'Biographical Details'.

[92] Roland Oliver and Anthony Atmore, *Africa Since 1800*, 5th edn (Cambridge: Cambridge University Press, 2004), pp. 211–368.

[93] BKMKP Confidential Information Department (MP/29) 'Biographical Details'.

Figure 5.4 Benedicto Kiwanuka (far right) with Archbishop Kiwanuka (centre), c. early 1960s
Source: BKMKP

produced a thirty-five point manifesto in Luganda entitled, 'If you want to be Free (or have freedom) on the Earth', within which he argued that political peace was contingent upon spiritual fulfilment.[94]

After returning to Uganda, Kiwanuka married Maxencia Zalwango, whom he met after mass.[95] A devout Catholic, Zalwango was also educated at Villa Maria. Zalwango, however, was from Bunyoro, Buganda's precolonial rival. Her ethnic heritage caused considerable tension within the Kiwanuka family.[96] In a culture that valued filial negotiation, Kiwanuka's insistence upon the wedding was peculiar, informed

---

[94] BKMKP In Memoriam [. . .] *'Oba Oyagala Okuba n'Eddembe mu Nsi'*, [c. early 1940s]: *'Tyanga okunyiza mikwongyo wamu ne Katonda'*.
[95] Bade, *Benedicto Kiwanuka*, p. 7.
[96] Interview, Josephine Kiwanuka, 7 July 2011, London. Josephine, the eldest daughter of Benedicto and Maxencia, recalled considerable tension between her father's extended family in Buddu and her mother.

by a sense of Catholic universality. For Kiwanuka, Zalwango's zeal for Catholicism outweighed the importance of her ethnicity and parentage. Indeed, Catholic priests played a more decisive role than either family in negotiating dowry across the Buganda–Bunyoro border.[97]

Benedicto applied to read law at Pius XII Catholic University College in Basutoland (National University of Lesotho) after the wedding, where he studied from 1950 to 1952.[98] Catholic Sotho colleagues and friends shaped Kiwanuka's political sensibilities. In a Christmas letter, one friend, a priest, evoked God's blessing on Kiwanuka before affectionately recalling their participation in the Eucharist: 'I shall have a special remembrance of you in my midnight Communion on Dec. 25th. Please pray for me also.'[99] Near the end of his time in Basutoland, Pius XII's registrar called upon the Blessed Mother to guide Kiwanuka: 'You may rest assured that I will keep praying for you. May our Blessed Mother be your guide and your strength. And if you find time, a letter from you will always be welcome.'[100] In an earlier letter, the registrar talked to his Ugandan friend about difficult days to come and the challenge of rigorous study over an extended period of time. The letter concluded with an exhortation. From southern Africa, where societies and states were being reorganised according to settler policies and Apartheid pass laws, Kiwanuka was exhorted to create a social and political organisation in eastern Africa inspired by Catholic hierarchy and tradition. Moved by the registrar's encouragement, Kiwanuka underlined the section of the letter that called him to work toward shaping society according to Catholic order:

As for your plans for the future, I cannot but endorse them fully. I do hope that you will find the financial assistance you need to pursue your law studies, and I pray Our Lord to make things easy for you in these difficult matters. Yes, go ahead. The way in front of you is still long; you will probably on certain days find the journey simply exhausting. But keep on! Africa needs men who shall give her a social and political organisation thoroughly

---

[97] Bade, *Benedicto Kiwanuka*, pp. 8–10.
[98] BKMKP Confidential Information Department (MP/29) 'Biographical Details'.
[99] BKMKP [Undesignated A] Brother Ignatius M.S. Phakwe, St Augustine's Seminary, Basutoland, to B.M. Kiwanuka, 19 December 1951.
[100] BKMKP the Honourable Chief Justice – Ranch Scheme Registrar, Pius XII Catholic University College, to B.M. Kiwanuka, 16 May 1952.

inspired by the message of Our Lord as interpreted by His Vicar on earth, Our Holy Father the Pope.[101]

Following his studies in South Africa, Kiwanuka studied law in London between 1952 and 1956.

From the mid-1950s up until the mid-1960s, Kiwanuka adapted the social theology of the Oxford Tractarian John Henry Newman to think about Catholic society in Uganda's late colonial politics. A Fellow of Oriel College, Oxford, Newman had been a prominent Anglican priest who converted to Catholicism in the nineteenth century.[102] Newman's principal work was an autobiographical account of his conversion, *Apologia Pro Vita Sua, A Defence of One's Life*, which was authored to make a theological and historical defence of Catholicism to Oxbridge Protestants. For Kiwanuka, Newman's volume was serendipitous: it recounted the story of an Anglican priest's conversion to Catholicism. Kiwanuka drew from the work to generate a theological and political vocabulary with which to persuade Protestants in Uganda to stop hampering Catholic political movement.

Portions of Kiwanuka's annotated copy of *Apologia* (autographed on 9 June 1953) interrogated the topic of social authority. For Newman, functional societies were organised around multiple nodes of power: conscience, the Bible, Church, antiquity, words of the wise, hereditary lessons, ethical truths, historical memories, legal saws, state maxims, proverbs, sentiments and presages. To index his reading of Newman's interpretation of authority, Kiwanuka annotated the question 'what is authority?'[103] Legitimacy in Newman's theology was interconnected with a Catholic mandate to confront social injustice. 'The infallibility lodged in the Catholic Church', argued Newman, derived from the fact that it constituted 'a supereminent prodigious power sent upon earth to encounter and master a giant evil': the Protestant body politic. Kiwanuka in his annotations noted that the cardinal's argument captured the 'reason for the existence of the Catholic Church'.[104]

---

[101] BKMKP the Honourable Chief Justice – Ranch Scheme Registrar, Pius XII Catholic University College, to B.M. Kiwanuka, 5 April 1952.
[102] Owen Chadwick, *The Spirit of the Oxford Movement: Tractarian Essays* (Cambridge: Cambridge University Press, 1992).
[103] BKMKP Library Newman, *Apologia Pro Vita Sua*, p. 194, annotation.
[104] Ibid., p. 168, annotation.

Kiwanuka outlined Newman's criticism against Protestant dogma and practice throughout the work. In his reflection on the moral theology of the Italian lawyer St Alphonsus Maria De'Liguori (1696–1787), Newman underscored the philosopher's proposition that justice existed in a society to the extent that cultural or political conditions hampered falsification or evil. Kiwanuka appropriated Newman's reading of De'Liguori, whose work had been shaped by the teleology of Thomas Aquinas (1225–74). It suggested that governments are legitimate to the degree that they embody moral virtue. And after reading this section, Kiwanuka reminded himself to 'listen to the soundness of argument here'.[105] Kiwanuka noted that 'veracity is for the sake of society', without which 'we should be doing society great harm'.[106] In turn, Kiwanuka inferred, 'On a matter of Principle never draw back –'.[107] And when Kiwanuka read Newman's reflection on Moses and the liberation of the Hebrews, he noted that 'we shall say this'.[108]

Kiwanuka did 'say this'. He incorporated *Apologia* into his political pamphlets by the early 1960s. In a political manifesto on Uganda's independence election, Kiwanuka reminded his Baganda readers about a period of time nearly 'a hundred years ago' when Protestants valued 'manliness, openness, consistency, truth', which were metaphors that he extracted from Newman.[109] Kiwanuka used Newman to castigate cronyism and political hypocrisy in KY: 'But now where is this openness? Where is consistency in policy? Where is truth in ordinary dealings? Where is manliness? Expedience has replaced principle and this has been the cause of all our troubles here. If we are to have democracy, let us have it in full.'[110] Kiwanuka not only directly cited Newman; the argument was clearly Thomistic. And by using Newman to develop his articulation of Ganda politics, Kiwanuka hoped to show his Protestant opponents that they did not possess the moral authority to govern Buganda or Uganda.

---

[105] Ibid., p. 227, annotation.
[106] Ibid., p. 225, annotation.
[107] Ibid., p. 87, annotation.
[108] Ibid., p. 177, annotation.
[109] Newman, *Apologia*, p. 85, in RDA 904.4 Kiwanuka '1962 Uganda Elections', p. 42.
[110] RDA 904.4 Kiwanuka '1962 Uganda Elections', p. 42.

Kiwanuka 'turned to the Holy Bible for guidance' to further inform his reading of Newman.[111] In the Luganda press, the commentator Mr Ssebuko used biblical references to denounce Kiwanuka and the DP for their inability to defend the political and economic interests of the state's citizens.[112] In response, Kiwanuka adapted St Mark's gospel to call for political unity in Buganda and to persuade patriots to become nationalists: 'Mr. Ssebuko seems to love the Bible. But remember that in this Bible the Lord warns us that "Kingdoms with Internal disputes will never last". If we Baganda continue to fight among ourselves, I am sure we shall not yield anything but more and more disputes.'

The debate between Kiwanuka and Ssebuko raised larger questions about the sanction of kingship in Ganda society. Ssebuko reminded the DP's liberal president about a time when Hebrew communities in ancient Palestine wished to be ruled by kings. This was a request, after all, that God had honoured through the prophet Samuel in 'Samuel I Chapter 8'. Kiwanuka in response castigated Ssebuko for the format of his citation: 'Mr. Ssebuko, you referred to words in the Bible, which you said are in Samuel I Chapter 8. I want to put you right that according to the Catholic Bible, we state, "I Samuel, Chapter 8". But I am surprised that you quoted this chapter yet you claim to love the Kabaka more than all of us.' Kiwanuka challenged Ssebuko to return to I Samuel, to reread its contents. Contrary to what Ssebuko had suggested, Samuel's history did not legitimise the institution of kingship; it robustly critiqued it. According to the biblical story, Samuel prophesied that Israel's kings would exploit and ravage families, local villages and the state. Samuel bleakly declared: 'And ye shall cry out in that day because of your king which ye shall have chosen you; and the Lord will not hear you in that day.'[113] The chapter concluded by chronicling Israel's disobedience: 'Nevertheless the people refused to obey the voice of Samuel; and they said, Nay; but we will have a king over us.'

By challenging his readers to critically reread Samuel's prophecy, Kiwanuka focused biblical exegesis to cloud the clarity of KY's political gaze. Whereas activists in the King Alone Party marketed

---

[111] Ibid., p. 26.
[112] '*Democratic Party N'entegeka Y'obufuzi bwa Uganda*', *Munno* 23 October 1958, p. 3.
[113] I Samuel 8.

themselves as defenders of Buganda's precolonial kingship, the prophet Samuel and Kiwanuka talked about a state governed by stubborn royalists and monarchs who through disobedience to God destroyed local communities. By returning to I Samuel 8, Buganda's foremost Catholic intellectual showed that he served God faithfully and sought to both challenge autocratic rule and save Uganda from political pandemonium.

Catholic spirituality permeated Kiwanuka's political thought throughout the 1950s and 1960s, but it was not the only intellectual tradition from which he drew. Far more than Musazi, Mulira or Mayanja, Kiwanuka was a political theorist. And he is likely one of the few politicians in late colonial Africa, who, after winning a presidential party election, committed to privately and critically studying natural law and Enlightenment constitutional theory. Like I.K. Musazi, Benedicto Kiwanuka was an avid reader. By late 1947, he was the assistant librarian in the High Court Library in Kampala.[114] In early 1951, while still in Basutoland, he joined the Catholic Literary Foundation, an international Catholic reading and publishing society.[115] Albert Bade's research showed that by the mid-1950s, Kiwanuka had begun to work through dozens of volumes in the English literary canon, from Rudyard Kipling to H.G. Wells.[116] My own work with Kiwanuka's personal library supports Bade's findings.[117] Kiwanuka's library contained several autographed and dated volumes, including: W.N. Weech

---

[114] BKMKP [Undesignated A] Registrar, [High Court Library], to Director of Education, Makerere, 1 December 1947; Bade, *Benedicto Kiwanuka*, pp. 12–14.

[115] BKMKP [Undesignated A] Catholic Literary Foundation, Milwaukee, to B.M. Kiwanuka, 30 January 1951.

[116] Additional works included Charles Dickens; Gustav Doré's illustrations of *Don Quixote* (1863); Sir Arthur C. Doyle (*Sherlock Holmes*, 1890s–1920s); Anthony Hope (*The Prisoner of Zenda*, 1894); Henrik Ibsen; Jerome K. Jerome (*Three Men in a Boat*, 1889); Fridtjof Nansen (*Farthest North*, 1897); Sir Walter Scott; William M. Thackeray; George L.P. Busson du Maurier (*Trilby*, 1895); Mark Twain (late nineteenth century) (Bade, *Benedicto Kiwanuka*, pp. 13–14).

[117] Non-autographed volumes included Homer (*The Iliad*, eighth century BCE); Frederick W. Faber (*The Creator and the Creature*, 1857); T. Tyfield and K.R. Nicol, editors (*The Living Tradition: An Anthology of English Verse from 1340 to 1940*, c. 1946); Mortimer J. Adler (*Development of Political Theory and Government*, 1959); K.M. Panikkar (*Asia and Western Dominance*, 1961); L.W. White and H.D. Hussey (*Introduction to Government in Great Britain and the Commonwealth*, 1965).

(editor), *History of the World* (1905, autographed 20 December 1945); E. M. Forster, *A Passage to India* (1924, annotated 28 February 1951); Fulton J. Sheen, *Peace of Soul* (1949, annotated 16 June 1953); and Viscount John Simon, *Retrospect* (1952, autographed 8 July 1955). Kiwanuka's library also shows that he was keenly interested in political philosophy and the history of European political thought, a passion he cultivated while studying law.

Kiwanuka pored over volumes of Robert Maynard Hutchins' edited series, *Great Books of the Western World* (Encyclopaedia Britannica, 1952),[118] some of which are still maintained in Kiwanuka's private collection, to imagine kingdoms whose subjects were constitutionally empowered to create states unencumbered by royalist politics. Underscored and annotated volumes include: *Plato* (volume 7), *Descartes/Spinoza* (volume 31), *Locke/Berkeley/Hume* (volume 35), *Kant* (volume 42) and James Boswell's *Life of Samuel Johnson* (volume 44). In particular, Kiwanuka's private notes show that from October to December 1958, he worked critically and systematically through John Locke and Jean-Jacques Rousseau.[119] In his annotations on Locke's *Two Treatises*, dated 28 October 1958,[120] Kiwanuka reflected on the 'origin of slavery'.[121] He noted that 'freedom from absolute, arbitrary power is so necessary to, and closely joined with, a man's preservation, that he cannot part with it but by what forfeits his preservation and life together'.[122]

In his notes on *The Social Contract*, which Rousseau drafted to contest political kingship,[123] Kiwanuka noted that Europe's early modern kings and hereditary bureaucrats 'had taken too much power and enslaved people', which demanded social revolt. 'Such people need not obey the Government', Kiwanuka noted.[124] Rousseau's solution to political monarchy prescribed social and economic 'liberty,

---

[118] JLEP Ambassador Maurice P.K. Kiwanuka to Jonathon L. Earle, 18 July 2011.
[119] BKMKP [Personal Notes], 28 October 1958–3 December 1958.
[120] BKMKP [Personal Notes], 'John Locke', 28 October 1958.
[121] BKMKP Library John Locke, 'Concerning Civil Government', in *Great Books of the Western World*, ed. by Robert Maynard Hutchins, p. 30, annotation.
[122] Ibid., p. 30, underscore.
[123] Victor Gourevitch, 'Introduction', in Jean-Jacques Rousseau, *"The Social Contract" and Other Later Political Writings*, ed. by Victor Gourevitch, 2 vols (Cambridge: Cambridge University Press, 1997), II, p. xxiv.
[124] BKMKP [Personal Notes], 'Jean Jacques Rousseau', 28 October 1958–3 December 1958.

equality, and universal suffrage',[125] a vision that resulted in Rousseau's banishment from France. Kiwanuka summarised: 'The <u>Social Contract:</u> caused a stir – expelled from France.'[126] The creation of states without disruptive sovereigns was costly, ominous insight for a political activist working to secure, according to KY propagandists, 'the end of [Buganda]'.[127]

Rousseau translated easily enough for Kiwanuka. When he defined his 'cardinal principles to observe', it was concluded that both 'Kings should <u>never</u> and should be prevented, by force if necessary, to meddle in politics',[128] and that it is 'better to get rid of Kings then have them who interfere with the smooth running of democracy'.[129] In October 1958, precisely when he was studying Rousseau, Kiwanuka drafted a lengthy diatribe against *Katikkiro* Mikaeri Kintu. The argumentative overtones of Kiwanuka's letter resonated with Rousseau's social commentary. Kiwanuka stated to the prime minister that the kingdom's nobility exploited their subjects through overtaxation and economic corruption.[130] 'So that the Katikkiro may understand better', began Kiwanuka, the 'common people are those the Katikkiro's lot mistreats day and night, making them kneel in puddles of mud to greet the nobility; they are the people they overtax or imprison for failure to pay; the ones they retrench from their jobs in favour of their relatives'.[131] Buganda's kingdom was a state where its citizens 'were not heard', where activists were 'detained without trial'. In Kintu's Buganda, authority was being used to confiscate property and exploit Catholics and Muslims, 'whom you regard as worthless and whose tax you use in sending your own people for studies overseas'. In Buganda,

---

[125] Ibid.

[126] Ibid., 'Rousseau', 11 November 1958.

[127] ICS PP.UG.KY 'Kabaka Yekka'.

[128] BKMKP [Undesignated D] Loose paper, n.d. While the manuscript is not dated, Kiwanuka's writing matches the style of the material that he was producing during the late 1950s and early 1960s.

[129] BKMKP [Undesignated D] Loose paper, n.d.

[130] Kiwanuka also used Rousseau's language in the early 1960s to publicly criticise Uganda's hereditary rulers: the kings of Buganda, Ankole and Toro. In a press release, Kiwanuka castigated Uganda's monarchs and called upon them to create kingdoms within which subjects were free to 'choose their Governments without fear or prejudice' (BKMKP [19] [Designated] B.K. Kiwanuka, 'Press Release', 21 February 1960).

[131] BKMKP [Undesignated] B.K. Kiwanuka to *Ow'Ekitibwa Katikiro*, 14 October 1958. I am using Bade's translation in this paragraph (pp. 40–1).

Amazima n'obwekanya was no longer extended to 'the ones who pay homage to the Kabaka'.

Articulated in the DP's political manifesto, *Forward to Freedom*, Kiwanuka aimed to 'transform Uganda into a state in which people can live in harmony without fear, want or discrimination based on tribe, religion or race'.[132] To develop this social vision, he used biblical metaphor and the ideologies of classical liberalism in tandem to advocate for self-rule: 'Blessed are they who struggle and toil for the sake of self-government, for they will have everlasting self satisfaction in a self-governing Buganda.'[133] Like Musazi, Mulira and Mayanja, Kiwanuka was pressed to recast regional pasts and particular claims upon the state by using religious texts and global intellectual history. In doing so, he showed just how mouldable colonial knowledge could be. But whereas Musazi, Mulira and Mayanja used the past to maintain the political function of Buganda's kingship – at least to some extent – Kiwanuka was willing to see it abrogated if necessary.

Conclusion: Religious Politics and the Creation of Uganda's Postcolonial Government

In March 1961, the Democratic Party disregarded the *Lukiiko*'s demand for an electoral boycott, which was designed to prevent Baganda from being appointed to the National Assembly on the eve of independence. Due to patriotic violence and intimidation tactics organised by KY, only 3.5 per cent of Buganda's electorate registered to vote.[134] Even in Catholic Buddu, only 2.7 per cent of the county's population registered.[135] Outside of Buganda, electoral registration looked very different – approximately 75 per cent of Uganda's electorate registered to vote.[136] During the election, the DP secured forty-three seats (nineteen from Buganda), while Milton Obote's UPC secured thirty-five. In consequence, Kiwanuka was appointed Minister without Portfolio on 14 April 1961 and Prime Minister on 1 March

---

[132] MUA AF PSF 329.96671 B.M. Kiwanuka, 'Forward to Freedom, Being the Manifesto of the Democratic Party', 11 April 1960, p. 3.
[133] Ibid., p. 12.
[134] Welbourn, *Religion and Politics in Uganda*, p. 22.
[135] Ibid., p. 66.
[136] The Right Honourable the Earl of Munster, 'Report of the Uganda Relationships Commission' (Entebbe: Government Printer, 1961), p. 26.

1962. Buganda's king, government and subjects were placed under the constitutional authority of a Catholic commoner from Buddu.

Kiwanuka's appointment instigated mass political protest throughout Buganda. When I interviewed A.D. Lubowa, who represented the government of Buganda during Uganda's constitutional negotiations in London, he recalled Protestant ministers railing against political Catholicism openly on the floor of Buganda's parliament. Lubowa recalled:

I used to hear talk in Mmengo, people talking *openly without any fear*, when Kiwanuka had become the Prime Minister – the first Prime Minister of Uganda. They would say, 'We can't have a Catholic to rule us'. They were *saying that openly, in Mmengo*. During the pre-Independence period they were saying that, 'We can't! For goodness sake, we can't have this Catholic to rule us' [. . .] 'Now we are reaching Independence, self-government; [. . .] and a Catholic takes over. *For goodness sake, we can't have this*'. That sort of feeling used to come out.[137]

In rural Buganda, disgust translated into open violence; patriots and DP supporters engaged in brutality and retaliation.[138] After being attacked by royalists, one DP activist in Kyaggwe concluded that it 'is quite obvious that Kabaka Yeka was created in order to do evil actions [. . .]'.[139] To a colonial officer, he recalled that 'a sub-county chief on 25/2/62 came with a mob of people during day time to destroy and wipe up my home and people'. With spears, shields and large knives in hand, he continued, patriots pronounced that it 'was now time for the Kabaka to kill the red ant[s]'.

Throughout the early 1960s, KY and DP activists engaged in a flurry of pamphleteering. *Kabaka Yekka* activists such as Abubakar Mayanja warned patriots that if 'the party supported by the Roman Catholic Church comes into power that will be the end of this

---

[137] Interview, A.D. Lubowa, 23 November 2009, Maya, Mpigi District. Inflections are Lubowa's.

[138] Simon Mwebe indicated that one of the primary goals of the Party's Youth Wing was to retaliate against physical attacks. By responding to Protestant violence, he noted, the Party was implementing the teaching of Moses: 'An eye for an eye, a tooth for a tooth' (Interview, Simon Mwebe, 17 March 2010, Kampala).

[139] BNA CO 822/2125/6 Gilbert Mulindwa, Mukono, to Colonial Secretary, 6 April 1962.

Figure 5.5 Left to Right (foreground): Prime Minister A. Milton Obote;
Kabaka Muteesa II, c. 1962
Source: DRUM Magazine

Kingdom'.[140] Subjects were called to demonstrate 'unshaken loyalty
to the throne' and to 'hit back at [the Democratic Party]'.[141] Royalists
charged communities to ensure that '[impenitent] [hungry-for-power-
politicians] do not get into power', those who sought to 'destroy
[our] national heritage'. Catholic leaders such as Archbishop Joseph

---

[140] ICS PP.UG.KY 'Kabaka Yekka'. See also ICS PP.UG.KY A.K. Mayanja,
'*Kabaka Yekka Amulisa Obulimba bwa D.P.*', [c. 1962]; ICS PP.UG.KY
'*Kabaka Atta Nabbe*', [c. 1962].
[141] MUA KY/71(D) 'Kabaka Yekka, Aims and Objectives', 12 June 1961.

Kiwanuka, by contrast, openly condemned KY. In a Pastoral Letter, Archbishop Kiwanuka argued that when 'the king still mixes up in politics the kingship is on the way to digging its own grave'.[142] The head of Uganda's Catholic Church pronounced that '"Kabaka Yekka" and the others who flatter themselves that they are the defenders of the Throne and of the King, are the one who will spoil our royalty by dragging the king in the backwash of politics'.[143]

By October 1962, the Democratic Party lost Buganda's pamphleteer war. In the context of two Constitutional Conferences – Lancaster (September–October 1961) and Marlborough (June 1962) – and a second election, Buganda's government secured sixty-five seats for KY in the *Lukiiko* to the Democratic Party's three.[144] This enabled the *Lukiiko* to send twenty-one KY representatives to the National Assembly. Throughout the country's remaining constituencies, the UPC secured thirty-seven seats in the National Assembly; the Democratic Party, twenty-four.[145] With fifty-eight seats to the Democratic Party's twenty-four, Uganda's UPC/KY coalition secured parliamentary majority. On 28 April, after one year in office, Benedicto Kiwanuka vacated the premier's residence.[146] Uganda's first president would be a king, *Kabaka* Muteesa II; her prime minister, Apolo Milton Obote. After fifty years, Kiwanuka is the only elected prime minister or president of Uganda to have democratically vacated office (Figure 5.5).

---

[142] RDA 81.4 Archbishop Joseph Kiwanuka, 'Pastoral Letter: Church and State, Guiding Principles', November 1961, p. 14.

[143] Ibid.

[144] D.A. Low, *Buganda in Modern History* (Berkeley: University of California Press, 1971), p. 219.

[145] 'Report of the Uganda Independence Conference, 1962' (London: Her Majesty's Stationery Office, July 1962), p. 3.

[146] RDA 904.4 Kiwanuka, '1962 Uganda Election', p. 1.

Conclusion: Textual Production and Historical Imagination in Postcolonial Buganda

[I] passed a resolution and said thus far and no further. That is why, on the 22nd of February, 1966, we had to act to put a stop to all this nonsense. And from there we moved rapidly. We started with cleaning our own house: arresting our own people, and then we moved to others. And I tell you that if anything shoots up tomorrow or the next day we will wipe them up because we want a clean road instead of something which is dirty. Today we have the black book – the Republican Constitution. It is on the basis of that book that we want to destroy the memory of the Indirect Rule System. We must build one country and this country must have only one Government, not several governments scattered in every corner of the country. We must consider ourselves as the people of Uganda so that there can be no room for anybody to leave this country to go abroad and when he is asked to sign his name in a book he signs Chief Minister, Busoga, Chief Minister, Ankole or Chief or Prime Minister, Buganda.

President A. Milton Obote[1]

Far from uniting the country, Obote had decisively split it, and I can only say here, as so often, that he must have known what he was doing; the results of his actions cannot have come as a surprise. In this case he purposefully antagonised the ablest and richest unit in the country, presumably already planning to destroy them as he had destroyed the party that represented them [*Kabaka Yekka*]. His method of building a united nation has been to destroy those that do not agree with him.

Kabaka Edward Muteesa II[2]

I have argued in this book that competing interpretations of the past propelled public politics in colonial Buganda in ways that have been largely overlooked in eastern Africa's nationalist historiography. There

---

[1] BNA FCO 31/186 'Speech by the President of Uganda People's Congress Delegates' Meeting, Introducing the Constitutional and Political Report', 8 June 1968.

[2] Kabaka Edward Mutesa II, *Desecration of My Kingdom* (London: Constable, 1967), p. 180.

did not exist simply one political vision to which all Ganda activists aspired. Local historians and political thinkers reworked colonial knowledge to recast and reinforce older ways of talking about state and society. This is important because it challenges us to avoid the extensive narrowing or distillation of late colonial political discourses. Buganda's colonial elites were not merely the products of missionary education. They were political historians who were the inheritors of competing regional historiographies. The proliferation of historical pluralism precipitated the end of formal empire in Uganda.

But this book has not only made a case for political and historical pluralism in southern Uganda, it has raised larger questions about colonial literacy and the methodologies with which textual historians explore the late colonial period. The production of marginalia in annotated libraries challenges the tenability of using European literary classifications to explore textual practices in twentieth-century eastern Africa. It suggests that 'secular' and 'sacred' epistemological boundaries were tremendously blurred in colonial southern Uganda, if they existed at all. Ignatius Musazi, Eridadi Mulira, Abu Mayanja and Benedicto Kiwanuka reread multiple genres to imagine political alternatives, from John Locke to Harold Laski, or from Hamu Mukasa to the Christian Old Testament. Whereas scholars such as J.D.Y. Peel and Adrian Hastings argued that the Bible was the foundational text of nationalism in colonial Africa, this study has challenged this assertion by showing the extent to which reading practices in colonial Buganda were far more cosmopolitan.

The proliferation of colonial literacy and vernacular history writing in Buganda raised far-reaching challenges for producing national histories and stable states in the postcolonial period. It has been approximately 50 years since Uganda attained independence. Since then the country has undergone extensive political and economic rupture. In February 1966, at the end of a short-lived alliance between *Kabaka Yekka* and Milton Obote's Uganda People's Congress, Prime Minister Obote ordered Uganda's army under the command of General Idi Amin to apprehend *Kabaka* Muteesa II, who was unwilling to return land to the kingdom of Bunyoro that Buganda had incorporated in 1900 (the 'Lost Counties'). For Obote, Muteesa had violated his constitutional responsibility to protect the republic of Uganda against ethnic partisanship. After fleeing Kampala during the attack, Muteesa II resettled in London and died in exile in November 1969. More broadly, though, the proliferation of competing political visions during the end of empire meant that Buganda's centre could not hold.

Obote was an avid reader. Kenneth Ingham's biography shows that he spent extensive periods of time throughout his life in Uganda's libraries.[3] Like Musazi, Mulira and Kiwanuka, he read his Bible and European legal history in tandem.[4] Obote used colonial literacy to reinforce much older conceptions of Langi republicanism, which became the foundation for his vision of Uganda's socialist order. It is not without coincidence, then, that when Obote restructured Uganda's constitution in 1967 that he used the language of literacy or 'books' to legitimise the abolition of kingship and to rewrite the memory of Uganda's colonial past: 'Today we have the black *book* – the Republican Constitution. It is on the basis of that *book* that we want to destroy the memory of the Indirect Rule System. We must build one country and this country must have only one Government, not several governments scattered in every corner of the country.'[5] Uganda's hereditary monarchies remained legally dismantled until 1993, when President Yoweri Museveni reinvested them as cultural institutions, allegedly without political power.[6]

If Obote saw the abolition of kingship as a necessity for statebuilding, Buganda's monarch saw it as an act of desecration while in exile in London. Muteesa published a 194-page book in 1967 to delegitimise Obote's republican agenda, *Desecration of My Kingdom*. For Muteesa, the production of a ghostwritten book was part of a larger international campaign to solicit the intervention of Great Britain and the United Nations.[7] To some extent, Muteesa's book is best read as *Bildungsroman*, which explores the coming of age of Buganda's king in a Protestant empire. To this end, the novel used choice images to recount the story of a king's rise to power: an adolescent *kabaka* at

---

[3] Kenneth Ingham, *Obote: A Political Biography* (London: Routledge, 1994), pp. 10 & 21.

[4] Ibid., pp. 24 & 31.

[5] BNA FCO 31/186 'Speech by the President of Uganda People's Congress Delegates' Meeting, Introducing the Constitutional and Political Report', 8 June 1968. The emphases are mine.

[6] The fullest treatment of Buganda's interregnum politics is Mikael Karlström, 'The Cultural Kingdom in Uganda: Popular Royalism and the Restoration of the Buganda Kingship, Volume I' (unpublished PhD, The University of Chicago, 1999).

[7] 'The Kabaka asks for UN Intervention', *London Times*, 3 May 1966, p. 8.

King's College, Budo; coronation by an Anglican bishop; and a picture of three of Muteesa II's children playing with British youth. Additional photographs were used to capture key moments of high politics: the signing of the Namirembe Agreement in 1955; a conversation in state regalia with Milton Obote; and the hosting of Queen Elizabeth The Queen Mother with the *Nnabagereka*.

More than chronicling the biography of an exiled king, though, *Desecration* adapted biblical metaphors to remind a Christian audience in Great Britain of a common past, intertwined with reflections on missionary preaching, a Cambridge education and discussions about the universality of the body of Christ. To charm his audience, Muteesa had his writer include a three-paragraph essay that he drafted at the age of nine. The essay was entitled, 'Christ and World Friendship'.[8] The essay drew from three texts in the New Testament, each of which called Christian communities to love their neighbours. A young Muteesa noted, 'a neighbour does not only mean the next-door person, but the nearest nation'.[9] Buganda's prepubescent potentate developed the point further by calling Christians in Great Britain to support their spiritual brothers and sisters in Uganda: 'All His [Jesus'] friends should love each other, so world friendship really means loving Jesus and His friends.'

It is not clear to what extent Muteesa redacted the content of his earlier essay in the book (if at all). But in any case, Muteesa had hoped to move British powerbrokers to action, much as the *Lukiiko*'s delegation had 10 years earlier. This is why the book contained two pictures related to the 1955 Agreement. Muteesa emphasised this juncture to illustrate British support of southern Uganda's constitutional, post-1955 monarchy.[10] He also did this to recall a time when the Westminster government responded to Buganda's political demands, which Muteesa highlighted further by recounting the interdependence between the London government and Apolo Kaggwa and Hamu Mukasa, whose cordial experiences in Westminster were accentuated in the book.[11] But unlike Kaggwa, Mukasa and Mulira's delegation,

---

[8] Mutesa II, *Desecration of My Kingdom*, p. 78.
[9] Ibid.
[10] Ibid., p. 148.
[11] Ibid., p. 66.

Muteesa was unsuccessful. Buganda's colonial order had finally unravelled. *Kabaka* Muteesa II died in exile.

Uganda's military was not only a powerful tool for pushing kings off their thrones. General Idi Amin wielded the army in 1971 to successfully remove from power his former commander, Milton Obote. Amin's Second Republic lasted for nearly a decade. While the 1970s attracted the earlier attention of scholars such as Ali Mazrui, who published no fewer than five pieces throughout the 1970s,[12] this period has been largely understudied.[13] Amin's Uganda was a period of both tremendous ambiguity and extensive literary production. In the early 1970s, Ignatius Musazi drafted letters to Idi Amin to explain that communities throughout rural Buganda were beginning to discuss the possibility of coronating a new king, 'which may lead to greater misunderstandings, and possible blood baths if not plots and counter plots, with dire consequences to our country'.[14] Much as he had decades earlier, Musazi reworked passages from his Bible to encourage Amin to emulate Jesus Christ: 'Whatever ye would that men should do to you, to ye also unto them.'[15] For Musazi, letter production provided space to weave theological and cultural history into a cohesive political discourse. In doing so, he presented himself to Amin as a necessary commentator on Ganda politics.

E.M.K. Mulira's private archive shows that he used this period to author some of his most lengthy and penetrative theological essays,[16] including elaborate diagrams on Buddhist philosophy.[17] Mulira's most extensive textual production from this period was *How to Know God and Man*, a two-volume history that reworked the history of human redemption in the Bible, from the creation story in Genesis to the story of Jesus' apocalyptic return. The prologue of the book called readers to reflect on the teachings of James Aggrey, much as Mulira's plays had nearly 40 years earlier. Mulira recounted the legend of an eagle

---

[12] Mazrui's fullest historical treatment is 'Religious Strangers in Uganda: From Emin Pasha to Amin Dada', *African Affairs*, 76 (1977), 21–38.
[13] To survey recent studies on 1970s Uganda see Derek R. Peterson and Edgar C. Taylor, 'Rethinking the State in Idi Amin's Uganda: The Politics of Exhortation', *Journal of Eastern African Studies*, 7 (2013), 58–82.
[14] RDA D.923.1 I.K. Musazi to General Idi Amin Dada, 15 March 1971.
[15] Ibid.
[16] See EMKM/CT, boxes 2–5.
[17] EMKM/CT/1/3.

that could not fly because it was repeatedly told that it was a chicken. Aggrey recounted the fable in public forums to implore western Africans to 'stretch forth [their] wings and fly'![18] Mulira now used this western African story and biblical passages to empower readers to blossom 'in the years of wilderness' and to 'read and re-read it [the book] several times, pondering each word and trying to understand every sentence and paragraph'.

Like Mulira, Benedicto Kiwanuka was engaged in textual production throughout the 1960s and early 1970s. His private papers show that, up until his assassination in September 1972, he was cutting and archiving hundreds of newspaper clippings and creating extensive marginalia in his personal copies of the English, Luganda and Swahili press. The production of annotation accompanied a large body of legal expositions that he authored as the chief justice of the Uganda Supreme Court. In his letters to Obote in the mid-1960s, he incorporated the case studies of Napoleon, Hitler, Mussolini and Nkrumah to critique the erosion of constitutional power.[19] Throughout 1972, he incorporated the Bible and the biography of Martin Luther in his letters to castigate dissenters in the Catholic Church, just as local Catholic leadership was beginning to expand its critique of national politics.[20] For his public criticism of both the Asian expulsion in August 1972 and the detention of the British businessman Donald Stewart, which was also condemned by Uganda's Catholic archbishop,[21] Kiwanuka was summarily executed at the Makindye military base in late September.

Idi Amin presented himself to the public as a pan-African nationalist, economic reformer and international champion of African rights. As Derek Peterson has shown, Amin's administration was to be 'a government of action'.[22] The demand of administrative superiors upon low-level bureaucrats resulted in prolific documentary production.[23] Amin

---

[18] EMKM/CT/1/3 *E.M.K. Mulira, How to Know God and Man: The Story of God and Man on Earth: Book I: The First Man: Adam* ([c. 1982]), prologue.

[19] BKMK Confidential Benedicto Kiwanuka to Milton Obote, 3 March 1966.

[20] BKMK Mr Kiwanuka Personal Benedicto Kiwanuka to Revd Fr Dr A.M. Lugira, 5 February 1972.

[21] 'President Amin is Told to Ensure Safety of British Citizens', *London Times*, 8 September 1972, p. 2.

[22] Idi Amin, early 1970s, quoted in Derek R. Peterson, '*Archive Work in Uganda*' (unpublished manuscript, 2015), p. 6.

[23] Peterson, '*Archive Work in Uganda*', pp. 6–7.

too was compelled to articulate his political vision through the creation of books.[24] Throughout his presidency, he published numerous literary pieces. Following the Yom Kippur War, Amin had authored under his name a fifty-two-page book on the 'Middle East Crisis'. Within its pages, Amin described himself as an able negotiator and called upon 'all other Arab states, Palestinian liberation fighters, and other just and peace-loving nations of the world, to give you [Palestine] their fullest and undiluted moral and material support, co-operation and confidence'.[25] The book is comprised of no fewer than fourteen images that portray Amin as an astute international diplomat working alongside Muslim statebuilders to stabilise world politics. Thus was the rationale for Amin's penchant for credentialism. By using photography and textual nomenclatures Amin positioned himself as an energetic leader who had successfully assailed multiple arenas of local and international power: Uganda's presidency, al-hajji, field marshal, military general, Victoria Cross, Distinguished Service Order, Military Cross and Conqueror of the British Empire (CBE).

Amin also used books to create the historical logic of his aggressive military policies in central and eastern Africa. In 1976 Amin used colonial records to argue that Uganda's peripheral territories had been illegally transferred to Kenya, Sudan and Zaïre in the mid-twentieth century, which, he argued, necessitated military intervention. The cover of Amin's book, *The Shaping of Modern Uganda and Administrative Divisions*, illustrated a brightly coloured map that outlined the neighbouring territories that he was preparing to militarily repossess. The seventy-five-page book was filled with historical analyses, charts, photographs and maps that Amin used to 'inspire us in our tireless endeavour to improve the quality of life in our human settlements'.[26] Milton Obote with Ugandan insurgents and the Tanzanian military,

---

[24] The fullest survey of documentary production during the 1970s is Cherry Gertzel, *Uganda: An Annotated Bibliography of Source Material* (London: Hans Zell Publishers, 1991).

[25] His Excellency Al-Hajji General Idi Amin Dada, VC, DSO, MC, President of the Republic of Uganda, *On the Middle East Crisis* (Kampala: Edited by the Office of His Excellency the President, Parliamentary Buildings, January 1974), p. 2.

[26] Al-Hajji Field Marshal Dr Idi Amin Dada, VC, DSO, MC, President of the Republic of Uganda, *The Shaping of Modern Uganda and Administrative Divisions: Documents 1900–76* (1976).

though, interrupted Amin's tireless endeavour in early 1979. Like Muteesa, in 2003, Amin died in exile.

Uganda was ruled by seven administrations between the toppling of the Amin government and 1986; each was removed by force, excluding the presidency of Yoweri Museveni, whose tenure is uncertain.[27] Museveni, like his predecessors, is a bibliophile and student of global history. In a recent speech, Uganda's ruler contended that Buganda should emulate Japan, whose emperors, unlike the rulers of the Qing dynasty, survived because they removed themselves from the arena of national politics following the Second World War.[28] In his autobiography, Museveni recalled studying the history of state formation in nineteenth-century Europe.[29] And his reading of the French revolution provided a powerful framework for envisioning the toppling of Obote's second government.[30] Like Musazi, Museveni studied France's political history alongside his Bible. Unsurprisingly, then, he used a biblical proverb to title his memoir and legitimise the ethos of the National Resistance Movement: 'To pursue the metaphor of the biblical quotation, before the "mustard seed" of freedom and democracy could be sown in Uganda, the land first had to be cleared of the rocks and weeds of a corrupt system, which had given rise by the 1970s to sectarian dictatorship and violence.'[31]

After two decades of contentious politics, Abu Mayanja helped draft Museveni's new constitution during the late 1980s. During the late 1960s he had been an open critic of the Obote government, especially after the formation of the National Association for the Advancement of Muslims, whose purpose was to break the political back of Buganda's

[27] Anna Reuss and Kristof Titeca, 'Museveni Got More Votes than Love in Uganda's Election', *Washington Post*, 20 February 2016.
[28] 'President Museveni's remarks before handing over Ebyaffe to Buganda Kingdom's delegation on April 15, 2014, at State House Entebbe', State House, Entebbe, 16 April 2014 <www.statehouse.go.ug/media/presidential-statements/2014/04/16/president-musevenis-remarks-handing-over-ebyaffe-buganda-ki> [accessed 7 July 2014].
[29] Yoweri Kaguta Museveni, *Sowing the Mustard Seed*, ed. by Elizabeth Kanyogonya and Kevin Shillington (London: Macmillan Education Ltd, 1997), p. 14.
[30] Ibid.
[31] Ibid., p. xiii.

Muslim community.[32] Throughout this period, Mayanja was an active writer in the pan-African magazine *Transition*, which was established in the early 1960s. During Uganda's constitutional crisis in the late 1960s, Mayanja looked toward western Africa, reminding his audience that the 'fact that Nkrumah had a detention law did not prevent him from being overthrown in a coup; clearly the men who overthrew him were plotting all the time, detention or no detention'.[33] One year later, Mayanja interpreted Uganda's postcolonial politics in the *longue durée* to argue that 'far from wanting to change the out-moded colonial laws, the Government of Uganda seems to be quite happy in retaining them and utilising them, especially those laws designed by the Colonial Regime to suppress freedom of association and expression'.[34] Mayanja's argument for historical continuity resulted in his incarceration, which lasted until Idi Amin released him in 1971.

After serving as the Minister of Education in Amin's government for a few years, Mayanja left formal politics until the mid-1980s. Much of his later social commentary was published in the government press, the *New Vision*. Between 2004 and his death in November 2005, Mayanja published no fewer than thirty-nine articles. In his final piece, published just 3 days before his passing, Mayanja once again returned to the history and impact of sedition laws in late colonial Uganda to criticise the Movement government for arresting the *Lukiiko* minister David Ntege on charges of 'promoting sectarianism'.[35] Much as he had in his diatribe against the Obote government, Mayanja argued that Uganda's postcolonial presidents (including Museveni) have radicalised colonial policies; they have not departed from them.

Mayanja's argument in 2005 was indicative of a much larger discursive shift unfolding in contemporary Buganda. Shortly after President Museveni secured military control of Kampala, the Ganda historian Phares Mutibwa suggested that 'Museveni has a golden opportunity,

---

[32] RDA D.128.5 Varied correspondence between the national government and Uganda Muslim Community, Kibuli, late 1960s. See also BNA FCO 31/202 Islam in Uganda.

[33] Abu Mayanja, 'The Government's Proposal for a New Constitution of Uganda', *Transition*, 32 (1967), 20–5 (p. 23).

[34] Abu Mayanja, 'The Fact that We Hate Apartheid Should Have No Relevance in the Way We Punish Traffic Offenders', *Transition*, 37 (1968), 14–15 (p. 15).

[35] Abu Mayanja, 'The Sentence Imposed on David Ntege was Excessive', *New Vision*, 1 November 2005, p. 10.

with the people's goodwill behind him, to lift Uganda finally out of its abyss of agony'.[36] Sixteen years later, Mutibwa no longer effuses his earlier optimism. He writes that 'the relations between Mengo and the NRM Government (including and above all Museveni himself) are no longer as warm as they used to be', with the 'relationship between Mengo and the NRM Administration [becoming] blurred every day'.[37]

In ways that are more poignant, *Katikkiro* Charles Peter Mayiga uses his recent book to argue that '[h]istory reveals that the people of Buganda carefully choose when to draw their swords, and when to negotiate'.[38] Written by a practising Catholic, Mayiga's history incorporates the earliest motto of *Munno*, *Katonda ne Buganda, Omwoyo Gumu n'Emmeeme Emu*, 'God bless Buganda, with her people together as one in spirit', to reinforce 'Buganda's nationalism, which seems immutable'.[39] Today, as in the 1950s, activists look toward different pasts to envision competing political alternatives. Mayiga's past recalls a time when 'the Kingdom enjoyed sovereignty and military might [. . .]'.[40] But also like the 1950s, during the end of formal empire, there are other histories, biographies and stories that need to be heard and critically studied – in Buganda and throughout Uganda.

[36] Phares Mutibwa, *Uganda since Independence: A Story of Unfulfilled Hopes* (Trenton, NJ: African World Press, Inc., 1992), p. 202.

[37] Phares Mutibwa, *The Buganda Factor in Uganda Politics* (Kampala: Fountain Publishers, 2008), pp. 251–2.

[38] Charles P. Mayiga, *King on the Throne: The Story of the Restoration of the Kingdom of Buganda* (Kampala: Prime Time Communication, 2009), p. 274.

[39] Ibid., p. 418.

[40] Ibid., p. 274.

Glossary and Orthography

The term Buganda is used to describe the kingdom and place of the Baganda. The singular and plural forms of the people of Buganda are Omuganda/Abaganda, or Muganda and Baganda. In adjectival form, Kiganda or Ganda is used. To facilitate readability and consistency, Luganda word constructions in this book follow John D. Murphy's *Luganda-English Dictionary* (Washington, DC: Catholic University Press, 1972). Each chapter explores numerous Luganda etymologies. These are defined and explored in due course. Here, I have provided a list of vocabulary that recur throughout the entire volume.

Ggombolola	sub-county
Kibuga	capital
Mailo	approximately one square mile, implemented after 1900
Mmengo	a specific location in contemporary Kampala; a term that is used loosely to refer to the parliament of the kingdom of Buganda and the ruling government of the kingdom
Muganda (plur. *–Baganda*)	citizen/subject of Buganda (or, brother/brothers)
Mukopi (plur. *–bakopi*)	commoner; a person of no particular distinction (royal or otherwise)
Mukungu (plur. *–bakungu*)	high-ranking chief
Mulangira (plur. *–balangira*)	prince
Mutaka (plur. *–bataka*)	hereditary clan head
Muwanika	treasurer
Kabaka	king of Buganda

Katikkiro	prime minister
Lubaale (plur. *–balubaale*)	deity, hero-god
Lukiiko	Buganda parliament
Mulamuzi	chief justice
Nnabagereka	wife of the king of Buganda
Nnamasole	queen mother of the kingdom of Buganda
Ssaza	Buganda county

Bibliography

The following archival material was consulted during the research of this book.

Institutional Archives

Archives in Italy

Archives des Missionnaires d'Afrique, Rome
With the assistance of the photography archivist of the collection, Father François Richard, I located numerous photographs of early colonial Buddu, some of which have been included in this book. The photographs from the collection are signified: *Photothèque Missionnaires d'Afrique Rome.*

Archives in Uganda

King's College, Budo
The File Records of Budo highlight the educational performance of the school's former students. They also provide insight into the College's relationship with eastern Africa's Islamic political institutions, including the East African Muslim Welfare Society and the Young Men's Muslim Association.

Makerere University Africana Archives
At the time of my research, the Africana Archives was in the process of being reclassified. In addition to consulting the papers of Apolo Kaggwa and Hamu Mukasa, I worked closely with the material in the Buganda Government files, *Kabaka Yekka* files, and Extra Mural records.

Files: AF PSF; AF UC; Unmarked Buganda Government Files; KY Files; Hamu Mukasa Papers AR/BUG/78

Hamu Mukasa Library, Kwata Mpola House, Mukono

The personal library of Hamu Mukasa includes an extensively annotated library, manuscripts, and photographic images from early colonial Buganda.

Rubaga Diocesan Archives, Kampala

The Rubaga Archives provide extensive amounts of material concerning Catholic politics in late colonial Uganda. The library also houses
the most complete collection of both *Munno* and the bounded records
of Uganda's postcolonial parliamentary assemblies.
   Files: 31; 81; 99; 128; 904

Uganda Christian University Archives, Archives
of the Bishop of Uganda, Mukono

This is the most extensive collection of sources regarding local
Protestant activism during the colonial period.
   Files: 1/41; 1/66; 1/72; 1/112; 1/113; 1/136; 1/179

Uganda Museum Library, Kampala

The library maintains an extensive, unpublished volume of the early
Luganda press, with English translations. At the time of this project,
the volume was found on the regular bookshelves.

Uganda National Archives, Library

The library houses copies of the Agreed Recommendations of the
Namirembe Conference; and an extensive amount of constitutional
documents and government reports.

Uganda National Archives, Secretariat Minute Papers

At the time of my research the National Archives was housed in Entebbe,
the colonial capital of Uganda. The Archive is now in Kampala. It houses
district reports, correspondence between Uganda's and Buganda's
respective statebuilders, economic studies, and material related to the
general operation of the colonial government.
   Files: A43; A44; A45; A46

Archives in United Kingdom

British National Archives, Colonial Office Records Series, Kew Gardens

Material includes intelligence reports, commissions of inquiry, dispatches, interview transcriptions, political party manifestos, petitions, newspaper clippings, court records, and academic summaries provided by the East African Institute of Social Research.

Files: CO 536; CO 537; CO 822; MP K122

Centre of African Studies, University of Cambridge

During the 1960s, the Centre acquired a series of studies and governmental records through Audrey Richards and the East African Institute of Social Research.

Files: 676

The papers of E.M.K. Mulira include an unpublished biography, unpublished essays, personal correspondence and political pamphlets. Large portions of the collection are now accessible through Apollo, the digital repository of the University of Cambridge. The classifications for the Mulira papers have been moderately revised since the completion of this book.

Church Missionary Society Papers, Cadbury Research Library, University of Birmingham

Material produced by Anglican missionaries and Buganda's early Christian converts offered important insights into the area's competing regional interests. The CMS Papers also include material produced by E.M.K. Mulira and his father, Nasanaeri Ndawula Kiwomamagaaya.

Files: ACC 265; ACC 549; ACC 549–50

Institute of Commonwealth Studies, University of London

The ICS contains a number of pamphlets and manifestos produced by Uganda's political parties in the late 1950 and early 1960s. The collection also includes the private papers of Professor Keith Hancock, which illuminates the inner workings of the Namirembe Conference and the *Lukiiko's* international delegation. The delegation was a committee that was charged with securing the return of *Kabaka* Muteesa II from exile during the 1950s.

> Files: PP.UG
> Professor Keith Hancock Papers (Files: 29)

King's College, Cambridge

The Annual Reports of the College highlight Abubakar Mayanja's studies at Cambridge during the mid-1900s. The papers of the broadcaster Sir George Reginald Barnes contain correspondence to and from the Ganda intellectual Erisa Kironde.

> Files: Annual Reports
> George Reginald Barnes Papers (Files: GRB 2)

Museum of Archaeology and Anthropology, University of Cambridge

The Museum contains records surrounding the acquisition of the remains of the Ganda hero-god, Kibuuka, and the return of his remains to Uganda in the early 1960s. This material was removed from the final book.

Dame Margery F. Perham Papers, Bodleian
Library of Commonwealth and African Studies,
Rhodes House, University of Oxford

The papers of Margery Perham include personal correspondence with Ugandan activists and Colonial Reports.

> Files: 514; 515; 529

Professor Audrey Richards Papers, London School of Economics

The papers of Audrey Richards include field notes and correspondence from her work in Uganda in the 1950s.

> Files: 6; 7

Royal Commonwealth Society Collections,
University Library, University of Cambridge

In addition to providing English translations of *Munno* in the early 1900s, the papers of Sir John Gray include copies of letters that illuminate political negotiation and conflict between Buganda's competing religious communities in the late nineteenth century.

> Files: 126; 150

School of Oriental and African Studies, Archives and Special Collections

The library of SOAS contains one of the most extensive collections of early Luganda grammars and dictionaries. The Special Collections provide insight into E.M.K. Mulira's work on a Luganda grammar and dictionary during the mid-twentieth century. It also houses a copy of Mulira's play, 'Mackay the Dauntless: A Play in Three Acts' (c. 1944).

Files: MS 380474

Archives in United States

James Aggrey Papers, Moorland-Spingarn Research Center, Howard University, Washington, D.C.

During the course of my research on E.M.K. Mulira, I spent time conducting research with the papers of the Ghanaian intellectual James Emman Kwegyir Aggrey, whose career influenced Mulira's philosophy of co-education. Ultimately, much of this material was removed from the final draft.

Series B   Box 147: 1–3
Series C   Box 147–3
Series E   Box 147: 3–4
Series H   Box 147: 5 & 7

Eliot Elisofon Photographic Archives, Smithsonian National Museum of African Art

The Elisofon collection includes a rich assembly of photographs from early twentieth-century Uganda. Richard H. Leakey assembled the collection in the early 1900s.

Lloyd A. Fallers Papers, Special Collections Research Center, University of Chicago

The collection, comprised of 28 linear feet of material, includes correspondence and field notes from Fallers' work in Uganda. It also contains a copy of John Rowe's English translation of Ali Kulumba's *Ebyafayo By'obusiramu mu Uganda*.

Fallers' material on Buganda is contained largely in boxes: 29; 30; 54.

National Archives and Records Administration,
College Park, Maryland
The records of the National Archives concern Uganda's postcolonial politics, which is largely beyond the scope of the current volume. The site in College Park also maintains the CIA's declassified searchable database, which highlights the involvement of the American government in central and eastern Africa during the late 1950s and early 1960s.

Private Papers (not institutionally deposited)

Throughout the duration of this project, numerous private collections were revewied.

Buganda Lukiiko Archives
The collection contains the parliamentary assembly minutes, between 1894 and 1918.

Neal Ascherson Papers, United Kingdom
In the late 1950s, the journalist and writer Neal Ascheron worked with the Uganda National Congress in Uganda, a movement with which he became familiar through Abubakar Mayanja at King's College, Cambridge. Mr Ascherson graciously made his Uganda field notes from this period available.

Erieza Bwete Papers, Uganda
The tin-trunk archive of the trade unionist Erieza Bwete, which I unearthed in the former county of Ssingo, contains loose manuscripts, letters, petitions and memoirs. The collection deals mostly with farmers' and cooperative activism from the mid- to late twentieth century.

Jonathon L. Earle Papers
This modest collection includes correspondence between the author and anti-colonial activists and their families; printed Luganda pamphlets; audio and video recorded interviews and ethnographic material.

Canon Harold Myers and Mollie Grace Papers, United Kingdom
The private collection of the Graces includes correspondence, political pamphlets, and photographic sources. These chronicle the Grace's work in Ankole, Buganda and Achimota.

Benedicto K.M. Kiwanuka Papers, Uganda

In partnership with the Kiwanuka family, I digitised Prime Minister Benedicto Kiwanuka's personal papers. In this book, I use the folder titles originally designated by Kiwanuka. The collection includes letters, journals, government records, course notebooks, photographic sources and an annotated library. The files and loose papers comprise approximately 5900 artefacts.

Jolly Joe Kiwanuka Papers, Uganda

The papers are comprised of bounded volumes of the Luganda press, mostly chronicling Joseph Kiwanuka's output during the late 1950s and the activism of the Uganda National Congress and its successor: Uganda People's Congress.

Ignatius K. Musazi Library, Uganda

The annotated library of Ignatius Musazi, located in northern Buganda, contains approximately 100 volumes.

Ssemujju Ibrahim Nganda Papers, Uganda

This collection includes notes and transcripts taken from interviews with Abubakar Mayanja. Before his passing, Mayanja had begun the process of co-authoring an autobiography with Nganda.

Interviews

Assorted, 13 July 2010, Kkungu
Ascherson, Neal, 17 August 2010, London
Barlow, Hugo, 11 November 2010, Munyonyo (Kampala)
Bonabana, Euginia, and Rose Nakimera, 19 January 2010, Mutundwe
Guwedeko, Fred, 25 February 2010, Makerere University
Kaggwa, Kawalya, Interview by Audrey Richards, 8 February 1954, in ARP 7/6/69 Audrey Richards, Field Notes
Kakyama, Asiya, 9 December 2009, Kampala
Kalema, Rhoda, 5 & 7 January 2010, Kampala
Kajubi, William S., 2 December 2009 & 17 February 2010, Kampala
Kayunga, Sallie S., 25 November 2010, Makerere University
Kisitu, Gideon, 14 January 2010, Nakulabye
Kiwanuka, Josephine, 7 July 2011, London

Kiwanuka, Maurice P.K., 29 May 2010, Kampala

Kiwanuka, Semakula M., 9 November 2010, Muyenga (Kampala)

Kiwanuka, Yusufu, Interview by Arye Oded, 12 November 1967, Lwanjaza, Singo County, in Arye Oded, *Islam in Uganda: Islamization through a Centralized State in Pre-Colonial Africa* (New York: Israel Universities Press, 1974)

Laetitia, Kinyingi, 7 January 2010, Kampala

Lubowa, A.D., 23 November 2009, Maya, Mpigi District

Lukwago, Al-Hajj Isa, 11 February 2010, Kampala

Mugwisa, Samuel, 16 December 2009, Kampala

Mukasa, George Kasedde, 23 June 2010, Kampala

Mulira, Eve, 10 November 2009, Kampala

Mulira, James, 25 June 2010, Kampala

Mulira, Mary, 11 June 2010, Kampala

Mulira, Peter, 3 November 2009, Kampala

Musazi, E.N., 11 December 2009, Timina (Luwero)

Musazi, Elizabeth, 10 February 2010, Kampala

Musazi, I.K., Interview by Neal Ascherson, 9 June 1956, Uganda Club, Kampala, in Neil Ascherson Papers

Musazi, I.K., Interview by Simba S. Kayunga, June 1988, Tinda (Kampala), in Sallie S. Kayunga, 'Uganda National Congress and the Struggle for Democracy: 1952–1962' (Working Paper No. 14, Centre for Basic Research Publications, Kampala, 1995)

Musoke, Kintu, 26 February 2010, Masaka

Mutiaba, Al-Hajj Mustafa, 3 March 2010, Kampala

Mwebe, Simon, 11 February & 17 March 2010, Kampala

Naniskombi, Rita, 11 & 16 November 2009, Luteete, Wakiso District

Nganda, Ssemujju I., 22 & 27 July 2010, Kampala

Nsambo, Shaikh al-Islām Ahmad, Interview by Arye Oded, 11 November & 16 December 1967, Natete, in Arye Oded, *Islam in Uganda: Islamization through a Centralized State in Pre-Colonial Africa* (New York: Israel Universities Press, 1974)

Sempebwa, Ernest, Interview by Gordon P. McGregor, March 2002, Makerere, in Gordon P. McGregor, *King's College Budo: A Centenary History, 1906–2006* (Kampala: Fountain Publishers, 2006)

Ssali, Nick, 17 November 2009, Radio One (Kampala)

Tyaba, L. Mathias, and Simon Mwebe, 30 July 2010, Kampala

Wamala, Osmani, Interview by Amin Mutyaba, A.K. Kasozi, Noel King, and William M. Watt, May & September 1967, Buyanga, Butambala County, in Noel Quinton King, A.B.K. Kasozi and Arye Oded, *Islam and the Confluence of Religions in Uganda, 1840–1966* (Tallahassee, FL: American Academy of Religion, 1973)

Newspapers

African Pilot. Uganda Information Department: Summary of the Local Press

Bukedde. Personal collection; www.bukedde.co.ug/

Daily Herald. British Library

Daily Mail. British Library

Daily Telegraph. British Library

Dobozi lya Buganda. Makerere University Africana Archives; Uganda Information Department: Summary of the Local Press

Drum. In, *Uganda: The Bloodstained Pearl of Africa and its Struggle for Peace: From the Pages of Drum*, ed. by Adam Seftel (Kampala: Fountain Publishers, 1994)

East Africa and Rhodesia. Rare Books Room (University Library, Cambridge)

Ebifa mu Buganda (Ebifa mu Uganda). Makerere University Africana Archives

Evening News. British Library

Emambya Esaze. Makerere University Africana Archives

Gambuze. Makerere University Africana Archives; Uganda Information Department: Summary of the Local Press

Guardian. The Guardian and Observer Digital Archives: archive http://archive.guardian.co.uk/Default/Skins/DigitalArchive/Client.asp?Skin=DigitalArchive&enter=true&AW=1330161867594&AppName=2

Ggwanga. Personal collection

Independent. British Library

Monitor. Personal collection; Digital Archives: www.monitor.co.ug/

New Vision. Personal collection; Digital Archives: www.newvision.co.ug/Archive.aspx

Munno. British Library; Rubaga Diocesan Archives; Sir John Gray Papers; Uganda Information Department: Summary of the Local Press

Ndimugezi. Uganda Information Department: Summary of the Local Press

New Times of Burma. British Library

Obugagga. Makerere University Africana Archives; Uganda Information Department: Summary of the Local Press

Observer. The Guardian and Observer Digital Archives: archive http://archive.guardian.co.uk/Default/Skins/DigitalArchive/Client.asp?Skin=DigitalArchive&enter=true&AW=1330161867594&AppName=2

Sekanyolya. Uganda Information Department: Summary of the Local Press

Taifa Empya. Makerere University Africana Archives; Uganda Information Department: Summary of the Local Press

Times. The Times Digital Archives: http://gale.cengage.co.uk/times.aspx/

Transition. West Room (University Library, Cambridge)

Uganda Empya. Makerere University Africana Archives; Uganda Information Department: Summary of the Local Press

Uganda Express. Personal collection of Sam Kiwanuka; Uganda Information Department: Summary of the Local Press

Uganda Eyogera. Makerere University Africana Archives; Uganda Information Department: Summary of the Local Press

Uganda Herald (Uganda Argus). British Library; Makerere University Africana Archives

Uganda Mail. Uganda Information Department: Summary of the Local Press

Uganda Post. Makerere University Africana Archives; Personal Collection of Sam Kiwanuka; Uganda Information Department: Summary of the Local Press

United Asia [Bombay]. Rare Books (University Library, Cambridge)

Washington Post. Digital Archives

Published Primary Sources

Books

60 Years of Uganda Muslim Education Association (UMEA) (Kampala: New Limited).

Abdel Haleem, M.A.S., trans., *The Qur'an* (Oxford: Oxford University Press, 2004).

Amin, Dada, His Excellence Al-Hajji General Idi, VC, DSO, MC, President of the Republic of Uganda, *On the Middle East Crisis* (Kampala: Edited by the Office of His Excellence the President, Parliamentary Buildings, January 1974).

Amin, Dada, Al-Hajji Field, Marshal Dr Idi, VC, DSO, MC, President of the Republic of Uganda, *The Shaping of Modern Uganda and Administrative Divisions: Documents 1900–76* (1976).

Ashe, Robert P., *Two Kings of Uganda (Life by the Shores of Victoria Nyanza: Being an Account of a Residence of Six Years in Eastern Equatorial Africa)* (London: Sampson Low, Marston, and Company, 1890).

Ashton, E.O., E.M.K. Mulira, E.G.M. Ndawula, and Alfred N. Tucker, *A Luganda Grammar* (London: Longmans, Green & Co., 1954).

Atkins, Beryl, ed., *Collins Robert French-English, English-French Dictionary*, 3rd edn (Glasgow: Harper Collins Publishers, 1993).

Blackledge, G.R., *Luganda-English and English-Luganda Vocabulary* (London: Society for Promoting Christian Knowledge, 1904).

Du Bois, W.E.B, *The Souls of Black Folk*, ed. by Brent H. Edwards (Oxford: Oxford University Press, 2007).

Bunyan, John, *Omutambuze*, trans. by E.C. Gordon, 3rd edn (Kampala: Uganda Bookshop, 1927).

Pilgrim's Progress (New York: P.F. Collier & Son, 1909).

Chesswas, J.D., *The Essentials of Luganda*, 4th edn (Nairobi: Oxford University Press, 1967).

Cook, Albert C., *A Doctor and His Dog in Uganda*, ed. by H.B. Cook (London: The Religious Tract Society, 1903).

Crabtree, W.A., *A Manual of Lu-Ganda* (Cambridge: Cambridge University Press, 1921).

Elements of Luganda Grammar: Together with Exercises and Vocabulary (Kampala: Uganda Bookshop, 1923).

Duta, Henry W., *Engero Za Baganda* (London: Society for Promoting Christian Knowledge, 1902).

Elements of Luganda Grammar Together with Exercises and Vocabulary (London: Society for Promoting Christian Knowledge, 1902).

Gorju, P. Julien, *Entre Le Victoria l'Albert Et l'Edouard: Ethnographie De La Partie Anglaise Du Vicariat De l'Uganda* (Rennes: Imprimeries Oberthur, 1920).

Grammar Enganda (Kampala: Uganda News Press, 1927).

Grammar Ey'oluganda (Bukalasa, Uganda: White Fathers' Printing Press, 1926).

Grammar Ey'oluganda, 2nd edn (Bukalasa, Uganda: White Fathers' Printing Press, 1930).

Grammar Eyo Lungereza. Eyalongosebwa H.T.C. Weatherhead Nga Aberwa S.M. Bazongere Esomero Budo (Kampala: Uganda Bookshop, 1936).

Grant, James A., *A Walk Across Africa (Domestic Scenes from My Nile Journal)* (Edinburgh: William Blackwood and Sons, 1864).

Harrison, Alexina M., *A.M. Mackay: Pioneer Missionary of the Church Missionary Society in Uganda* (London: Hodder and Stoughton, 1890).

Hattersley, Charles W., and Henry W. Duta, *Luganda Phrases and Idioms: For New Arrivals and Travellers in Uganda* (London: Society for Promoting Christian Knowledge, 1904).

Hughes, Christopher, *The Federal Constitution of Switzerland* (Oxford: Clarendon Press, 1954).

Jensen, Mark K., *Emile Zola's J'Accuse! A New Translation with a Critical Introduction* (Soquel, CA: Bay Side Press, 1992).

Kaggwa, Apolo, *Bassekabaka Be Buganda (The Kings of Buganda)*, trans. by Semakula Kiwanuka (Nairobi, Dar Es Salaam, Kampala: East African Publishing House, 1971 [1901]).

   Ekitabo Kye Bika Bya Baganda (The Book of the Clans of Buganda) (Kampala: Uganda Bookshop and Uganda Society, 1949 [1908]).

   Ekitabo Kye Kika Kya Nsenene (The Book of the Grasshopper Clan), trans. by John A. Rowe, 2nd edn (Mengo, Uganda, 1905).

   Ekitabo Kye Mpisa Za Baganda (The Book of the Customs of Buganda), ed. by May M. Edel, trans. by Ernest B. Kalibala (New York: Columbia University Press, 1934 [1905]).

   The Reign of Mwanga II (A Later Addition to Ekitabo Kya Basekabaka Be Buganda), trans. by Simon Musoke (Kampala: Typescript found in the University of Cambridge Library, 1953).

   The Tales of Sir Apolo: Uganda Folklore and Proverbs, trans. by F. Rowling (London: The Religious Tract Society, 1934).

Kakungulu, Badru, and A.B.K. Kasozi, *Abaasimba Obuyisiraamu Mu Uganda* (Kampala: Equator Books, 1977).

Kavuma, Paulo, *Crisis in Buganda, 1953–55: The Story of the Exile and Return of the Kabaka, Mutesa II* (London: Rex Collings, 1979).

Kiingi, K.B., Deo Kasiriivu, Douglas K. Nkonge, Deo Kawalya, Ibrahim Ssentongo, and Anatole Kiriggwajjo, eds., *Enkuluze y'Oluganda Ey'e Makerere* (Kampala: Fountain Publishers, 2007).

Kirwan, B.E.R., and P.A. Gore, *Elementary Luganda* (Kampala: Uganda Bookshop, 1951).

Kitching, A.L., and G.R. Blackledge, *A Luganda-English and English-Luganda Dictionary* (London: Society for Promoting Christian Knowledge, 1925).

Kulumba, Ali, *Empagi Z'obusiramu Mu Luganda* (Kampala: Sapoba Book Press, 1953).

Kulumba, Ali, and Mustafa Mutyaba, *Nuhu Kalema N'Obusiraamu Mu Buganda* (Kampala: Crane Publishers Ltd., 1994).

L'ouganda et les Agissements de la Compagnie Anglaise "East-Africa" (Paris: Missions D'Afrique, 1892).

Layer, Ernest, *Les Pères Blancs Et La Civilisation Dans l'Ouganda* (Rouen: Imprimerie Cagniard, 1909).

Legum, Colin, *Must We Lose Africa?* (London: W.H. Allen, 1954).

LeVeux, R.P., *Premier Essai De Vocabulaire Luganda-Français d'Après l'Ordre Étymologique* (Alger: Maison-Carrée, 1917).

Livinhac, L., and C. Denoit, *Grammaire Luganda*, ed. by P.A. Wolters (Alger: Maison-Carrée, 1921).

Lugard, Frederick D., *The Rise of Our East African Empire: Early Efforts in Nyasaland and Uganda*, 2 vols (London: Frank Cass and Co. Ltd., 1968 [1893]).

Manuel de Langue Luganda, Comprenant La Grammaire et un Recueil de Contes et de Légendes, Par Les P.P. L.L. Et C.D. Des Pères Blancs, Missionnaires Dans Le Buganda, 2nd edn (Einsiedeln, Suisse: Benziger & Co., 1894).

Mayiga, Charles P., *King on the Throne: The Story of the Restoration of the Kingdom of Buganda* (Kampala: Prime Time Communication, 2009).

Miti Kabazzi, James Kibuka, *Buganda, 1875–1900: A Centenary Contribution*, trans. by G.K. Rock, 2 vols (London: United Society for Christian Literature, n.d.).

Mugwanya, Stanislaus, *Ekitabo eky'Olugendo Olulungi Nga Zawabu (The Book of the Golden Journey)*, 1914.

Mukasa, Ham, *Simuda Nyuma: Ebiro Bya Mutesa (Do Not Turn Back: The Reign of Mutesa)* (London: Society for Promoting Christian Knowledge, 1938).

Simuda Nyuma: Ebiro Bya Mutesa, Unedited (Makerere University Africana Archives, 1938).

Uganda's Katakiro in England: Being the Official Account of His Visit to the Coronation of His Majesty King Edward VII, trans. by Ernest Millar (London: Hutchinson & Co., 1904).

Mukasa, Revd Reuben Spartas, *History* (Makerere University Africana Archives, 1946).

Mulira, E.M.K., *Aligaweesa: Omuvubuka Wa Uganda Empya* (Kampala: Uganda Bookshop Press, 1955).

Government Gyennonya: Abakopi Okuba N'eddobozi Mu Buganda (Kampala: Uganda Bookshop Press, 1944).

Kiribedda Ne Balizzakiwa: Abavubuka Ababiri Ab'omulembe (Nairobi: East African Printers Ltd., 1963).

Sir Apolo Kaggwa, KCMG, MBE, trans. by John A. Rowe (Kampala: Uganda Bookshop Press, 1949).

Teefe (Kampala: Uganda Publishing House, 1968 [1950]).

The Vernacular in African Education (London: Longmans, Green & Co., 1951).

Thoughts of a Young African (London: Lutterworth Press for the United Society for Christian Literature, 1945).

Troubled Uganda (London: Fabian Publications, 1950).

Mulira, E.M.K., and E.G.M. Ndawula, *A Luganda-English and English-Luganda Dictionary*, 2nd edn (London: Society for Promoting Christian Knowledge, 1952).

Mullins, J.D., and Ham Mukasa, *The Wonderful Story of Uganda* (London: Church Missionary Society, 1904).

Murphy, John D., *Luganda-English Dictionary* (Washington, DC: Consortium Press for Catholic University of America Press, 1972).

Museveni, Yoweri Kaguta, *Sowing the Mustard Seed*, ed. by Elizabeth Kanyogonya and Kevin Shillington (London: Macmillan Education Ltd., 1997).

Musoke, D.S.K., '*Buganda Nyaffe*, Part I: A Descriptive Booklet about Land and Its Users', [c. June 1944].

Mutesa II, *Kabaka* Edward, *Desecration of My Kingdom* (London: Constable, 1967).

Mwebe, Simon, and Anthony Sserubiri, *Ebyafaayo Bya D.P., 1954–1984* (Kampala: Foundation for African Development, 1984).

Nakabiri, Hafiswa, and Mustafa Mutyaba, *Omulangira Nuhu Kyabasinga* (Kampala: Crane Books, 2009).

Nicq, Abbé, *Le Père Siméon Lourdel De La Société Des Pères Blancs Et Les Premières Années De La Mission De l'Ouganda*, 3rd edn (Maison-Carrée, Alger: Imprimerie des Pères Blancs, 1932).

Parma-Ntanda, Musa K., *Deposition of H.H. The Kabaka of Buganda: The Representative in London of the Women of Uganda Challenges Her Majesty's Government's White Paper and the Secretary of State's Decision* (Sussex: Grange Press for The Women's League of Buganda, 1954).

Pères Blancs, *The Manuel De Langue Luganda Comprenant La Grammaire Et Un Recueil De Contes Et De Légendes*, 3rd edn (Alger: Maison-Carrée, 1914).

Pilkington, George L., *Luganda-English and English-Luganda Vocabulary* (London: Society for Promoting Christian Knowledge, 1899).

Roscoe, John, *The Baganda: An Account of Their Native Customs and Beliefs*, 2nd edn (London: Frank Cass and Co. Ltd., 1965 [1911]).

Rousseau, Jean-Jacques, *"The Social Contract" and Other Later Political Writings*, ed. by Victor Gourevitch, 2 vols (Cambridge: Cambridge University Press, 1997).

Rowling, F., *A Guide to Luganda Prose Composition* (London: Society for Promoting Christian Knowledge, 1921).

Shepherd, George W., *The Early Struggle for Freedom and Unity in Uganda: I K Musazi and the Farmer's Cooperative Movement* (New York: The John Day Company, 1955).

Smith, Edwin William, *Aggrey of Africa: A Study in Black and White*, 2nd edn (London: Student Christian Movement Press, 1929).

Speke, John Hanning, *Journal of the Discovery of the Source of the Nile* (Edinburgh: William Blackwood and Sons, 1863).

Ssewagaba, Ssejjemba, *Lwaki Katikkiro; Martin L. Nsibirwa Yatemulwa Nga 5/9/1945.*

Stanley, Henry M., *Through the Dark Continent (The Sources of the Nile Around the Great Lakes of Equatorial Africa and Down the Livingstone River to the Atlantic Ocean)*, 2 vols (New York: Sampson Low, Marston, Searle, & Rivington, 1878).

Stuart, Andrew, *Of Cargoes, Colonies and Kings: Diplomatic and Administrative Service from Africa to the Pacific* (London: Radcliffe Press, 2001).

The Bible (Authorised Translation).

Tucker, Alfred R., *Eighteen Years in Uganda and East Africa*, 2 vols (London: Edward Arnold, 1908).

Ṭūsī, Naṣīr 'al-Dīn Muḥammad ibn Muḥammad, *The Nasirean Ethics*, trans. by G.M. Wickens (London: Allen & Unwin, 1964).

Walser, Ferdinand, *Luganda Proverbs* (Berlin: Reimer, 1982).

Washington, Booker T., *Up From Slavery: An Autobiography* (New York: Doubleday, Page & Co., 1902).

Wheare, K.C., *Federal Government* (London: Oxford University Press, 1953).

Wilson, C.T., *An Outline Grammar of the Luganda Language* (London: Society for Promoting Christian Knowledge, 1882).

Zimbe, B. Musoke, *Buganda and the King (Buganda Ne Kabaka)*, trans. by F. Kamoga (Mengo, Uganda, 1978 [1939]).

Chapters in Edited Books

Byron, Lord G.G., 'The Destruction of Sennacherib', in *Selected Poems*, ed. by Susan J. Wolfson and Peter J. Manning (London: Penguin Classics, 2006), p. 355.

Chwa II, Kabaka Daudi, 'Memorandum on the Proposed Federation of the British East African Dependencies. Its Effects on the Constitution of Buganda Kingdom', in *The Mind of Buganda: Documents of the Modern History of an African Kingdom*, ed. by D.A. Low (London: Heinemann Educational, 1971), pp. 73–81.

Fraser, Alek G., 'Notes on West African Education', in *The Future of the Negro: Some Chapters in the Development of Race*, ed. by Brig-Gen

Sir, Gordon Guggisberg and Alek G. Fraser (London: Student Christian Movement, 1929), pp. 101–49.

Kaggwa, Apolo to Captain Frederick Lugard, 4 July 1896, in *The Mind of Buganda: Documents of the Modern History of an African Kingdom*, ed. by D.A. Low (London: Heinemann Educational, 1971), p. 31.

Kayamba, Martin, 'The Story of Martin Kayamba Mdumi, M.B.E., of the Bondei Tribe', in *Ten Africans*, ed. by Margery Perham (London: Faber and Faber, 1963 [1936]), pp. 173–272.

Mukasa, Ham, 'The Life of Ham Mukasa', in *The Wonderful Story of Uganda*, trans. by Ven Archdeacon Walker (London: Church Missionary Society, 1904), pp. 173–208.

Mukasa, Samwiri, 'The Record of My Service to the Kingdom of Buganda and the Important Government of Britain, the Protector of This Nation Buganda', in *The Mind of Buganda: Documents of the Modern History of an African Kingdom*, ed. by D.A. Low (London: Heinemann Educational, 1925), pp. 57–61.

Mulira, Rebecca, 'Rebecca Muliira', in *A Rising Tide: Ugandan Women's Struggle for a Public Voice 1940–2004*, ed. by Winnie Byanyima and Richard Mugisha (Kampala: Forum for Women in Democracy, 2005), pp. 38–46.

Pius XI, Pope, 'On Atheistic Communism', in *Encyclical Letter* (London: Catholic Truth Society, 1937).

Wheare, K.C., 'When Federal Government Is Justified', in *Federalism: An Australian Jubilee Study*, ed. by Sawer Hughes (Melbourne: F.W. Cheshire, 1952), pp. 110–34.

Articles

Anonymous, 'A Background to the Political Scene in Buganda', *Uganda Church Review*, (Winter 1958), 21–6.

Chesswas, J.D., 'Notes from the Province: Buganda', *Uganda Teachers' Journal*, 5 (1950), 17–18.

Gava, R.K.K., 'Report on Muslim Schools', *Uganda Teachers' Journal*, 6 (1951), 9–10.

'Report on Muslim Schools', *Uganda Teachers' Journal*, 7 (1952), 12–14.

'Report on Muslim Schools', *Uganda Teachers' Journal*, 8 (1953), 10–12.

Gleave, J.T., 'Some Thoughts on Vernacular Teacher Training', *Uganda Teachers' Journal*, 6 (1951), 39–41.

Kisosonkole, Kupuliano Bisase, and Ignatius K. Musazi, 'Education in Uganda', *Uganda Church Review*, 18 (1930), 50–5.

Mayanja, Abu, 'The Fact that We Hate Apartheid Should Have no Relevance in the Way We Punish Traffic Offenders', *Transition*, 37 (1968), 14–15.

'The Government's Proposal for a New Constitution of Uganda', *Transition*, 32 (1967), 20–5.

'The Struggle for Democracy in Uganda', *United Asia [Bombay]*, 7 (1955), 97–101.

You and Your Vote: A Guide to the Lukiiko Election (Kampala: Kabaka Yekka Publication, 1962).

Mukasa, Hamu, 'The Rule of the Kings of Buganda', *Uganda Journal*, 10 (1946), 136–43.

Musoke, Musa, 'Muslim Education in the Uganda Protectorate', *Uganda Teachers' Journal*, 1 (1939), 242–3.

Owen, W.E., 'Influence of Dreams on the Baganda', *Uganda Notes*, (September 1910).

Pasha, Emin, 'The Diaries of Emin Pasha – Extracts I', *Uganda Journal*, ed. by John M. Gray, 25 (1961), 1–15.

Young Men's Muslim Association, *Prince Badru Kakungulu* (Kampala: Wood Printers & Stationers Ltd., 1990).

Official Publications

Anderson, J.N.D., *Islamic Law in Africa*, Colonial Research Publication, 16 (London: Her Majesty's Stationery Office, 1954).

'Annual Report of the Education Department for the Year Ended 31st December, 1930' (Entebbe: Government Printer, 1931).

'Annual Report of the Education Department for the Year Ended 31st December, 1935' (Entebbe: Government Printer, 1936).

'Annual Report of the Education Department for the Year Ended 31st December, 1949' (Entebbe: Government Printer, 1951).

Kabaka's Government, *Okwefuga Kwa Buganda* (Kampala: Uganda Printing & Publishing Co. Ltd., October 1960).

Munster, Right Honourable the Earl of, 'Report of the Uganda Relationships Commission' (Entebbe: Government Printer, 1961).

Parliamentary Debates (Hansard), House of Commons, Volumes 466, 524, 528, 533.

'Report of the Commission of Inquiry into the Disturbances in Uganda during April, 1949' (Entebbe: Government Printer, 1950).

'Report of the Commission of Inquiry into the Disturbances which Occurred in Uganda during January, 1945' (Entebbe: Government Printer).

'Report of the Cotton Commission', 1938 (Entebbe: Government Printer, 1939), in Apter, *The Political Kingdom in Uganda*, p. 189.

'Report of the Uganda Independence Conference, 1962' (London: Her Majesty's Stationery Office, July 1962).

'The Uganda Agreement of 1900', in *Buganda and British Overrule, 1900–1955: Two Studies*, ed. by D.A. Low and R.C. Pratt (London: Oxford University Press, 1960), pp. 350–64.

Uganda Protectorate: Buganda (London: Her Majesty's Stationary Office, 1954).

'Uganda Protectorate: Withdrawal of the Recognition from Kabaka Mutesa II of Buganda' (London: Her Majesty's Stationary Office, 1953).

Unpublished Manuscripts (Abridged)
'Abubakar Kakyama Mayanja' (Kampala: Crane Books, 2005).
The Aga Khan's Shia Imami Ismailia Education Department for Uganda, 'A Review of Islamilia Education in the Uganda Protectorate' (n.d.).
Ascherson, Neal, 'The History of the Uganda National Congress', n.d.
'*Okujjukira* Sheik Islaam-Ali Saad Kulumba', 2004.
'[YMMA] Certificate of Registration as a Corporate Body under the Trustees (Incorporation) Ordinance, 1959'.

Published Secondary Sources

Books
Alam, Muzaffar, *The Languages of Political Islam: India, 1200–1800* (London: Hurst & Co, 2004).
Anderson, Benedict, *Imagined Communities*, revised edn (London: Verso, 2006).
Anonymous, *A Short History of the Democratic Party*, ed. by Richard Muscat (Rome: Foundation for African Development, 1984).
Apter, David E., *The Political Kingdom in Uganda: A Study of Bureaucratic Nationalism*, 2nd edn (Princeton, NJ: Princeton University Press, 1967).
Bade, Albert, *Benedicto Kiwanuka: The Man and His Politics* (Kampala: Fountain Publishers, 1996).
Barber, Karin, *The Anthropology of Texts, Persons and Publics: Oral and Written Culture in Africa and Beyond* (Cambridge: Cambridge University Press, 2007).
Bayly, Christopher, *Recovering Liberties: Indian Thought in the Age of Liberalism and Empire* (Cambridge: Cambridge University Press, 2011).
Beattie, John, *Bunyoro: An African Kingdom, Case Studies in Cultural Anthropology* (New York: Holt, Rinehart and Winston, 1960).
The Nyoro State (Oxford: Clarendon Press, 1971).
Becker, Felicitas, *Becoming Muslim in Mainland Tanzania, 1890–2000: The Spread of Islam Beyond the Indian Ocean Coast* (New York: Oxford University Press for the British Academy, 2008).
Behrend, Heike, and Ute Luig, eds., *Spirit Possession, Modernity and Power in Africa* (Oxford: James Currey, 1999).
Cabrita, Joel, *Text and Authority in the South African Nazaretha Church* (Cambridge: Cambridge University Press).

Cannadine, David, ed., *What Is History Now?* (New York: Palgrave Macmillan Ltd., 2002).

Carey, Hilary M., *God's Empire: Religion and Colonialism in the British World, c. 1801–1908* (Cambridge: Cambridge University Press, 2011).

Carlyle, Thomas, *Past and Present*, ed. by Chris Vanden Bossche, Joel J. Brattin and D.J. Trela (Berkeley, CA: University of California Press, 2005).

Carr, E.H., *What Is History?*, ed. by R.W. Davies, 2nd edn (New York: Penguin Books, 1987).

Cassirer, Ernst, *The Philosophy of the Enlightenment*, trans. by Fritz C.A. Koelln and James P. Pettegrove (Boston, MA: Beacon Press, 1951).

Chadwick, Owen, *The Secularization of the European Mind in the Nineteenth Century* (Cambridge: Cambridge University Press, 1977).

The Spirit of the Oxford Movement: Tractarian Essays (Cambridge: Cambridge University Press, 1992).

Chakrabarty, Dipesh, *Provincializing Europe: Postcolonial Thought and Historical Difference* (Princeton, NJ: Princeton University Press, 2007).

Chatterjee, Partha, *The Black Whole of Empire: History of a Global Practice of Power* (Princeton, NJ: Princeton University Press, 2012).

The Nations and Its Fragments (Princeton, NJ: Princeton University Press, 1993).

Chartier, Roger, *L'ordre Des Livres: Lecteurs, Auteurs, Bibliothèques En Europe Entre XIVe Et XVIIIe Siècle* (Aix-en-Provence: Alinéa, 1992).

Colley, Linda, *The Ordeal of Elizabeth Marsh: A Woman in World History* (New York: Pantheon, 2007).

Collingwood, R.G., *An Autobiography* (Oxford: Oxford University Press, 1983).

The Idea of History (Oxford: Clarendon Press, 1946).

The Principles of History: And Other Writings in Philosophy of History, ed. by W.H. Dray and W.J. Van der Dussen (Oxford: Oxford University Press, 2001).

Comaroff, Jean and John, *Of Revelation and Revolution: Christianity, Colonialism, and Consciousness in South Africa*, 2 vols (Chicago, IL: University of Chicago Press, 1991).

Cooper, Frederick, *Africa since 1940: The Past of the Present* (Cambridge: Cambridge University Press, 2002).

Colonialism in Question: Theory, Knowledge, History (Berkeley, CA: University of California Press, 2005).

Coquery-Vidrovitch, Catherine, *Africa and the Africans in the Nineteenth Century: A Turbulent History* (Armonk, NY: M.E. Sharpe, 2009).

Cox, Richard, *Pan-Africanism in Practice: An East African Study: PAFMECSA 1958–1964* (London: Oxford University Press, 1964).

Cunningham, J.F., *Uganda and Its Peoples: Notes on the Protectorate of Uganda Especially the Anthropology and Ethnology of Its Indigenous Races* (London: Hutchinson & Co., 1905).

Daftary, Farhad, *Mediaeval Isma'ili History and Thought* (Cambridge: Cambridge University Press, 2001).

    The Isma'ilis: Their History and Doctrines, 2nd edn (Cambridge: Cambridge University Press, 2007).

Ddiba, J.L., *Eddini Mu Uganda*, 2 vols (Masaka, Uganda: St. Liberatum Printing Press, 1967).

Doyle, Shane, *Crisis and Decline in Bunyoro: Population and Environment in Western Uganda 1860–1955* (Oxford: James Currey, 2006).

Dray, William H., *History as Re-enactment: R.G. Collingwood's Idea of History* (Oxford: Oxford University Press, 1999).

Duffy, Eamon, *Marking the Hours: English People and Their Prayers, 1240–1570* (New Haven, CT: Yale University Press, 2011).

Durkheim, Émile, *Les Formes Élémentaires De La Vie Religieuse: Le Système Totémique En Australie* (Paris: Librairie Félix Alcan, 1912).

Eliade, Mircea, *Traité D'histoire Des Religions* (Paris: Payot, 1949).

Ellis, Stephen, and Gerrie ter Haar, *Worlds of Power: Religious Thought and Political Practice in Africa* (London: Hurst & Company, 2004).

Elton, Geoffrey, *The Practice of History*, 2nd edn (Oxford: Wiley-Blackwell, 2002).

Etherington, Norman, *Theories of Imperialism: War, Conquest and Capital* (London, Croom Helm, 1984).

Evans, Richard J., *In Defence of History*, 2nd edn (London: Granta, 2001).

Falola, Toyin, *Nationalism and African Intellectuals* (Rochester, NY: University of Rochester Press, 2001).

Fallers, Lloyd A., ed., *The King's Men: Leadership and Status in Buganda on the Eve of Independence* (London: Oxford University Press, 1964).

Feierman, Steven, *Peasant Intellectuals: Anthropology and History in Tanzania* (Madison, WI: University of Wisconsin Press, 1990).

Foucault, Michel, *The Order of Things: An Archaeology of the Human Sciences* (London: Routledge, 1989).

Freeden, Michael, *Ideologies and Political Theory: A Conceptual Approach* (Oxford: Clarendon, 1996).

Gadamer, Hans-Georg, *Truth and Method*, trans. by Joel Weinsheimer and Donald G. Marshall, 2nd edn (London: Sheed & Ward, 1989).

Gellner, Ernest, *Nations and Nationalism*, 2nd edn (Ithaca, NY: Cornell University Press, 2008).

Geertz, Clifford, *Islam Observed: Religious Development in Morocco and Indonesia* (New Haven, CT: Yale University Press, 1968).

    The Interpretation of Cultures (London: Fontana Press, an imprint of HarperCollins Publishers, 1973).

Gertzel, Cherry, *Uganda: An Annotated Bibliography of Source Material* (London: Hans Zell Publishers, 1991).

Geschiere, Peter, *The Modernity of Witchcraft: Politics and the Occult in Postcolonial Africa*, trans. by Janet Roitman and Peter Geschiere (Charlottesville, VA: University of Virginia Press, 1997).

Greene, Sandra E., *Sacred Sites and the Colonial Encounter: A History of Meaning and Memory in Ghana* (Bloomington, IN: Indiana University Press, 2002).

ter Haar, Gerrie, *Spirit of Africa: Healing Ministry of Archbishop Milingo of Zambia* (Trenton, NJ: Africa World Press, 1992).

Gilroy, Paul, *The Black Atlantic: Modernity and Double-Consciousness* (Harvard University Press, 1993).

Goody, Jack, *The Logic of Writing and the Organization of Society* (Cambridge: Cambridge University Press, 1986).

Hansen, Holger Bernt, and Michael Twaddle, eds., *Religion and Politics in East Africa: The Period since Independence* (London: James Curry, 1995).

Hanson, Holly E., *Landed Obligation: The Practice of Power in Buganda* (Portsmouth, NH: Heinemann, 2003).

Hastings, Adrian, *The Construction of Nationhood: Ethnicity, Religion and Nationalism* (Cambridge: Cambridge University Press, 1997).

la Hausse de Lalouvière, Paul, *Restless Identities: Signatures of Nationalism, Zulu Ethnicity and History in the Lives of Petros Lamula and Lymon Maling* (Pietermaritzburg: University of Natal Press, 2000).

Hayashida, Nelson O., *Dreams in the African Literature: The Significance of Dreams and Visions among Zambian Baptists* (Amsterdam: Rodopi, 1999).

Haydon, Edwin S., *Law and Justice in Buganda* (London: Butterworth, 1960).

Haynes, Jeffrey, *Religion, Globalization and Political Culture in the Third World* (Basingstoke: Macmillan, 1999).

Healey, Joseph G., and Donald Sybertz, *Towards an African Narrative Theology* (Nairobi: Paulines Publications Africa, 1996).

Hefner, Robert W., ed., *Conversion to Christianity: Historical and Anthropological Perspectives on a Great Transformation* (Berkeley, CA: University of California Press, 1993).

Heidegger, Martin, *Being and Time*, trans. by Joan Stambaugh, 2nd edn (Albany, NY: State University of New York Press, 1996).

Hobsbawm, Eric J., *Nations and Nationalism since 1780: Programme, Myth, Reality* (Cambridge: Cambridge University Press, 1990).

The Age of Extremes: A History of the World, 1914–1991 (New York: Pantheon, 1994).

Interesting Times: A Twentieth-Century Life (New York: Pantheon Books, 2002).

Hofmeyr, Isabel, *The Portable Bunyan: A Transnational History of "The Pilgrim's Progress"* (Princeton, NJ: Princeton University Press, 2003).

Holmes, Richard, *Coleridge: Early Visions, 1772–1804* (London: Pantheon, 1989).

Holt, P.M., *The Mahdist State in the Sudan: 1881–1898: A Study of Its Origins, Development and Overthrow*, 2nd edn (Oxford: Oxford University Press, 1979).

Hunter, Emma, *Political Thought and the Public Sphere in Tanzania: Freedom, Democracy and Citizenship in the Era of Decolonization* (Cambridge: Cambridge University Press, 2015).

Iliffe, John, *A Modern History of Tanganyika* (Cambridge: Cambridge University Press, 1979).

Honour in African History (Cambridge: Cambridge University Press, 2005).

Obasanjo, Nigeria and the World (Oxford: James Currey, 2011).

Ingham, Kenneth, *Obote: A Political Biography* (London: Routledge, 1994).

Jenkins, Keith, *Rethinking History*, 3rd edn (London: Routledge, 2003).

Johns, Adrian, *The Nature of the Book: Print and Knowledge in the Making* (Chicago, IL: University of Chicago Press, 1998).

Jørgensen, Jan Jelmert, *Uganda: A Modern History* (London: Croom Helm, 1981).

Kamali, Mohammad H., *A Textbook of Hadīth Studies: Authenticity, Compilation, Classification and Criticism of Hadīth* (Markfield: Islamic Foundation, 2005).

Shari'ah Law: An Introduction (Oxford: Oneworld Publications, 2008).

Kasirye, Joseph S., *Obulamu Bwa Stanislaus Mugwanya (The Life of Stanislaus Mugwanya)* (Dublin: Typescript found in Seeley Library, University of Cambridge, 1963).

Kasozi, A.B.K., *The Life of Prince Badru Kakungulu Wasajja: And the Development of a Forward Looking Muslim Community in Uganda, 1907–1991* (Kampala: Progressive Publishing House, 1996).

The Spread of Islam in Uganda (Nairobi: Oxford University Press, 1986).

Katznelson, Ira, and Gareth S. Jones, eds., *Religion and the Political Imagination* (Cambridge: Cambridge University Press, 2010).

Kedourie, Elie, *Nationalism* (London: Hutchinson, 1960).

Kibuuka, Ernest Z., *Omulembe Gwa Muteesa II* (Kampala: Crane Books, 2004).

Kiwanuka, Semakula, *A History of Buganda: From the Foundation of the Kingdom to 1900* (London: Longman, 1971).

Kodesh, Neil, *Beyond the Royal Gaze: Clanship and Public Healing in Buganda* (Charlottesville, VA: University of Virginia Press, 2010).

Kramnick, Isaac, and Barry Sheerman, *Harold Laski: A Life on the Left* (London: Hamish Hamilton, 1993).

Landau, Paul S., *The Realm of the Word: Language, Gender and Christianity in a Southern African Kingdom* (Portsmouth, NH: Heinemann Educational Publishers, 1995).

Lapidus, Ira M., *A History of Islamic Societies*, 2nd edn (Cambridge: Cambridge University Press, 2002).

Lodge, Tom, *Mandela: A Critical Life* (New York: Oxford University Press, 2007).

Low, D.A., *Buganda in Modern History* (Berkeley, CA: University of California Press, 1971).

Religion and Society in Buganda, 1875–1900 (Kampala: East African Institute of Social Research, 1956).

Low, D.A., and R.C. Pratt, eds., *Buganda and British Overrule, 1900–1955: Two Studies* (London: Oxford University Press, 1960).

Luig, Ulrich, *Conversion as a Social Process: A History of Missionary Christianity among the Valley Tonga, Zambia* (Hamburg: Lit Verlag, 1996).

Magaziner, Daniel, *The Law and the Prophets: Black Consciousness in South Africa, 1968–1977* (Athens: Ohio University Press, 2010).

Magesa, Laurenti, *African Religion: The Moral Traditions of Abundant Life* (Maryknoll, NY: Orbis Books, 1997).

Mair, Lucy P., *An African People in the Twentieth Century* (London: Routledge & Kegan Paul Ltd., 1965 [1934]).

Mamdani, Mahmood, *Citizen and Subject: Contemporary Africa and the Legacy of Late Colonialism* (Princeton, NJ: Princeton University Press, 1996).

Politics and Class Formation in Uganda (Kampala: Fountain Publishers, 1976).

Mana, Kä, *Christ d'Afrique: Enjeux Éthiques De La Foi Africaine En Jésus-Christ* (Paris: Karthala, 1994).

Marx, Karl, *Marx: Later Political Writings*, ed. by Terrell Carver (Cambridge: Cambridge University Press, 1996).

Mbembe, Achille, *On the Postcolony* (Berkeley, CA: University of California Press, 2001).

McCaskie, T.C., *State and Society in Pre-colonial Asante* (Cambridge: Cambridge University Press, 2003).

McGraw, Bryan T., *Faith in Politics: Religion and Liberal Democracy* (Cambridge: Cambridge University Press, 2010).

McGregor, Gordon P., *King's College Budo: A Centenary History, 1906–2006* (Kampala: Fountain Publishers, 2006).

McKitterick, Meredith, *To Dwell Secure: Generation, Christianity, and Colonialism in Ovamboland* (Portsmouth, NH: Heinemann, 2002).

McKitterick, Rosamond, *The Carolingians and the Written Word* (Cambridge: Cambridge University Press, 1989).

Médard, Henri, *Le Royaume Du Buganda Au XIXe Siècle: Mutations Politiques Et Religieuses D'un Ancien Etat d'Afrique De l'Est* (Paris: Karthala, 2007).

Meyer, Birgit, *Translating the Devil: Religion and Modernity among the Ewe in Ghana* (Edinburgh: Edinburgh University Press for the International African Institute, 1999).

Milbank, John, *Theology and Social Theory: Beyond Secular Reason* (Oxford: Blackwell Publishers, 1990).

Morris, Brian, *Anthropological Studies of Religion: An Introductory Text* (Cambridge: Cambridge University Press, 1987).

Mutibwa, Phares, *The Buganda Factor in Uganda Politics* (Kampala: Fountain Publishers, 2008).

   Uganda since Independence: A Story of Unfulfilled Hopes (Trenton, NJ: African World Press, Inc., 1992).

Nsimbi, M. B, *Amannya Amaganda N'ennomo Zaago* (Kampala: Published for the Uganda Society by the East African Literature Bureau, 1956).

Oded, Arye, *Islam in Uganda: Islamization Through a Centralized State in Pre-colonial Africa* (New York: Israel Universities Press, 1974).

Odhiambo, E.S. Atieno, and John Lonsdale, eds., *Mau Mau and Nationhood: Arms, Authority and Narration* (Oxford: James Currey, 2003).

Oliver, Roland, and Anthony Atmore, *Africa since 1800*, 5th edn (Cambridge: Cambridge University Press, 2004).

Ong, Walter J., *Orality and Literacy*, 2nd edn (London: Routledge, 2002).

Parker, John, and Richard Rathbone, *African History: A Very Short Introduction* (Oxford: Oxford University Press, 2007).

Parsons, Timothy, *The African Rank-and-File: Social Implications of Colonial Military Service in the King's African Rifles, 1902–1964* (Portsmouth, NH: Heinemann, 1999).

Peel, J.D.Y., *Religious Encounter and the Making of the Yoruba* (Bloomington, IN: Indiana University Press, 2003).

Perham, Margery, *Ten Africans*, 2nd edn (London: Faber, 1963 [1936]).

Peterson, Derek R., *Creative Writing: Translation, Bookkeeping, and the Work of Imagination in Colonial Kenya* (Portsmouth, NH: Heinemann, 2004).

   Ethnic Patriotism and the East African Revival: A History of Dissent, c. 1935–1972 (Cambridge: Cambridge University Press, 2012).

Peterson, Derek R., and Giacomo Macola, *Recasting the Past: History Writing and Political Work in Modern Africa* (Athens: Ohio University Press, 2009).

Philips, John, *Writing African History* (Rochester, NY: University of Rochester Press, 2006).

Pirouet, Louise, *Black Evangelists: The Spread of Christianity in Uganda, 1891–1914* (London: Collings, 1978).

Pocock, J.G.A., *Political Thought and History: Essays on Theory and Method* (New York: Cambridge University Press, 2009).

Prestholdt, Jeremy, *Domesticating the World: African Consumerism and the Genealogies of Globalization* (Berkeley, CA: University of California Press, 2008).

Ray, Benjamin C., *Myth, Ritual, and Kingship in Buganda* (Oxford: Oxford University Press, 1991).

Reid, Richard J., *Political Power in Pre-colonial Buganda: Economy, Society and Welfare in the Nineteenth Century, East African Studies* (Oxford: James Currey, 2002).

Richards, Audrey I., ed., *Economic Development and Tribal Change: A Study of Immigrant Labour in Buganda*, 2nd edn (Nairobi: Oxford University Press, 1973).

Roberts, Andrew, *A History of Zambia* (London: Heinemann, 1976).

Rosberg, Carl G., and John C. Nottingham, *The Myth of "Mau Mau": Nationalism in Kenya* (New York: F. Praeger, 1966).

Rublack, Ulinka, ed., *A Concise Companion to History* (Oxford: Oxford University Press, 2011).

Schoenbrun, David L., *A Green Place, a Good Place: Agrarian Change, Gender, and Social Identity in the Great Lakes Region to the 15th Century* (Portsmouth, NH: Heinemann, 1998).

Shorter, Aylward, *Cross and Flag in Africa: The "White Fathers" During the Colonial Scramble (1892–1914)* (Maryknoll, MD: Orbis Books, 2006).

Skinner, Quentin, *Visions of Politics: Regarding Method* (Cambridge: Cambridge University Press, 2002).

Sommerville, C. John, *The Secularization of Early Modern England: From Religious Culture to Religious Faith* (Oxford: Oxford University Press, 1992).

Sundkler, Bengt, *Bantu Prophets in South Africa* (London: Lutterworth Press, 1948).

  Bara Bukoba: Church and Community in Tanzania (London: C. Hurst & Company, 1980).

  Zulu Zion and Some Swazi Zionists (Oxford: Oxford University Press, 1976).

Taylor, John V., *The Growth of the Church in Buganda: An Attempt at Understanding* (London: SCM Press, 1958).

Thompson, E.P., *The Making of the English Working Class* (New York: Vintage Books, 1963).

Thompson, Gardner, *Governing Uganda: British Colonial Rule and Its Legacy* (Kampala: Foundation Publishers, 2003).

Thornton, John, *The Kongolese Saint Anthony: Dona Beatriz Kimpa Vita and the Antonian Movement, 1684–1706*, 2nd edn (Cambridge: Cambridge University Press, 1998).

Troeltsch, Ernst, *Die Bedeutung Des Protestantismus Für Die Entstehung Der Modernen Welt* (München: R. Oldenbourg, 1911).

Die Wissenschaftliche Lage Und Ihre Anforderungen an Die Theologie: Vortrag (Tübingen: Freiburg, 1900).

Twaddle, Michael, *Kakungulu and the Creation of Uganda, 1868–1928*, Eastern African Studies (London: James Currey, 1993).

de Vere Allen, James, *Swahili Origins: Swahili Culture and the Shungwaya Phenomenon* (London: James Currey, 1993).

Vinson, Robert Trent, *The Americans are Coming!: Dreams of African American Liberation in Segregationist South Africa* (Athens: Ohio University Press, 2012).

Ward, W.E.F., *Fraser of Trinity and Achimota* (Accra: Ghana Universities Press, 1965).

Weber, Max, *Die Protestantische Ethik Und Der Geist Des Kapitalismus* (Tübingen: Mohr, 1934).

Welbourn, Fred B., *East African Rebels: A Study of Some Independent Churches* (London: SCM Press, 1961).

Religion and Politics in Uganda: 1952–1962 (Nairobi: East African Publishing House, 1965).

West, Henry W., *The Mailo System in Buganda: A Preliminary Case Study in African Land Tenure* (Entebbe: Government Printer, 1965).

White, Luise *Speaking with Vampires: Rumor and History in Colonial Africa* (Berkeley, CA: University of California Press, 2000).

Wild, J.V., *The Uganda Mutiny, 1897* (Kampala: Uganda Bookshop, 1954).

Wild-Wood, Emma, *Migration and Christian Identity in Congo (DRC)* (Leiden: Brill, 2008).

Wittgenstein, Ludwig, *Philosophical Investigations*, trans. by G.E.M. Anscombe, 2nd edn (Oxford: Blackwell, 1997).

Wood, Laurence W., *God and History* (Lexington, KY: Emeth Press, 2005).

Wrigley, C.C., *Crops and Wealth in Uganda: A Short Agrarian History* (Kampala: East African Institute of Social Research, 1959).

Wrigley, Christopher, *Kingship and State: The Buganda Dynasty* (Cambridge: Cambridge University Press, 1996).

Zachernuk, Philip S., *Colonial Subjects: An African Intelligentsia and Atlantic Ideas* (Charlottesville, VA: University Press of Virginia, 2000).

Chapters in Edited Books

Barber, Karin, 'Introduction: Hidden Innovators in Africa', in *Africa's Hidden Histories: Everyday Literacy and Making the Self*, ed. by Karin Barber (Bloomington, IN: Indiana University Press, 2006), pp. 1–24.

Bayly, Christopher, 'History and World History', in *A Concise Companion to History*, ed. by Ulinka Rublack (Oxford: Oxford University Press, 2011), pp. 3–25.

Brett, Annabel S., 'What Is Intellectual History Now?', in *What Is History Now?*, ed. by David Cannadine (Palgrave Macmillan Ltd., 2002), pp. 113–32.

Breuilly, John, 'Introduction', in *Nations and Nationalism*, trans. by Ernest Gellner, 2nd edn (Ithaca, NY: Cornell University Press, 2008), pp. xiii–liii.

Chartier, Roger, 'Reading Matter and "Popular" Reading: From the Renaissance to the Seventeenth Century', in *A History of Reading in the West*, ed. by Guglielmo Cavallo and Roger Chartier, trans. by Lydia G. Cochrane (Cambridge: Polity Press, 1999), pp. 269–83.

Creppel, Ingrid, 'Secularisation: Religion and the Roots of Innovation in the Political Sphere', in *Religion and the Political Imagination*, ed. by Ira Katznelson and Gareth S. Jones (Cambridge: Cambridge University Press, 2010), pp. 23–45.

Earle, Jonathon L., 'Hamu Mukasa', in *Dictionary of African Biography*, ed. by Henry Louis Gates, Jr. and Emmanuel Akyeampong (Oxford: Oxford University Press, 2011).

'Nuhu Kyabasinga Mbogo', in *Dictionary of African Biography*, ed. by Henry Louis Gates, Jr. and Emmanuel Akyeampong (Oxford: Oxford University Press, 2011).

Evans, Richard J., 'Prologue: What Is History? – Now', in *What Is History Now?* ed. by David Cannadine (New York: Palgrave Macmillan Ltd., 2002), pp. 1–18.

Fallers, Lloyd A., 'Introduction', in *The King's Men: Leadership and Status in Buganda on the Eve of Independence*, ed. by Lloyd A. Fallers (London: Oxford University Press, 1964), pp. 1–19.

Feierman, Steven, 'African Histories and the Dissolution of World History', in *Africa and the Disciplines: The Contributions of Research in Africa to the Social Sciences and Humanities*, ed. by Robert H. Bates, V.Y.

Mudimbe and Jean F. O'Barr (Chicago, IL: University of Chicago Press, 1993), pp. 167–212.

Fortt, J.M., 'The Distribution of the Immigrant and Ganda Population within Buganda', in *Economic Development and Tribal Change: A Study of Immigrant Labour in Buganda*, ed. by Audrey I. Richards, 2nd edn (Nairobi: Oxford University Press, 1973), pp. 77–118.

Foucault, Michel, 'Nietzsche, Genealogy, History', in *The Foucault Reader*, ed. by Paul Rabinow (New York: Pantheon, 1984), pp. 76–100.

 'What Is an Author?', in *The Foucault Reader*, ed. by Paul Rabinow (New York: Pantheon, 1984), pp. 101–20.

Gilmartin, David, 'Customary Law and Sharī'at in British Punjab', in *Sharī'at and Ambiguity in South Asian Islam*, ed. by Katherine P. Ewing (Berkeley, CA: University of California Press, 1988), pp. 43–62.

Greene, Theodore M., in Immanuel Kant, *Religion within the Limits of Reason Alone*, trans. by Theodore M. Greene and Hoyt H. Hudson (New York: Harper Torchbooks, 1960), pp. ix–lxxviii.

Gourevitch, Victor, 'Introduction', in Jean-Jacques Rousseau, *'The Social Contract' and Other Later Political Writings*, ed. by Victor Gourevitch, 2 vols (Cambridge: Cambridge University Press, 1997), II, pp. ix–xxxi.

Hanson, Holly E., 'Queen Mothers and Good Government in Buganda: The Loss of Women's Political Power in the Nineteenth Century', in *Women in African Colonial Histories*, ed. by Jean Allman, Susan Geiger and Nakanyike Musisi (Bloomington, IN: Indiana University Press, 2002), pp. 101–34.

Holdrege, Barbara, 'What's Beyond the Post? Comparative Analysis as Critical Method', in *A Magic Still Dwells: Comparative Religion in the Postmodern Age*, ed. by Kimberley C. Patton and Benjamin C. Ray (Berkeley, CA: University of California Press, 2000), pp. 77–91.

Howell, Caroline, 'Church and State in Crisis: The Deposition of the Kabaka of Buganda, 1953–1955', in *Missions, Nationalism, and the End of Empire*, ed. by Brian Stanley and Alaine Low (Grand Rapids, MI: William B. Eerdmans Publishing Co., 2003), pp. 194–211.

Hufton, Olwen, 'What Is Religious History Now?', in *What Is History Now?*, ed. by David Cannadine (Palgrave Macmillan Ltd., 2002), pp. 57–79.

Iliffe, John, 'The Spokesman: Martin Kayamba', in *Modern Tanzanians: A Volume of Biographies* (Nairobi: East African Publishing House, 1973), pp. 66–94.

Lonsdale, John, 'Jomo Kenyatta, God and the Modern World', in *African Modernities: Entangled Meanings in Current Debate*, ed. by Jan G. Deutsch, Peter Probst and Heike Schmidt (London: James Currey, 2002), pp. 31–66.

'The Moral Economy of Mau Mau: The Problem', in *Unhappy Valley: Conflict in Kenya and Africa*, ed. by Bruce Berman and John Lonsdale (London: James Currey, 1992), pp. 265–314.

'Moral Ethnicity and Political Tribalism', in *Inventions and Boundaries: Historical and Anthropological Approaches to the Study of Ethnicity and Nationalism*, ed. by Preben Kaarsholm and Jan Hultin (Roskilde: International Development Studies, Roskilde University, 1994), pp. 131–50.

'The Moral Economy of Mau Mau: Wealth, Poverty and Civic Virtue in Kikuyu Political Thought', in *Unhappy Valley: Conflict in Kenya and Africa*, ed. by Bruce Berman and John Lonsdale (London: James Currey, 1992), pp. 315–504.

Low, D.A., 'The Making and Implementation of the Uganda Agreement of 1900', in *Buganda and British Overrule, 1900–1955: Two Studies*, ed. by D.A. Low and R.C. Pratt (London: Oxford University Press, 1960), pp. 3–159.

Mbembe, Achille, 'The Power of the Archive and Its Limits', in *Refiguring the Archive*, ed. by Carolyn Hamilton, Verne Harris, Michèle Pickover, Graeme Reid, Razia Saleh and Jane Taylor (London: Kluwer Academic Publishers, 2002), pp. 19–26.

Peterson, Bhekizizwe, 'The Bantu World and the World of the Book: Reading, Reading, and "Enlightenment"', in *Africa's Hidden Histories: Everyday Literacy and Making the Self*, ed. by Karin Barber (Bloomington, IN: Indiana University Press, 2006), pp. 236–57.

Peterson, Derek R., 'The Rhetoric of the Word: Bible Translation and Mau Mau in Colonial Central Kenya', in *Missions, Nationalism, and the End of Empire*, ed. by Brian Stanley and Alaine Low (Cambridge: William B. Eerdmans Publishing Co., 2003), pp. 165–79.

Peterson, Derek R., and Darren R. Walhof, 'Rethinking Religion', in *The Invention of Religion: Rethinking Belief in Politics and History*, ed. by Derek R. Peterson and Darren R. Walhof (New Brunswick, NJ: Rutgers University Press, 2002), pp. 1–16.

Powesland, P.G., 'History of the Migration in Uganda', in *Economic Development and Tribal Change: A Study of Immigrant Labour in Buganda*, ed. by Audrey I. Richards, 2nd edn (Nairobi: Oxford University Press, 1973), pp. 17–51.

Pratt, R.C., 'The Politics of Indirect Rule: Uganda, 1900–1955', in *Buganda and British Overrule*, ed. by D.A. Low and R.C. Pratt (London: Oxford University Press, 1960), pp. 163–316.

Ranger, Terence, 'The Invention of Tradition Revisited: The Case of Colonial Africa', in *Legitimacy and the State in Twentieth Century Africa*, ed. by

Terence Ranger and Olufemi Vaughan (Hampshire: Macmillan Press, 1993), pp. 62–111.

Richards, Audrey I., 'Epilogue', in *The King's Men: Leadership and Status in Buganda on the Eve of Independence*, ed. by Lloyd A. Fallers (London: Oxford University Press, 1964), pp. 357–94.

'The Assimilation of the Immigrants', in *Economic Development and Tribal Change: A Study of Immigrant Labour in Buganda*, ed. by Audrey I. Richards, 2nd edn (Nairobi: Oxford University Press, 1973), pp. 161–93.

'Traditional Values and Current Political Behaviour', in *The King's Men: Leadership and Status in Buganda on the Eve of Independence*, ed. by Lloyd A. Fallers (London: Oxford University Press, 1964), pp. 294–335.

Rubin, Miri, 'Religion', in *A Concise Companion to History*, ed. by Ulinka Rublack (Oxford: Oxford University Press, 2011), pp. 317–30.

Twaddle, Michael, 'Was the Democratic Party of Uganda a Purely Confessional Party?', in *Christianity in Independent Africa*, ed. by Edward Fasholé-Luke (Bloomington, IN: Indiana University Press, 1978), pp. 255–66.

Twaddle, Michael, and Holger Bernt Hansen, 'The Changing State of Uganda', in *Developing Uganda*, ed. by Michael Twaddle and Holger Bernt Hansen (Oxford: James Currey Ltd., 1998), pp. 1–18.

Vaughan, Megan, 'Culture', in *A Concise Companion to History*, ed. by Ulinka Rublack (Oxford: Oxford University Press, 2011), pp. 227–45.

Weber, Max, 'Politics as a Vocation', in *From Max Weber: Essays in Sociology*, ed. by H.H. Gerth and C. Wright Mills, trans. by H.H. Gerth and C. Wright Mills (New York: Oxford University Press, 1946), pp. 77–128.

Wittmann, Reinhard, 'Was There a Reading Revolution at the End of the Eighteenth Century?', in *A History of Reading in the West*, ed. by Guglielmo Cavallo and Roger Chartier, trans. by Lydia G. Cochrane (Cambridge: Polity Press, 1999), pp. 284–312.

Wong, R. Bin, 'Causation', in *A Concise Companion to History*, ed. by Ulinka Rublack (Oxford: Oxford University Press, 2011), pp. 27–54.

Wrigley, C.C., 'The Changing Economic Structure of Buganda', in *The King's Men: Leadership and Status in Buganda on the Eve of Independence* (London: Oxford University Press, 1964), pp. 16–63.

Articles

Adatia, A.K., and N.Q. King, 'Some East African *Firmans* of H.H. Aga Khan III', *Journal of Religion in Africa*, 2 (1969), 179–91.

Alam, Muzaffar, and Sanjay Subrahmanyam, 'Envisioning Power: The Political Thought of a Late Eighteenth-century Mughal Prince', *The Indian Economic and Social History Review*, 43 (2006), 131–61.

Bayly, Christopher, 'Rammohan Roy and the Advent of Constitutional Liberalism in India, 1800–30', *Modern Intellectual History*, 4 (2007), 25–41.

Berry, Sara, 'Hegemony on a Shoestring: Indirect Rule and Access to Agricultural Land', *Africa*, 62 (1992), 327–55.

Bowles, B.D., 'Economic Anti-Colonialism and British Reaction in Uganda, 1936–1955', *Canadian Journal of African Studies/Revue Canadienne Des Études Africaines*, 9 (1975), 51–60.

Brizuela-García, Esperanza, 'The History of Africanization and the Africanization of History', *History in Africa*, 33 (2006), 85–100.

Burguière, André, 'Histoire D'une Histoire: La Naissance Des Annales', *Annales. Histoire, Sciences Sociales*, 34 (1979), 1347–59.

Cabrita, Joel, 'Politics and Preaching: Chiefly Converts to the Nazaretha Church, Obedient Subjects and Sermon Performance in South Africa', *Journal of African History*, 51 (2010), 21–40.

Carter, Felice, 'The Education of African Muslims in Uganda', *Uganda Journal*, 29 (1965), 193–99.

Cobley, Alan G., 'Literacy, Libraries and Consciousness: The Provision of Library Services for Blacks in South Africa in the pre-Apartheid Era', *Libraries & Culture*, 32 (1997), 57–80.

Connan, Dominique, and Johanna Siméant, 'John Lonsdale, Le Nationalisme, l'Éthnicité Et l'Économie Morale: Parcours D'un Pionnier De l'Histoire Africaine', *Genèses*, 83 (2011), 133–54.

Cooper, Frederick, 'Africa's Pasts and Africa's Historians', *Canadian Journal of African Studies/Revue Canadienne Des Études Africaines*, 34 (2000), 298–336.

'The Problem of Slavery in African Studies', *The Journal of African History*, 20 (1979), 103–25.

Cox, A.H., 'The Growth and Expansion of Buganda', *Uganda Journal*, 14 (1950), 153–59.

Doyle, Shane, 'The Cwezi-Kubandwa Debate: Gender, Hegemony and Pre-colonial Religion in Bunyoro, Western Uganda', *Africa: Journal of the International African Institute*, 77 (2007), 559–81.

Earle, Jonathon L., 'Dreams and Political Imagination in Colonial Buganda', *Journal of African History*, 58 (2017), 85–105.

'Reading Revolution in Late Colonial Buganda', *Journal of Eastern African Studies*, 6 (2012), 507–26.

Ehrlich, Cyril, 'Cotton and the Uganda Economy, 1903–1909', *Uganda Journal*, 21 (1957), 162–75.

'The Economy of Buganda', *Uganda Journal*, 20 (1956), 17–25.

Ellis, Stephen, 'Writing Histories of Contemporary Africa', *The Journal of African History*, 43 (2002), 1–26.

Gee, T.W., 'A Century of Muhammedan Influence in Buganda, 1852–1951', *Uganda Journal*, 22 (1958), 139–50.

'Uganda's Legislative Council between the Wars', *Uganda Journal*, 25 (1961), 54–64.

Gray, John M., 'Ahmed Bin Ibrahim – The First Arab to Reach Buganda', *Uganda Journal*, 10 (1947), 80–97.

'Kakungulu in Bukedi', *Uganda Journal*, 27 (1963), 31–59.

'Kibuka', *Uganda Journal*, 20 (1956), 52–71.

'The Year of the Three Kings of Buganda', *Uganda Journal*, 14 (1949), 15–52.

Hancock, I.R., 'Patriotism and Neo-Traditionalism in Buganda: The Kabaka Yekka ('The King Alone') Movement, 1961–1962', *The Journal of African History*, 11 (1970), 419–34.

'The Kakamega Club of Buganda', *The Journal of Modern African Studies*, 12 (1974), 131–35.

Hughes, A., 'The Early Days of Education in the Protectorate: White Fathers' Mission', *Uganda Teachers' Journal*, 1 (1939), 18–23.

Huppert, George, 'Lucien Febvre and Marc Bloch: The Creation of the Annales', *The French Review*, 55 (1982), 510–13.

Jones, Colin, 'Peter Mandler's "Problem with Cultural History", or, Is Playtime Over?', *Cultural and Social History*, 1 (2004), 94–117.

Jones, James W., 'Religion, Health, and the Psychology of Religion: How the Research on Religion and Health Helps Us Understand Religion', *Journal of Religion and Health*, 43 (2004), 317–28.

Kajubi, W. Senteza, 'Coffee and Prosperity in Buganda: Some Aspects of Economic and Social Change', *Uganda Journal*, 22 (1965), 135–47.

Karlström, Mikael, 'Imagining Democracy: Political Culture and Democratisation in Buganda', *Africa: Journal of the International African Institute*, 66 (1996), 485–505.

Kasozi, A.B.K., 'The Impact of Islam on Ganda Culture, 1844–1894', *Journal of Religion in Africa*, 12 (1981), 127–35.

Katumba, Ahmed, and Fred B. Welbourn, 'Muslim Martyrs of Buganda', *Uganda Journal*, 28 (1964), 151–63.

Klagge, James C., 'Wittgenstein and Neuroscience', *Synthese*, 78 (1989), 319–43.

Kodesh, Neil, 'History from the Healer's Shrine: Genre, Historical Imagination, and Early Ganda History', *Comparative Studies in Society and History*, 49 (2007), 527–52.

Lonsdale, John, 'African Studies, Europe and Asia', *Afrika Spectrum*, 40 (2005), 377–402.

'Agency in Tight Corners: Narrative and Initiative in African History', *Journal of African Cultural Studies*, 13 (2000), 5–16.

'States and Social Processes in Africa: A Historiographical Survey', *African Studies Review*, 24 (1981), 139–225.

'The Emergence of African Nations: A Historiographical Analysis', *African Affairs*, 67 (1968), 11–28.

Mandler, Peter, 'The Problem with Cultural History', *Cultural and Social History*, 1 (2004), 94–117.

Mazrui, Ali, 'Religious Strangers in Uganda: From Emin Pasha to Amin Dada', *African Affairs*, 76 (1977), 21–38.

Maxwell, David, '"Sacred History, Social History": Traditions and Texts in the Making of a Southern African Transnational Religious Movement', *Comparative Studies in Society and History*, 43 (2001), 502–24.

Miller, Joseph C., 'History and Africa/Africa and History', *American Historical Review*, 104 (1999), 1–32.

Morefield, Jeanne, 'States Are Not People: Harold Laski on Unsettling Sovereignty, Rediscovering Democracy', *Political Research Quarterly*, 58 (2005), 659–69.

Morgan, A.R., 'Uganda's Cotton Industry: Fifty Years Back', *Uganda Journal*, 22 (1958), 107–12.

Morris, H.S., 'The Divine Kingship of the Aga Khan: A Study of Theocracy in East Africa', *Southwestern Journal of Anthropology*, 14 (1958), 454–72.

Mulira, James, 'Nationalism and Communist Phobia in Colonial Uganda, 1945–1960', *Mawazo*, 5 (1983), 3–16.

Mutongi, Kenda, '"Worries of the Heart": Widowed Mothers, Daughters and Masculinities in Maragoli, Western Kenya, 1940–60', *Journal of African History*, 40 (1999), 67–86.

Norval, Aletta, 'The Things We Do with Words—Contemporary Approaches to the Analysis of Ideology', *British Journal of Political Science*, 30 (2000), 313–46.

Oliver, Roland, 'The Baganda and the Bakonjo', *Uganda Journal*, 18 (1954), 31–3.

Peires, J.B., '"Soft" Believers and "Hard" Unbelievers in the Xhosa Cattle-Killing', *The Journal of African History*, 27 (1986), 443–61.

Peterson, Derek R., and Edgar C. Taylor, 'Rethinking the State in Idi Amin's Uganda: The Politics of Exhortation', *Journal of Eastern African Studies*, 7 (2013), 58–82.

Pirouet, Louise, 'Evangelists and Subimperialists', *Dini Na Mila*, 4 (1969), 28–41.

Plantinga, Alvin, 'Epistemic Justification', *Noûs*, 20 (1986), 3–18.
  'Positive Epistemic Status and Proper Function', *Philosophical Perspectives*, 2 (1988), 1–50.
  'Reliabilism, Analyses and Defeaters', *Philosophy and Phenomenological Research*, 55 (1995), 427–64.
Pocock, J.G.A., 'Present at the Creation: With Laslett to the Lost Worlds', *International Journal of Public Affairs*, 2 (2006), 7–17.
Revel, Jacques, 'Histoire Et Sciences Sociales: Les Paradigmes Des Annales', *Annales. Histoire, Sciences Sociales*, 34 (1979), 1360–76.
Ricoeur, Paul, 'History and Hermeneutics', *The Journal of Philosophy*, 73 (1976), 683–95.
Rigby, Peter, 'Prophets, Diviners, and Prophetism: The Recent History of Kiganda Religion', *Journal of Anthropological Research*, 31 (1975), 116–48.
Roberts, A.D., 'The Sub-Imperialism of the Baganda', *Journal of African History*, 3 (1962), 435–50.
Roscoe, J., '95. Kibuka, the War God of the Baganda', *Man*, 7 (1907), 161–66.
Rowe, John A., 'The Purge of Christians at Mwanga's Court: A Reassessment of This Episode in Buganda History', *Journal of African History*, 5 (1963), 55–72
  'Eyewitness Accounts of Buganda History: The Memoirs of Ham Mukasa and His Generation', *Ethnohistory*, 36 (1989), 61–71.
  'Myth, Memoir, and Moral Admonition: Luganda Historical Writing, 1893–1969', *Uganda Journal*, 33 (1969), 17–40, 217–19.
  'The Baganda Revolutionaries', *Tarikh*, 3 (1970), 34–46.
Roy, Étienne Le, 'L'évolution De La Justice Traditionnelle Dans l'Afrique Francophone', *Canadian Journal of African Studies/Revue Canadienne Des Études Africaines*, 9 (1975), 75–87.
Schiller, Laurence D., 'The Royal Women of Buganda', *The International Journal of African Historical Studies*, 23 (1990), 455–73.
Schoenbrun, David L., 'A Mask of Calm: Emotion and Founding the Kingdom of Bunyoro in the Sixteenth Century', *Comparative Studies in Society and History*, 55 (2013), 634–64.
  'Conjuring the Modern in Africa: Durability and Rupture in Histories of Public Healing between the Great Lakes of East Africa', *The American Historical Review*, 111 (2006), 1403–39.
  'We Are What We Eat: Ancient Agriculture Between the Great Lakes', *The Journal of African History*, 34 (1993), 1–31.
Spear, Thomas, 'Neo-Traditionalism and the Limits of Invention in British Colonial Africa', *The Journal of African History*, 44 (2003), 3–27.

Summers, Carol, 'Catholic Action and Ugandan Radicalism: Political Activism in Buganda, 1930–1950', *Journal of Religion in Africa*, 39 (2009), 60–90.

'Grandfathers, Grandsons, Morality, and Radical Politics in Late Colonial Buganda', *The International Journal of African Historical Studies*, 38 (2005), 427–47.

'Radical Rudeness: Ugandan Social Critiques in the 1940s', *Journal of Social History*, 39 (2006), 741–70.

'"Subterranean Evil" and "Tumultuous Riot" in Buganda: Authority and Alienation at King's College, Budo, 1942', *The Journal of African History*, 47 (2006), 93–113.

'Young Buganda and Old Boys: Youth, Generational Transition, and Ideas of Leadership in Buganda, 1920–1949', *African Today*, 51 (2005), 109–28.

Sykes, J., 'A Further Note on the Education of African Muslims', *Uganda Journal*, 30 (1966), 227–28.

Thomas, H.B., 'Capax Imperii–The Story of Semei Kakungulu', *Uganda Journal*, 6 (1939), 125–36.

Tuck, Michael W., and John A. Rowe, 'Phoenix from the Ashes: Rediscovery of the Lost Lukiiko Archives', *History in Africa*, 32 (2005), 403–14.

Twaddle, Michael, 'Ganda Receptivity to Change', *The Journal of African History*, 15 (1974), 303–15.

'On Ganda Historiography', *History in Africa*, 1 (1974), 85–100.

'The Emergence of Politico-Religious Groupings in Late Nineteenth-Century Buganda', *The Journal of African History*, 29 (1988), 81–92.

'The Muslim Revolution in Buganda', *African Affairs*, 71 (1972), 54–72.

Walsham, Alexandra, 'The Reformation and "The Disenchantment of the World" Reassessed', *The Historical Journal*, 51 (2008), 497–528.

Ward, Kevin, 'The Church of Uganda and the Exile of Kabaka Muteesa II, 1953–55', *Journal of Religion in Africa*, 28 (1998), 411–49.

Webster, J.B., 'Pioneers of Teso', *Tarikh*, 3 (1970), 47–58.

Welbourn, Fred B., 'Kibuuka Comes Home', *Transition*, 1962, 15–20.

Wrigley, C.C., 'The Christian Revolution in Buganda', *Comparative Studies in Society and History*, 2 (1959), 33–48.

Internet Sources

'Chronology of the Press in Burma', *The Irrawaddy* (May 1, 2004) <www.irrawaddy.org/research_show.php?art_id=3533> [accessed 1 January 2011].

'Deaths in Uganda Forest Protest', 12 April 2007, in *BBC* <http://news.bbc.co.uk/1/hi/world/africa/6548107.stm> [accessed 6 October 2011].

'Investigating Kasubi Fire: Masaka Traditional Healer Launch Own Probe', 21 March 2010, National Television, Kampala, <www.youtube.com/watch?v=ft4g6CxF9Rc&feature=youtube_gdata> [accessed 23 March 2010].

'President Museveni's Remarks Before Handing over Ebyaffe to Buganda Kingdom's Delegation on April 15, 2014, at State House Entebbe', 16 April 2014, State House, Entebbe <www.statehouse.go.ug/media/presidential-statements/2014/04/16/president-musevenis-remarks-handing-over-ebyaffe-buganda-ki> [accessed 7 July 2014].

Obote, Milton, 'Notes on Concealment of Genocide in Uganda', (1990) <www.upcparty.net/obote/genocide.htm> [accessed 25 March 2010].

'The Role of the UPC in Uganda's Independence', (n.d.) <www.upcparty.net/press/therole.htm> [accessed 3 September 2009].

'Ugandan Plan for Forest Suspended', 22 May 2007, in *BBC* <http://news.bbc.co.uk/1/hi/world/africa/6680637.stm> [accessed 6 October 2011].

Unpublished Secondary

Earle, Jonathon L., 'Political Theologies in Late Colonial Buganda' (unpublished PhD, Cambridge: University of Cambridge, 2012).

Kalibala, Ernest B., 'The Social Structure of the Baganda Tribe of East Africa' (unpublished PhD, University of Harvard, 1946).

Karlström, Mikael, 'The Cultural Kingdom in Uganda: Popular Royalism and the Restoration of the Buganda Kingship, Volume I' (unpublished PhD, The University of Chicago, 1999).

Katungulu, M.M., 'Islam in Buganda', trans. by J. Busulwa, n.d.

Kayunga, Sallie S., 'Uganda National Congress and the Struggle for Democracy: 1952–1962' (Working Paper No. 14, CBR Publications, 1995).

Musoke, W.S., 'Reverend George Baskerville's Work at Ngogwe and the Rest of Kyaggwe County' (unpublished Bachelor of Arts thesis, Makerere University, 1970).

Mutyaba, Amin, 'The Development of Islam in Uganda', n.d.

Peterson, Derek R., 'Archive Work in Uganda' (unpublished manuscript, 2015).

Rowe, John A., 'Lugard at Kampala', Makerere History Paper 3, 1969.

'Revolution in Buganda, 1856–1900. Part One: The Reign of Kabaka Mukabya Mutesa, 1856–1884' (unpublished PhD, The University of Wisconsin, 1966).

Sanders, Ethan R., 'The African Association and the Growth and Movement of Politics in Mid-Twentieth Century East Africa' (unpublished PhD, University of Cambridge, 2012).

Stonehouse, Aidan, 'Peripheral Identities in an African State: A History of Ethnicity in the Kingdom of Buganda since 1884' (unpublished PhD, University of Leeds, 2012).

Summers, Carol, 'All the Kabaka's Wives: Baganda Women, the Kabaka Crisis (1953–6), and the Politics and Perils of Loyalty', (2007, Draft Paper, New York: African Studies Association, 2007).

Waliggo, John M., 'The Catholic Church in the Buddu Province of Buganda, 1879–1925' (unpublished PhD, University of Cambridge, 1976).

Index

African Studies Series

For EU product safety concerns, contact us at Calle de José Abascal, 56–1°,
28003 Madrid, Spain or eugpsr@cambridge.org.

www.ingramcontent.com/pod-product-compliance
Ingram Content Group UK Ltd.
Pitfield, Milton Keynes, MK11 3LW, UK
UKHW020337140625
459647UK00018B/2187